Advance Praise for

I HEAR SHE'S A REAL BITCH

"Whatever Jen Agg says is worth listening to. As owner of Toronto's excellent The Black Hoof, she's one of the most vocal and interesting observers of the peculiar subculture of the restaurant business. *I Hear She's a Real Bitch* is the book a lot of us have been waiting for. A terrific, beautifully written, frank, and funny memoir, and a compelling argument for pulling down the long outdated system of 'bro' culture that has dominated the industry since what feels like the beginning of time." —ANTHONY BOURDAIN

"Jen Agg insists on being heard. Her plainspoken yet breathlessly disclosing memoir is compulsively readable, highlighting her natural gift for not just *telling it like it is*, but remembering with heart and with humour. Much like dining at one of her perfectly-lit restaurants, reading Agg is a full-blown experience of the senses. I am grateful for her voice and for how generously she storytells. I read *I Hear She's a Real Bitch* all the way through, in one sitting, only putting it down once near the end, so as to delay reaching its final pages." —DURGA CHEW-BOSE, author of *Too Much and Not the Mood*

"Jen Agg has produced a memoir every bit as distinctive as her extraordinary restaurants. It is equal parts steel, grit, sass, TMI, and analytic brilliance. Nobody is better at creating the modern bistro, a joint that's *someplace*, yet also relaxed; meticulous, but utterly without pretension. Agg, it turns out, has an ear to match her eye; she is a dismayingly good writer, and her book is a double how-to: how to be a garishly successful restaurateur; and how to be a semi-completed human being. She has brought every bit of her unique verve to *I Hear She's a Real Bitch*. (PS: She can be, but she really isn't.)" —STEPHEN METCALF, critic-at-large at *Slate*, and host of the *Culture Gabfest* podcast

I HEAR SHE'S A REAL BITCH

I HEAR
SHE'S A
REAL
BITCH

JEN AGG

 DOUBLEDAY CANADA

Doubleday Canada and colophon are registered trademarks of Penguin Random House Canada Limited.

Library and Archives Canada Cataloguing in Publication

Agg, Jen, author
I hear she's a real bitch / Jen Agg.

Issued in print and electronic formats.
ISBN 978-0-385-68687-7 (hardback).—ISBN 978-0-385-68688-4 (epub)

1. Agg, Jen. 2. Restaurateurs—Ontario—Toronto—Biography.
3. Women in the food industry—Ontario—Toronto—Biography.
I. Title.

TX910.5.A23A3 2017   647.95092   C2016-903071-7
C2016-903072-5

Jacket and text design: Leah Springate
Jacket photos: (front) Jenna Wakani; (back) Daniel Neuhaus

Printed and bound in the USA

Published in Canada by Doubleday Canada,
a division of Penguin Random House Canada Limited

www.penguinrandomhouse.ca

10 9 8 7 6 5 4 3 2 1

Penguin
Random House
DOUBLEDAY CANADA

For Roland, without whom I'd die.

1:   SERVICE HUMS

"HANDS, PLEASE."

Three beats.

"HANDS, PLEASE."

Servers quickly snap to and move toward the pass in that way that's almost running but looks very relaxed—like a swan elegantly floating through the room, all quick legs and small steps from the waist down and an incredibly calm upper body, as though you are walking at a normal pace. It's learned. The Black Hoof servers know how to extricate themselves graciously from whatever they are doing, be it greeting people, talking to tables, or stirring cocktails while taking orders from the bar. The pass—where the chef puts up the plated food for servers to pick up and deliver to tables—is always a priority, and the servers are so seasoned they can all calculate, at hyper-speed and with darting eye contact, who's doing the least pressing thing. Whoever it is quickly untangles themselves from their task so they can get to the pass and run the food before "hands" is called a third time.

"Can you go for hands, please?" sounds so strange, but if I'm working the floor and unable to get to the pass myself, I'll say it to the nearest server in a low but unmistakably demanding voice. There's a certain pitch you can land on, a lower register, that feels designed for giving orders to staff in a loud restaurant. For me, it's much lower than my normal speaking voice, and whatever pointed words I'm saying get wrapped up in the bass notes of a Cure song, so only the server can hear them. And if I can somehow keep my face looking its *most pleasant* (a Herculean task, believe me), then I've achieved management nirvana: gotten my point across quickly and clearly while leaving the customer completely oblivious to what's going on.

For some context, the pass, in our case, is a worn-down piece of two-by-six. I, years prior, installed that piece of wood myself and rubbed it down with dark stain. It now shines with the patina of a thousand plates crossing over from the kitchen to tables of hungry diners.

Drinks are made first, and if the entire room is seated all at once (very likely on Friday and Saturday nights) the bartender gets hit hard first. The servers will deal with wine and beer orders themselves, but since we are well known for our cocktails, for the bartender a frenzy of stirring and shaking ensues. Our best dishwashers will assist by reading the bar chits and setting up and chilling glassware in the order the drinks are being made, sometimes even prepping garnishes. When dishwashers are at that level, they never stay in the pit too long.

Almost every table orders charcuterie: it is the food upon which we've built our reputation (and it's what we have stamped on our awning). But, aside from being our "signature" item, it also happens to be a perfect starting point for an unapologetically meaty meal.

The eight or ten items on offer on the charcuterie board are constantly rotating—old salamis get sliced down to the nub and new ones cure and become ready to be plucked from our *secret curing room*. This is a small walk-in fridge in the very dark recesses of the farthest corner of the basement, kept at just the right temperature and humidity to slowly turn raw, ground meat into perfect, salty tubes.

The concept at the Black Hoof is simple—we offer great everything, including service and atmosphere—but our reputation rests, fundamentally, on the quality of this board. And the quality has never wavered, though each new chef brings their own personality to it. Some are more traditional, sticking to the drier saucissons secs of France, the somehow creamy *and* crumbly chorizos of Spain, and the long-cured kings of charcuterie, the famous whole-muscle prosciuttos of Italy. Some are more wild, focusing on infusing old traditions with new flavours—like spicy horse, whose perfect marriage of sweet horse meat and fiery chili flakes might even make timid eaters forget what they're eating; or curried goat, a match as obvious as it is delicious; or blueberry bison—tart, dried blueberries the perfect foil to the gamy meat. The fundamental reliability and consistently great sameness of the board has kept the menu anchored for almost ten years. And we always serve it with the explanation that the charcuterie is precisely laid out—each slice cut specifically to best highlight whatever style salumi it is—ranging from least to most intense flavour: "We recommend you start here"—points at bottom—"and work your way toward the handle." Never "Chef recommends" . . . UGHHH to "Chef recommends"! Nothing gets my hackles up quite like servers (in other restaurants, obviously) referring to the chef as "Chef." It's come to indicate an old-guard mentality that is mostly unchecked reverence for someone who is good at cooking food. Plus, it's hyper-cheesy. "Doctor recommends you take your pill every day"; "Judge recommends you go directly to jail—do not pass Go," etc., etc. I call my doctor by his first name, and I'd be tempted to call a judge Peter instead of "Your Honour," so, in general, I'm not really into honorifics.

"It's not a hard and fast rule, but you'll find the flavours get a little more intense as you go along." This explanation takes only five seconds, and I must have said it a thousand times, but I'm always conscious to keep it sounding fresh, as though each utterance is somehow the first time those words have tumbled from my lips in that particular order. "On the corner"—gestures to it—"country terrine wrapped in bacon, whipped schmaltz"—gesture follows items, never coming too close, but close enough that the diner can see what you're pointing at—"capicollo from the shoulder, across here, sopressata, beef heart and dill, red wine and clove, pistachio-studded mortadella"—still with the pointing (always say "pistachio" in case they've neglected to mention their severe nut allergy, which happens more than it ought to)—"then this is one of my favourites, smoked summer sausage, and across the top spicy horse, and finally some chorizo. And, of course, our house grainy mustard" (because you'd be shocked how many people ask what that one is while plopping their finger in its thousands of tiny, sticky orbs).

That's how I deliver—or drop—boards, anyway. I speak quickly, but not too quickly, and try to keep my interruption of their conversation as unobtrusive as possible, while still letting people know what they're eating.

We used to serve every board with a side of pickles, and we built the cost into the price, but half the time the pickle plate would come back untouched. Infuriating! First of all, who doesn't like pickles? Especially when they are the perfect counterpoint to fatty, salty charcuterie? And pickles aren't *just* pickles; you can pickle literally anything, so there's always an array of colours and flavours: bright-pink, sharply acidic beets, cooked to remove the skins and kept just slightly softer than raw; curried cauliflower; stinky turnips, which smell like rotting corpses but somehow manage to taste heavenly; spicy green beans, whose crispness and bracing acidity perfectly follow a fatty slice of salumi. As a result of this sad wastefulness, many years ago I decided to lower the price of the board and charge a very nominal $3 for a side of pickles. This does two things. It makes it so if you want pickles, you have to pay for them, which in turn makes you far more likely to consume them. And it ensures that we are spending all that time and energy (and labour cost) on a food that is actually going to get eaten. It's the same thing with bread. We could build the cost of bread into our boards, but we make sure people actually want it by charging them separately, which greatly reduces waste. People are sometimes annoyed by the extra charges, which I don't understand. I wish they would recognize the pricing's inherent choice and, therefore, its value. But it's all about *perceived* value, a very different thing from *actual* value. We'd make more money if we just charged $26 for the board and included bread and pickles, but the waste would horrify me.

"And would you like a plate of pickles? Really helps cut through all that lovely fat." I ask this very quickly when I'm dropping a board if I notice the table hasn't ordered a pickle plate, and they almost always say yes, which gives me an opportunity to remind the server to always offer pickles, in that low, vaguely ominous "talking to servers" voice. Because the cooks know I want every charcuterie board ordered to have a side of pickles, they stock up on them on nights when I'm working. Occasionally the customer will make some joke about upselling, which, yes, I'm doing, because this *is* a business. But for us, it's not so much about the three little dollars as it is about maximum enjoyment of the board, and cured meat needs pickles!

"HOW DO YOU MAKE A SMALL FORTUNE in the restaurant business?"

"Start with a large one."

This isn't so much a joke as it is sage advice. The reality is that the Game of Restaurants isn't for the faint of heart. Unless you find a way to dominate and command it, it will destroy you. Try, though, to not lop off anyone's head in the process.

The Black Hoof doesn't serve coffee, mostly because we don't have any room, anywhere at all, for the set-up required to produce great coffee—and why do something unless you're at least aiming for great? But, also, I don't want to serve coffee. It just isn't worth it. If people order coffee they tend to linger over it and take up the table for far longer than necessary, and for what? An extra six bucks? I know, I know, it sounds so cold and calculating when you put it that way, but anybody who's owned a restaurant knows you can have all the passion and hospitality of a $5,000-a-night escort service run by artists and opera singers, but it all comes down to a numbers game: if you don't do just slightly over breaking even, then all of your passion and hospitality is useless, because you won't have a room to paint it on.

I've learned that the best way to survive this business is to pick a side. You can go with basic and mundane, with a little bit of something that will please everyone, probably make money, and excel at mediocrity. Or you can have vision and do something with a narrow focus that surely won't please everyone—but that's the point: you can't please everyone, so why try? That's literally what shitty restaurant chains were designed for. My restaurants are about focus, linear vision, doing a few things really well, etc. But, still, I kick myself once a week for not just selling burgers instead, and having an easy-to-control one-item restaurant that would essentially print money. So much money—just ask Danny Meyer (owner of Shake Shack via Gramercy Tavern/Union Hospitality for all you non-restaurant peeps). Everybody loves a good burger. Actually, everyone loves a burger, period; it doesn't even need to be good. But I chose to base my first restaurant around charcuterie instead.

As the charcuterie gets torn into by hungry diners, everything starts to amp up. This is the beginning of the *first push*. Cooks listen to the commands of the chef and work so quickly and in such harmony it's like watching a ballet, a really fast one—*Sweaty Swan Lake*. The chef reaches into the fridge as the *garde manger* instinctively senses this and moves to make room almost before he bends down. The stove cook passes over protein just as the chef is placing whatever he grabbed and turns to allow space for the meat pass. The chef checks the meat for doneness, plates it, and moves on to the next thing as a server responds to the call for "hands, please" and whisks it away, somehow allowing a customer to get by without knocking down the plate or the customer. All while the prep cook is dropping off freshly cleaned bone marrow from the prep kitchen across the street—it's a literal miracle no one's been hit by a car yet since we all run back and forth across the street, day and night. Minutes later that same plate, having only just been served to table 2, is now licked clean and gets taken to the pit (a very generous word for a dishwasher, both machine and human, and a small sink wedged in between the back bar and the stove). The dishwasher reaches for the plate, saving the server half a precious second, and the bartender places freshly shaken cocktails that the server somehow turns and grabs in one fluid motion. This all happens in an extremely tiny workspace (like, however small you're imagining it is? It's smaller), and it's beautiful to watch. The room hums with that crackling energy of everything happening all at once, and then I realize it's only twenty minutes into service.

I've watched this dance from behind the bar, feeling like I'm inside the vortex rather than watching the spin; I've watched it from the back of the room on the rare occasions I'll sit down with my friends or family for dinner. Eating at your restaurant is an incredibly necessary thing to do as an owner. You'll feel weird and conspicuous, but you'll discover where that draft is coming in from, as well as a better way to clear table 8. I do it much more now than I ever did in the first six or seven years. It is essential to real quality control as it gives you the perspective of the customer, and it will 100 percent make your restaurant better.

Nothing, though, gives you a better perspective than hosting. You can greet and say goodnight to every single patron, and you know exactly what's going on at every single table.

When the manager texts me, usually between 6:00 and 6:30, I rush to tie my shoes and run over to the restaurant. It's around the corner in the truest sense, and if I move fast I can be there in under thirty seconds. I usually aim for 6:30 for my Saturday night hosting shift—that's the time when the first seating is peeling slices of charcuterie off the board and there is just the beginning of a wait-list.

After years of working full bar services and trying to manage an ever-growing company, I've finally built an amazing staff, and I've learned that my skills are better used in management, but I can't give up that Saturday shift. I burst into the restaurant and shove my bag into the tiny slot beside the stereo that isn't littered with staff snacks and ChapSticks, just behind the bar near the front, next to a woefully under-stocked first-aid kit that I really try to keep filled with Band-Aids—that's right, Band-Aids, none of that off-brand shit. If you happen to be lucky enough to find something to stop the bleeding after being careless enough to cut yourself in the first place, then you can be comforted in the fact that it'll damn well stay on.

As I stand up from behind the bar I am already mentally plugged into work mode, and I immediately make eye contact with the couple at the first two bar stools. They're scraping a bone marrow clean and spreading thick slices of pork blood and bison heart terrine on toasted rye bread. They aren't talking much but they look happy. I scan the rest of the bar and in an instant can see all the things that need to happen. I automatically fill all the half-empty water glasses, and I catch a couple opening the front door out of the corner of my eye. I smile at them and put down the bottle before seating them at the last two available bar stools.

"Everything tasting nice here?" I ask the couple at the bar—which plays a lot better spoken than read on the page. It's tough to figure out the language of a quality check, but this wording allows for a simple nod, and doesn't interrupt too much. And I don't do it for every course, just once. They seem happy for the interaction, and both look up smiling, chins greased with marrow fat.

I really like hosting.

HOOF CHARCUTERIE BOARD

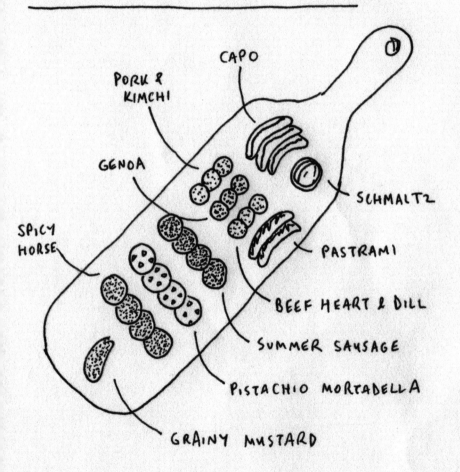

PORK & KIMCHI

CAPO

GENOA

SPICY HORSE

SCHMALTZ

PASTRAMI

BEEF HEART & DILL

SUMMER SAUSAGE

PISTACHIO MORTADELLA

GRAINY MUSTARD

2: F AND B IN HARMONY

THE IMPORTANCE OF A GREAT STAFF, managed by great leaders, cannot be overstated, the virtues of such having been extolled to us by so many people in this industry, over and over. Certainly, empire-building luminaries like Momofuku emperor David Chang and Danny Meyer understand it. Hell, In-N-Out Burger understands it. *Your staff is everything.* When a staff is in perfect shape, it should have the kind of leadership that is an extension of your vision. It should be headed up by people who actually give a shit and understand the motivations behind the "weird" rules and points of service that may seem crazy to someone less detail-oriented. The leadership is what's most important. Even a staff of long-time professional servers will slowly degrade and fall apart without strong leadership and someone to say, "Hey, don't do it that way." Which isn't to say everyone's role isn't important—the Hoof would grind to a halt without good hosts and dishwashers, and a server who brings both skill and personality will mark a diner just as much as perfectly seared foie gras will. It's the same with cooks, they need a strong leader to produce beautiful food; even the ones who might go on to be leaders themselves still need someone to hold it all together—the glue. Teams need captains.

We always drop drinks first, and always at the same time for the entire table. It's so annoying when places don't do that and the drinks trickle over one or two at a time, and you can't "Cheers!" It's awkward, and you're like, "I want to drink my drink right now, because these people I'm with are excessively boring, but now I have to wait?" So if the board has to sit on the pass for forty-five seconds while drinks are dropped off, then it will just have to. Normally this would not be okay with the kitchen staff, but when things are working right there is an understanding that this is fine because the kitchen respects the front of house enough to trust their judgment. Rules, exceptions to them . . . etc. Running service is a prolonged series of quick decisions about what happens when. Harmony helps, but it can only exist under good leadership, and this is where great communication between front and back of house comes in handy.

Having the front and back function as a team rather than opponents begrudging each other at every opportunity isn't just important, it's essential, but it's a new model, completely opposed to how it's always been done. Even as recently as ten years ago, it was shockingly common for the cooks and the servers to be at odds with each other, if not engaged in all-out war. The friction arises primarily from discrepancies in wages and hours worked that are too great to ignore—cooks historically work much longer hours for far less money. But it's also about how cooks saw themselves—through a lens of struggle, entwining with and magnifying food as art—while they tended to see servers as transient and lacking their training, much of it gained through unpaid apprenticeships known as "stages," which isn't necessarily wrong. Conversely, servers as a whole probably spent a lot of recent history thinking of cooks as

uneducated, or rather *specifically* educated, torturous brutes—
and they weren't necessarily wrong either.

If you've worked in the restaurant business, you've heard
the horror stories about front and back of house that start
with glaring and whispering in a dragged-out cold war and
end at the hospital. It's awful when the servers and cooks hate
each other. The goal ought to be harmony, respect, and the
whole team working together; it's a better experience for
the customer and a better shift for the staff. And this kind of
amity is mainly achieved economically. I've learned that by
paying the cooks well and tipping them out generously, the
great financial divide that fosters resentment between cooks
and servers is closed a bit. This is a model that works for the
Hoof because we do enough turns that the servers make
plenty of money. The cooks' hours, as mentioned, are gruelling, so I make an effort to ensure that the front of house is
fully aware of that. New servers are taught to be sensitive to
the kitchen's long days, and to be tactful enough not to wander in for their shift at 5:00, lazily lay out their snacks, and yak
about the awesome day they had hanging out in the park. As
the night goes on they are encouraged to keep their hunger
pangs to themselves—just eat a snack and shut up about it—
and are instantly hushed if they start complaining of being
tired. It just isn't polite, or thoughtful. And the cooks, in turn,
won't do things like heating up a plate to molten temperatures
just to chuckle as a hapless server grabs it. It's a happy environment, which helps make seven-hour services fly by—because
as waiters in most other restaurants are serving their last
espressos and mentally ordering a pint and a shot at the local
watering hole, the Hoof staff is hitting its halfway point and

looking for the energy to keep up standards of service, even after a busy four hours.

How difficult front of house work can be is a thing that doesn't get discussed much in restaurants, as cooks generally don't have much respect for how mentally exhausting being nice and getting people stuff for seven hours can be. While there's no doubt that the cooks technically work much longer days, serving people can really wear you down, and when cooks occasionally make the transition from BOH to FOH, they very quickly learn just how much. In fact, one of the cooks at the Hoof recently went over to the other side because of his interest in bartending (and, presumably, spending more time with his wife). After two nights, he lost his voice and was shocked at how much talking he had to do. He also couldn't believe how much energy it took just to be pleasant and nice to people for seven straight hours, so much so that he seriously questioned his decision to leave the kitchen. He opted to stick it out, and he's become an invaluable member of the Cocktail Bar crew, someone who happens to have a real knack for all the prep work and syrup-making that goes on behind the scenes—best of both worlds.

I've worked hard to cultivate an environment that doesn't feel riddled with sparks about to burst into angry explosions between art and commerce. Why can't front and back just get along? Adding just a little more art in service and a little more commerce for the cooks seemed like a pretty logical fix. Now, with full autonomy as an owner, I push a friendlier, more fair approach by paying cooks well, having a portion of the tips go toward all the back of house, and not standing for abusive garbage. And to encourage even more cohesiveness, the kitchen is always invited to the wine and spirits tastings held primarily for FOH. This is a little thing, but it helps blur the line between front and back, and it allows everyone working to see themselves as part of a whole team instead of two separate halves.

I am so careful with hiring new employees. When you choose to bring someone into the restaurant world you created, when you know you'll be spending many hours together, prudence is paramount, but often there is no time for thoughtfully hemming and hawing over whether or not someone will be a good fit. Sometimes, when someone quits to pursue their master's, even if you've had six weeks' notice, you just have to take the best person interviewed from a weak pool. I believe in promoting from within, too. Not only does the person already understand the complex ebbs and flows of the restaurant, but *I* already know this person, which I like. Restaurant staff are very transient, but we are lucky in being able to keep turnover—and keep the risk of not-good people mucking everything up—to a minimum.

My hiring process has always been based on gut instinct, and wow, has my gut been off at times. But every single person who's worked at the Hoof for more than a few weeks—even the ones who sometimes looked like mistakes—has, at some point, made me very happy. Now, as an established restaurant, the Hoof has a staff made up of people who've been working together for years, people I genuinely love.

When I worked full services and took care of all the front of house hiring, it would fill me with dread, the idea of placing an ad and talking to way too many strangers about their industry experience. The whole thing just feels so awkward and phony. I could always tell right away if it was going to be a good personality fit, but if it very obviously wasn't I'd still, out of a sense of kindness, feel obligated to go through the motions: "And how long did you work there?" "Oh, interesting, and why did you quit?"—things I couldn't possibly have cared less about. Do men feel it necessary to finish an interview when it's so obviously a bad match? Because I definitely do. Even with all my protestations to the contrary, there is a part of me that feels at least a little connected to the status quo for women (nurturing, kind, polite), and I would have a really hard time cutting an interview short based on probably correct instincts. So I basically refuse to participate in them any more, and I rely on the good judgment of my managers to weed out the baddies.

As time went on and the hirings became less frequent, I would usually find a new person through someone already working for me. "If Justine and Julia say you're all right, then you're all right." But even when they come with the endorsement of two senior staff members, training new people is excruciating. I just want to be able to Vulcan mind meld our *complete training process* to the newbie so that I can stop feeling bad/guilty for how on edge *they* make *me* feel, and in turn stop taking that edginess out on them for what are normal learning-curve fuck-ups. "THIS HURTS ME MORE THAN IT HURTS YOU!"

I'm fortunate and happy that we rarely have to train anyone new these days, because I really hate change. I'm such a creature of habit that I can't stand having new people around, though I do try very hard to hide it, because I realize how ridiculous it is, and how much "hating change" ages me. Everyone I love at my restaurants was the new guy at some point, and I love them all now, so, presumably, I'll learn to love the idiot in front of me who keeps dropping plates *all wrong.*

There are only a few things that irk me more than sloppy drops. One is "octopus hands," when a server delivers your drink clutching it from above like an octopus, but so assured that *this* is the right way to carry a drink to a table. It is not. The right way is to hold the glass as close to the base as it's possible to carry it with no spills. Who knows where your grubby little fingers have been? I know where mine have been (basically, if it's a hole, I've been poking around there in the recent past), and that's enough to make me not want to place my mouth on the lip of a glass you've smeared with finger goop. Octopus hands are a thing I see all the time at other restaurants, and especially at bars, so when I see the new guy doing it, I just coolly whisper, "Watch your fingers" at him. He looks up, jolted, all confused, and I explain it in "correcting server mistake voice" while keeping my face its *most pleasant self*, always aware of how on display we are in the tiny room. It's a hard habit to break, though, so he'll do it again, but when it happens all I have to do now is look at his fingers hovering over a glass like a dirty alien about to clamp down. As training goes on, his response to my look becomes Pavlovian, and eventually he never does it again. But it takes time. And if that's one of his terrible habits, have no doubt, there are plenty more. Like the absolutely cringe-inducing fine-dining-style arm, held stiffly behind the back. How did this become a go-to for servers? It looks (particularly in a casual restaurant) out of place, falsely fancy, and just plain dumb. And you'd be surprised what a hard habit it is to break.

So, I'm the bad guy for a bit, which doesn't bother me in the least; it's my business, I sign the paycheques, and I want things done how I want them done. It's such a gendered expression, to be "the bad guy," but it's not too accusatory, as it smacks of a universal understanding that even good people must occasionally be bad guys for the sake of some greater good. In this case, it's only "greater-*ish*" good—the smooth running of a restaurant. But, as far as I know, there is no equivalent common-usage expression that is more oriented to women, and if there is, it's probably a nasty slur, like "she-devil" or, y'know, "bitch."

It takes a long time to properly integrate someone new into the Hoof family, slowly moulding his or her service into our style so it becomes seamless, second nature. I'm grateful to have a staff that consists of enough leaders and long-term employees—like Jake, David, Stu, Julia, and Lee—to take care of most the training now, as I'm both amazing and terrible at it. My expectations are ludicrously high and my patience, in contrast, lacking. But, like the Mafia, once you're in, you're in. When trust has been earned, I trust my staff so much, and over time I become a lot less "Iron Lady" and a lot more "Your Mom"—sometimes to my emotional detriment, as my involvement in their lives can cause me stress when they are going through something stressful. It's hard to care about the minutiae of the lives of your whole staff, but even harder not to. I fuss and worry about the Hoof kids and would do anything to help any of them in need (including lending money or a place to stay, or just an ear—okay, the ear usually comes with advice, solicited or not), and hey, if I don't ever have children of my own, I've at least touched the outer rays of motherhood.

The service at the Hoof is exactly the type of service I want but so rarely get when dining out. The servers are trained to, above all else, read their tables. Some people want to pull apart the wine list, carefully dissecting the merits of an Arbois versus a Cru Beaujolais, and others want to be left alone to hold hands and make googly eyes at each other. You have to know who you're dealing with and provide appropriate service, because it isn't just service, it's psychology. Obviously, food and beverage knowledge is hugely important, and the basic steps of actually serving the food and clearing the plates must be mastered, too. But those are skills you can teach. You can't teach someone to give a shit.

A smooth-running, efficient, seamless team like the Hoof's doesn't happen overnight; it takes time, a slow building, culling where needed, nurturing, to make sure your vision is being executed by like-minded people, which is probably why I'm so inclined to hire artists. When I was doing all the hiring by myself, my thoughts ran a gamut that was similar to the mental questionnaire I'd check off while meeting someone in a social setting: Do I like this person? Are they an it-getter? (Meaning, do they see the world at least a little bit the way I do, and do they understand things like social justice, beautiful music, and art?) Are they voracious readers? Are they in possession of a ridiculous, dark, well-nourished sense of humour? Are they smart and (fingers crossed) quick-witted? Do they really, really enjoy food and drink? Are they enough like me that I can teach them how I want them to be in my restaurants? But are they different enough from me so that my restaurants won't be fully staffed by skinny, brunette, white women? Do they dress well? (As horribly judgmental as it sounds, how someone chooses to present themselves can offer at least a little insight into what kind of person they are. And we can work with bad jeans—we will have you in good jeans inside of six months.) A couple of any of these qualities is a starting point. And I can say, without a doubt, that hiring for the right personality fit is always a better option than prioritizing a high level of experience.

It usually takes at least a couple of months to integrate a new person. During service I watch their every move. One new server just couldn't figure out how to elegantly drop the plates, and it was driving me crazy watching him clumsily try to place a charcuterie board at a table of four. There was nothing I could do from across the room but helplessly watch and chew my lip like a Molly-ed up teen. It would have looked even worse if I'd rushed over there and taken over, so I tried to just keep my face its *most pleasant self*. He walked away from the table and somehow sent a fork clattering to the floor, and it was like the record scratched in my head and the room went black except for a spotlight on the fork, which he was WALKING AWAY FROM. How did I hear it through the pulsing strains of "Back in the New York Groove" from ACROSS THE ROOM, but he didn't? I quickly dropped off the plates I'd been clearing, rushed over to the wait station, and in practically one movement replaced the diner's fork and picked up the one from the floor. This all happened in less than thirty seconds, but it was twenty-five too long for me.

I pick on everything, literally everything. How they move in the room is always a starting point. Some people are just completely unaware of how much space they are taking up. I've worked with bigger people who can exist in the tiniest spaces and tiny people whose clumsiness and wide movements make them seem twice as large. And it's such a weird thing to say to someone—how do you even explain that? For starters, I remind them to always, always say "behind" when approaching a co-worker whose back is turned. You get so used to it you find yourself muttering "behind, behind" to strangers at the mall. As soon as a new person understands to announce their presence (lest they end up getting hot stock spilled all over them) they start to subconsciously think about how they fit in the room, and most people naturally get it from there. But sometimes I've had to remind servers to always move aside for the customer, yes, even if they are carrying plates. Of course, most of the time, in that circumstance the customer will let the server pass, and that's nice.

Next is how they are talking to people. I have a mental (and actual) list of phrases I absolutely hate hearing, either as a diner or as an owner.

- "You still working on that?" Food is not work. Find another way to say it, or just use your eyes and your good sense to know when to clear a plate. (Also, please clear all the plates *after* everyone is finished. It's really true that if you clear as each diner is done it puts an unpleasant subconscious pressure on the slow eater to hurry the fuck up.)
- "How's everything going over here?" Like, assume they are having a good time! One quality check is always nice, most especially if you, as the server, encouraged the table to order a certain

menu item. By all means, ask them if they are enjoying it, but not how it's going.

- "Sorry, no more tables, we only have these bar stools." Why are you under-selling the awesomeness that is sitting at the bar? If you spin it negatively, they will start their meal thinking they could have had a better seat. Be positive: "Yes, we have these amazing spots at the bar where all the action is . . . best seats in the house."

- "I'm Jane, I'll be taking care of you tonight." Honestly, as a diner I probably don't care what your name is. It's such a weird affectation, and then if the customer actually calls you by name it's even weirder: "Jane, could we have some more water, please?" Never mind the connotations of "taking care of": "Am I sick?" "Will you be tucking me in?" "Does this come with a hand job?" If you and the customer are destined for a lifelong friendship, at some point your name will come up in a naturally, unforced way.

- "No problem." Why would anything be a problem? Just say "You're welcome" or "Absolutely" or literally anything other than "No problem."

There is so much effort that goes into training people to be great at serving in general, and at the Hoof in particular, it feels like such a big investment, so it's always hard to see any of them leave (mainly because of the unfortunate/ridiculous "hating new people" thing), but I am always happy for my staff when they start focusing on their passions as a career instead of something they do in between shifts. For a few of them, this business *is* their passion. These people are the core of the company, and they will be rewarded with partnerships, Oprah-style: "You get a restaurant! You get a restaurant!" and so on. I can't actually wait until I can just build restaurants, make them right, and then sit back in my Eames rocker scarfing ketchup chips, laughing hysterically and collecting cheques from all over the country. This is literally my dream, and I'm getting closer to it. (I can practically taste those chips—so sweet, so salty, so red. That "nutrition" info for thirty chips is useless to me, though; I need info on thirty *minutes* of chips. Although I'm very sad to report that, as of recently, eating a bag, a large bag, obviously—thirty *minutes*, not seconds—of ketchup chips causes me extreme stomach discomfort, to the point of keeping me up all night, full of MSG and regret.)

Working closely with people didn't come that easily to me. At the beginning I wanted to do everything myself, and despite being busy bartending and hosting I would sometimes take over serving table 1, the one in the front window right next to the bar, if I overheard the server using the wrong language or being too meek, or just generally not doing a good enough job. I'd quickly take them aside and tell them in my "talking to servers bass" to "focus on tables 2 through 5 and leave table 1 to me," making it very clear that there was no discussion to be had, that this was what was happening. It's a real pet peeve of mine, servers who let the table run roughshod over them. It's such a delicate art, that of charming a table into believing said table is making all the decisions, while they are actually, unknowingly, happily, following your orders. Why would you let a table of six order one of everything? Be smart about it. Of course they want to try as much as possible, but it absolutely won't be the best experience—everyone fighting for their share of thirty-six pieces of cavatelli pasta, with all the garnishes, cutting hen-of-the-woods mushrooms in half so all can taste? It's crazy. Make them have two pastas. Of course with something like our half-sweet and half-savoury foie gras—currently served with French toast, sour cherries, and a dollop of white chocolate cream, an insanely delicious combo that will make you weep with joy—one or two bites each is plenty (although I have definitely seen one person easily put down a foie on their own). So it's about understanding the menu well enough to make educated decisions on the diner's behalf, but also about understanding the diner; again, it's really about psychology. Obviously some diners are very alpha and don't want to listen to a server's suggestions, but the vast majority of patrons actually want you to guide them. And I'm very good at this part, the guiding, so it frustrates me when my staff is less that way.

When the Hoof was in its first year, that frustration led to me overworking, plus sustaining an incredibly high stress level for way too long. This caused me to drop fifteen pounds and develop what felt like chronic bronchitis, which I didn't have time to properly deal with, so it took months to go away. I only noticed the weight loss near the start of year two when my husband and I took a trip to Cuba over the Hoof's winter closure. I caught a glimpse of my legs in the angled mirror in our suite and was dumbfounded. I had somehow gotten stick-thin. It took my mental and physical health to be hanging by a thread before I finally started to let go and delegate, but it was also finding the right people to trust. I kissed a lot of frogs before I found my managerial Prince Charmings.

Jen Agg's Ten Commandments of Restaurant Service

1. No fine-dining-style arm stiffly behind back. It looks out of place and falsely fancy, and just dumb

2. No lifting water glasses to pour water. Figure out how to pour while leaving glasses on bar or table

3. No perfume

4. No saying "no problem." Why would anything be a problem? Just say "you're welcome" or "absolutely" or anything but "no problem"

5. No saying "you guys still workin' on that?" This should be so obvious but I still hear servers say it. Food isn't work

6. Always be positive about bar stools. Like, don't say in an apologetic way, "sorry, no tables, but I can put you at the bar," like it's somehow worse. It isn't. Make it sound like a win. "Lucky you, I have these lovely bar stools available"

7. Wipe tables/bar surface properly after every clear. Always. No exceptions. And before dropping bill. Do not drop a bill on a dirty table

8. Be nice to people

9. Accommodate reasonable food requests. Always check with kitchen

10. No octopus hands. Do not grab and carry glasses from the top. Keep fingers as far away from the rim as possible. I don't know where yours have been, but I know where mine have been

3: TREES IN SCARBOROUGH

THE RESTAURANT BUSINESS was never the job I dreamed about as a young girl growing up in Scarborough, Ontario. I was argumentative enough to have my sights set on being a lawyer—a long-term addiction to *Law and Order* had only fuelled my naive idea that somehow it was all just winning an argument, and one you *believed* in. But I probably would never have made it through law school—too much memorizing involved, when I can barely remember yesterday. There's no chance I'd have been able to pull out some *Daniels v. Big Pharma* precedent in front of a judge who'd probably already have held me in contempt a bunch of times, and whose politics I'd have a fifty-fifty chance of finding repugnant.

But somewhere along the way, whether it was picked up from my dad's entrepreneurial spirit—he was a teacher, but he was always doing other stuff where he could be his own boss—or just built into my DNA (kind of the same thing), I decided that working for myself should be my main goal, that being a boss was way better than having a boss.

Unlike my mom—who was a natural educator and forever changed people's lives as an ESL teacher who, as a point of fact and honour, actually gave a shit about her students—my dad didn't really enjoy teaching. He thought the kids were mostly lazy and tuned-out, and he especially hated the politics of the school system: essentially a microcosm of any structure with a leader under the control of the state's mandates. The red tape was endless, the freedom limited, and the pay, frankly, crap. His interest was in winning, and that seed had been planted when he was a young man at the University of Western Ontario (now Western University), furiously peeling potatoes deep in the bowels of the kitchen, just to put himself through school, and always trying to better his record. He only recently told me how much he wanted to "leave those rich, snobby bastards in the dust," and he knew that the first step toward the goal line was an education. He has never been prone to reveal himself, and I've spent my life prodding him open and poking at his natural stoicism. I've peppered him constantly with inappropriate questions about his marriage (I just want to know EVERYTHING), his life as a teenager, and what a drag it is getting old, while taking long walks through Scarborough's Rouge Valley, a lovely place surrounded by a sprawling mess of strip malls, samey homes, and endless nothingness, or sometimes on the balcony at the family cottage way north, outside Mattawa, Ontario.

The cottage was a wonderful place and the backdrop for many happy summers as my younger brother, Jonathan, and I grew up. My brother is seven years my junior, and he was a good sport about my merciless teasing and endless jokes about how he was "an accident." Seriously, though, "Mom, Dad: seven years is too big a gap between your only two children!" Dad helped build the cedar-clad cottage in the early 1980s after getting the lakefront property for a song in a Crown lottery. I have potent memories of games of Monopoly that would stretch out past my bedtime, with first my mother, then my brother dropping off, dad and I fighting it out to the end. He never *let* me win, but when I occasionally did, I felt invincible. More recently, with the cottage sold—beauty spot though it was, it was also a five-hour drive, and my parents just couldn't do it into their sixties—these talks have been taking place at their property near Cobourg, the kind of place that inspires descriptives like "rolling hills." It's quiet, and everyone who lives there is either over sixty or a drunk teen. We talk and watch the sun inch into the hills, always from the front porch, always with rosé.

For most of my childhood in the suburbs of Scarborough, fields and trees surrounded our quiet street. It felt idyllic—not that ten-year-old me was thinking, "Wow, this is *great!*" but I was able to take for granted the many nooks and crannies and creeks that were everywhere, before suburban sprawl swallowed everything up, spreading across the fields like a raging inferno fuelled by trees and foliage. It probably happened over the course of five or ten years, starting when I was eight or maybe a couple of years older, and that first big development in our neighbourhood (that buried a once bucolic golf course in little boxes made of ticky-tacky) when I was fourteen felt like a sea change. Like it would all be different. And it was: for one thing, there was finally a bus stop right at the top of my street.

In 1973 my parents had purchased a modest bungalow for $27,000 to go with their little puppy mutt and their future baby, still two years off. There was a two-acre plot of land attached to the property that cost an additional $7,500 that they had to scrape and borrow for—a line of credit and a small loan from my maternal grandfather, an ornery man who wasn't always kind to my mother but sincerely loved her. It would prove a wise investment for my parents.

There's a picture of me as a plump little baby playing with Toby the mutt on a plaid blanket in the "big backyard" (my mother's pet name for the land—she had pet names for everything). My dad is in the shot too, lying back on the blanket, Ray-Bans making him appear cooler than he'd actually register in person, admiring the hundreds of pine trees he'd planted in two long double rows, with well-tended grass in between. In a strange twist of my parents' mostly traditional roles (they both worked), my mother insisted on cutting the grass, a chore she took great pride in. The trees look so small in that picture, like you could pluck them up for a bouquet, but by the time I was a teenager, they were tall and bushy, and every year, one would be chosen by my mother and sacrificed for Christmas. I always felt a bit bad for that tree, like it had drawn the short straw just for being the most beautiful, its lush branches and emerald sparkle a death sentence. I tend to feel similarly about girls whose eyelids outshine their wit (not that both can't or shouldn't *sparkle sparkle*). So on the occasional lucky year when I was trusted with picking the tree for our house, I'd point at the slouchy one with a few bald patches, figuring it was time to put it out of its misery. My dad, egalitarian that he was, would just look at my mother and say, "She wants that one." The whole thing amused him— my mother trying to hide her disappointment at my terrible choice, and me insisting this was definitely *the one*. He'd take it down with a hacksaw while I held back the branches. My mother would stand a few yards back, staring at the tree, irritated, trying to find its good side.

I was a tomboy and a big risk-taker, and the "big backyard" was the perfect place to exhaust those particular personality traits. When I was seven my dad built me adorable gazebo in the back corner, his first of many. After that one, he was obsessed, and each new property he'd acquire—whether it was our cottage or a house to tinker with, rent out, then flip—got a gazebo, but over time, they seemed to become less resilient. And as Alzheimer's began creeping into his life and mind, so did he. The last one, at my parents' retirement property in Cobourg, couldn't stand up to the long, rolling winds. And it still hasn't been dealt with, an ugly emblem marring a beautiful property: weakened, withered, broken . . . but still, somehow, floppily standing.

This first gazebo, built just for me, was sturdy. Dad had painstakingly added in that cross-hatched wood that decorates the tops of middle-class fences in suburban neighbourhoods everywhere. He'd also included a marble bench and table, presumably for tea parties, but all I was interested in was jumping off the roof onto the grass below. My dad could have secured a big ladder in the field and I would have been just as pleased. I've spent my whole life jumping off gazebos.

The gazebo was only about eight feet high, but at eight or nine, when I was somewhere north of four feet tall, it was basically twice my height. I'd scramble up the adjacent crabapple tree to the roof, ready myself (I was always a little scared, just a little), pump my arms a few times for showmanship (for whose benefit I don't know; I often performed this ritual alone), and jumped, somehow always making a good landing on the soft grass that would eventually, over time, wear down to a hard sheen of dirt.

I couldn't get enough. I dreamed of higher heights, of becoming Mary Poppins with an umbrella that would surely let me coast down to safety. I made several attempts from the roof of the gazebo with several umbrellas of several sizes, but none floated me gently to the ground. I was either smart or scared enough never to take it up a higher tree, ignoring the Mother Superior's urging to "climb every mountain," a refrain that constantly ran through my head due to an alarming number of *Sound of Music* viewings. Honey-sweet musicals have been a lifelong, if now neglected, love, one I shared with my mother. (She couldn't carry a tune, but man she loved to sing.)

To satiate my cravings for higher highs, my dad helped me and a few of the neighbourhood kids build a platform about fifteen feet up a red pine. It was just high enough to feel secret, hidden among the branches, but not quite so high that any of us would break our ankles if we tumbled. The grouping of pines was so tall and old that the base boughs had all fallen away. We had to throw up a rope ladder just to reach the lowest branch, but from there it was an easy climb up to the platform. Sometimes I'd keep going and find myself thirty feet up in the sky, exhilarated and out of breath. I'd hang there for a bit, relishing the effort of the climb, feeling the slight fear the height brought, and just catching my breath. I loved the particular quiet of being in a tree surrounded by hundreds of soft, full pine branches (of course they were only soft if you stroked them the right way). Eventually I'd have to gingerly pick my way down, and it was always harder and a bit scarier climbing backwards, but I couldn't get enough. I loved being with friends and equally loved climbing away from them. This would become a baseline for all my friendships, and my 50/50 split between extro- and introversion.

My connection to trees—either learned, inherited, or both—was intense, and I attributed to them human qualities and even names, in a rich, anthropomorphic fantasy of imaginary "friends." Of two maples, along the property line of the backyard, the shorter one represented the maternal figure and the taller, sturdier one the dad (great young feminist I was!). Perhaps it was their silence I liked when I'd escape to them to be alone, sometimes to have a little cry, or the comfort of their trunks, the perfect spot to nestle in with a book, where I could lose hours and hours on a Saturday.

Everything a child could want surrounded me. But I was always trying to get to the end of the road, to peek around the corner, to expand my little Scarborough world. I'd zoom around the neighbourhood on my one-speed bike with back-pedal brakes, seeing who was around. By the time I was ten, a little cul-de-sac development of about twenty houses had sprouted off the top of our street where there had once been a barn. I'd loved sneaking into that old barn at sunset, when families were tucking into their under-seasoned, over-cooked dinners. I'd just poke around, imagining it was mine despite its ill-repair, its boards peeling away with more intent every winter. Any place I could find that was inherently somewhere I wasn't supposed to be was exactly where I'd run to. (I am fully expecting a dissection of this line as evidence of my admitted bourgeois, white-girl feminism.)

As a cynical grown-up I'm hard-pressed to recall what was so exciting about a sheltered square with dirt floors that smelled like an outdoor basement, but maybe it was just being able to trespass that was so exciting to me. And though I was sad about the barn being torn down, it was nice that there were new houses and finally some more kids to play with, because up until that point there had only been a few. One was a girl two years my junior who had a pool, so of course I wanted to hang out there all summer long. We would play "husband and wife," a "game" that involved me putting a stick down my pants and us lying beside each other "in bed." It sounds so weird now, but the prudish purity and lack of plot, although seemingly pointless, was actually a variation of a game of house with an attempt to untangle the stuff we didn't understand about marriage and sex. There were no rules and no one ever won; let's just call it an early exploration of gender roles. Two houses down were the twin girls who were mentally disabled, one more than the other, who we definitely called "the retarded twins"—this was in the 1980s, just before the decade got respectably politically correct while remaining drenched in intolerance. The twins were friendly and extremely generous with their toys and just wanted to play, so they were folded into our local gang, which included a couple of other girls from the neighbourhood. Somehow, despite their obvious differences and us being terrible children, we found common ground, and their strengths were what we focused on, because man they could run. They always won the disorganized races we would set up at the top of the cul-de-sac, the former barn, now some developer's kid's college fund.

My childhood obsession with outside play was balanced, and balanced well, by my fixation on television, likely brought on by the insane restrictions my parents placed on TV consumption when I was a preteen: half an hour on school nights and not a minute more. My mother was especially not into TV. I only ever remember her watching *Jeopardy*, keeping a proper score of her many correct answers (she was a wealth of information) and shushing you if you interrupted. I'd have to sneakily watch *Three's Company* and *WKRP in Cincinnati*—shows she thought of as the height of trashy—upstairs in my parents' bedroom while everyone else was down in the kitchen or living room. And many decades later, as she lay in the hospital dying of kidney failure, I couldn't even convince her to watch some silly comedy to take her mind off her dreadful surroundings. She was stubborn to the end. While you can't really buy better health care than what we have in Canada—which, philosophically, I think is amazing—it's actually really shitty and hard when it's your parent dying in a semi-private room beside an old man with a dreadful cough.

Sometimes, even well into my preteens, we'd watch *Disney* together on Sunday nights, and maybe *Life Goes On*, the show that taught North America to be a little more sensitive to the mentally challenged, even though it seemed like Corky burned down the family restaurant every other week, so it was kind of a mixed message. Otherwise, my mom entertained herself with crosswords—only cryptics (which still awes me)—games of Scrabble, and weekly trips to the theatre, ballet, symphony, or opera. She had season tickets to everything, and I was often her date.

My mother's downtown Toronto was a very conservative idea of culture, but I'll be forever grateful she took me, sometimes against my will, to all those shows, plays, and symphonies; it was the first spark igniting a lifelong adoration of performance art, especially music. I loved our monthly trips to Young People's Theatre, at Front and Sherbourne, where I'd sit, mesmerized by the action unfolding right in front of my eyes. We'd get a pack of wine gums, her favourite, and black cherry sodas, and if we had time, she'd take me somewhere for brunch, often Le Papillon, a serviceable French restaurant nearby on Front Street. I'd always get eggs Benedict, which came on a croissant. By the time I was ten, I'd finally grown out of a childhood aversion to eggs and could not believe something so delicious as eggs Benedict on a croissant existed. Later, in my late teens, when I taught myself how to make hollandaise and found out it was basically egg yolks and butter, I had a hard time reconciling the idea of eggs with egg sauce, but I got over it.

The profound influence all those trips to see the Toronto Symphony Orchestra had on me was undeniable; even as I would sometimes squirm in my seat, praying for intermission, the beauty and the spectacle of it seeped into me. So much so that from grade 5 until 8, I spent a month every summer excelling at the French horn as part of Scarborough's very impressive Music Camp, which as it turns out was way less cool than Art Camp, or so I heard. I'd chosen the French horn in grade 4 when they started us on instruments as part of the school curriculum, back in the days when the arts were a thriving, natural part of education. I liked it on sight because it looked complicated and different and untamable, but when I tried to play it nothing came out but sputtery air; I'd have to learn proper embouchure and so much more. I wanted to master it at first kiss, and I got really good, really fast. Eventually I took private lessons from a formidable woman named Caroline Spearing, whose disciplined, take-no-prisoners teaching style was both formative and oppressive. I became so good that after my audition for camp, an incredibly nerve-racking experience for a ten-year-old, they placed me as second chair in the top symphony, out of five possible bands and at least thirty French horn players. But that still wasn't good enough for me. I wanted to be first chair. I have always wanted to be first everything: why bother doing something if you aren't going to win at it? The orchestra was mostly made up of kids almost twice my age, so while it was a proud achievement to be chosen at all, it was also one that would prove extremely alienating. I was a precocious kid for sure, but developing crushes on real sixteen-year-old boys when I was ten or eleven wasn't good for anyone. Kyle Jones was going to ruin me—I couldn't think of anything or anyone else, but he was busy tossing Frisbees and chatting up Leah* and Lucy, the impossibly cool (by music camp standards) blond twins. Leah's Depeche Mode shirt was my first glimpse of a different road. I was intrigued.

In the late 1980s, indie rock was called "alternative," and I was just starting to understand it existed. With the help of Leah and Lucy's many band T-shirts and exploratory trips to the local Sam the Record Man, I became pretty well-versed in the music of The Smiths, REM, The Cure, and all the other '80s stalwarts, so that by the time I started high school I was quickly falling out of my nerdy music camp leanings. I'd even traded in my beloved French horn for singing, which I fell hard for, going so far as to join the church choir. I hated church, but I just wanted another opportunity to sing, even though I was already in the school choir and the all-Scarborough choir. My natural soprano voice lost a lot of its range as I hit my early teens—more like thirteen going on thirty-four—which was fine because, by that point, choir practice had become band practice, because *of course* I joined a band (with a future boyfriend and another pal) where I slapped a tambourine on my hip and tried to make like Bilinda (Butcher, not Belinda Carlisle). The culmination of many Sunday afternoon practices was a show at Lee's Palace, the combination band venue and dance club where I spent most of my teen nights, near Bloor and Bathurst, on the eastern edge of Koreatown. I couldn't hear myself in the monitor and was horribly off-key. It was devastating, though I always knew I wasn't close to talented enough to make it as a musician, in spite of my deep, endless love for music.

A MAGICAL DISCOVERY I MADE AROUND THE TIME I was twelve was my mother's "personal massager," which she kept, possibly hidden, under her bed. I immediately found a much quicker route to bliss than I could achieve with even the most rapid squiggles of my middle finger. It plugged in and had all these attachments, all made of hard rubber, and to twelve-year-old me all unnecessary as they just interfered with the maximum hum of the hard plastic tip. So after learning that the massager wouldn't, in fact, electrocute me, I preferred it bareback. And it was an addiction. The moment everyone was out of the house, I'd run upstairs to my mother's room (my parents slept in separate bedrooms, which I thought was totally weird until I'd been married for ten years, and trust me it's the way to go—we fuck all the time and sleep like babies, sometimes together, sometimes not) and hit it. The orgasms were so quick and forceful, I'd be done in under a minute, and some days I'd try to sneak in as many as possible, just for the challenge.

One regular afternoon, I had a bath and was still in my robe, and, figuring that my mom wouldn't be home for a while, I did what I always did when alone in the house: I made a beeline for the vibrator. I got into position, face down on the towel I laid out on the hard floor of her bedroom, and went to town. When I heard the stair outside creak in the way it only did when it was stepped on, I dismissed it as impossible . . . until I strained my neck to look up and saw my mother's horrified expression in the doorway. As she stood there, everything slowed down and it felt like minutes instead of seconds. I instinctually tossed the vibrator under the bed, but neglected to switch it off.

PRRRRRRRR, it sounded, as it rattled against the hardwood floor.

I waited for my mother to speak first. Because what was there to say?

PRRRRRRRR.

I assume she also didn't really know what to say, because what she eventually came up with was, "Why are you doing that?"

PRRRRRRRR.

I clutched at my robe and wrapped it tighter, a flush pushing up to my cheeks, while my mother just kept standing there, I guess wanting an answer. I thought about it and what would be the quickest way to shut down what was my most awkward conversation to date, and said, "Because it feels—"

PRRRRRRRR.

"—better." This was essentially true.

My mom finally left the room, and after putting the beast back in its box and under the bed, I got the hell out of there. And my mother and I didn't speak about it again.

To this day, I haven't found a battery-operated vibrator that can hold a candle to the awesome power of that plug-in.

This *incident* happened around the time that my mom and I started having a harder and harder time communicating with one another. Everything was a metaphor for everything else: dropping the French horn for singing, learning about music that wasn't from a musical—I was gaining my independence, reaching for it, grabbing at it. I was turning more to my friends for approval and for my sense of identity, the normal path for most western teens, and my mother and I just couldn't seem to agree on anything. For my mom, this would manifest itself in ways that at the time seemed really petty to me, like her saying, "Don't wear that shirt, it's trashy," which only made me want to wear it more. Or, "Don't hang out with that Michelle, she's trashy," which had the same effect. We'd row occasionally, but mostly I just went out of my way to be a bratty, insolent teenage girl so full of angst it made Robert Smith look like the star of the track team, if you took away the gothishness and heavy makeup.

It's not that my parents were particularly oppressive—if anything, they gave me a lot of leeway—but I wanted out.

The bus stop nearest my childhood home was four suburban blocks away—long blocks that were full of life in the same way taxidermy is. The houses, each one more like the last than the next; all so very much the same that you'd need to know your friend's exact address for the first few visits, as there were few clues to guide you to the above-ground pool party. Even the happy splashes and shrieks of punch-drunk preteens were sucked into damp cedar fences and dense cedar hedges. And any of the life brought by pool parties and the like would fade out by 7:00 p.m., as if by dimmer switch garages closed, voices hushed, and blue TV light filled up living rooms and eerily flickered through slits in closed curtains.

It took at least fifteen minutes to walk to the bus loop, even at a quick step. We were actually three blocks east of the place the bus turned around for much of my childhood, yet I'd still do it all the time, no matter how cold or rainy it was. I just wanted to. And then, for the entire year leading up to my sixteenth birthday, all I could talk about was getting my driver's licence, which meant the city would only ever be thirty minutes away. By the time I was sixteen, all I wanted to do was trade in the endless tedium of suburban life in Scarborough for the endless possibilities of downtown Toronto.

The day I took the test I got out of the car, legs still shaking a bit. I had to orient myself as the rows upon rows of station wagons and minivans blurred into each other. The examiner had already moved on to his next appointment after a half-hearted "congratulations" and I squinted into the sun trying to figure out which door my dad had gone in to wait for me. Despite being an avid reader, he'd never read in those circumstances, in the time before cellphones; he'd just sit. After locating the "waiting area," finally I saw the back of his head and ran up to him practically shrieking with excitement, "I passed! I passed it!!"

"That's my girl," he said. He paid the bored-looking teller in cash, and we headed out to the '89 Mercury Sable that I'd nicknamed the "Silver Bullet," because despite it being, without question, a family car, it had pretty good pickup when you gunned it. I tried to get in the passenger side, but my dad stopped me. "Nope. You're driving."

Even though I'd driven tons of times while I was learning I was still really nervous to actually get behind the wheel and take my father home. Something about it now being official made it something to lose, something to fuck up, feelings I'd never had tearing up the dirt roads at the cottage with perfect three-point turns and a total fearlessness of approaching cars. My nerves perked up even more when he told me to take the highway home. I'd driven quick on/offs with my instructor a few times, but merging into traffic still scared the shit out of me, so I protested.

He wouldn't have it. "I taught you to drive, so you'd better know how to merge properly! You've got precious cargo." *Precious cargo.* He'd repeat those two words to me many times over the years.

Despite my shaky nerves, I didn't argue with him. We approached the ramp and I desperately wanted to not veer onto it, to just take Sheppard (the long east-west street just north of highway 401 that bisects Scarborough), but I even more desperately didn't want to disappoint my dad. So I tossed aside my fears, somehow turning them into silly little garbage thoughts it would be embarrassing to heed, and slid onto the highway like a pro. I haven't been afraid to merge since.

A year later, at seventeen, I found myself back at Young People's Theatre, this time not in the audience with my mom but in the set department, as part of a grade 12 work-study program. I absolutely loved all the tools, the smell of sawdust, and making something out of nothing. I had a natural ease with raw materials and within a month was using big equipment like the band and table saws on my own. I loved seeing pieces of wood I'd carefully measured, cut, sanded, and painted become part of the sets that had so thrilled me as a child. I very quickly became a part of the crew family. They didn't treat me like a kid, and it was a blast—plus I got two school credits!

The head set designer was a really cute guy in his late twenties or early thirties who was always nice to me but never paid me any special attention—until the end-of-year company party. I'd borrowed a friend's very flattering dress and strolled into the main room knowing I looked great, and knowing I was still half a year shy of eighteen. He kept close to me all night, passing me spiked punch and sneaky beers. He never crossed any line, but the unspoken flirtation was the first time I started to understand the burgeoning power of my sexuality and the dangers of cute, older men. It didn't feel weird to have him flirt with me; it felt like a reward, like I'd earned his attentions. I know now that is so illustrative of how normal our culture thinks it is to sexualize teenage girls. I'm positive that if he'd tried to kiss me that night I would have been too flattered to reject him. That's fucked up.

To get to YPT, I'd take I'd take a long, complicated public transit journey with lots of waits and transfers by myself (it was a different time), something I'd been doing since I was twelve. Even though I had my driver's licence, I didn't have the use of the family car during the day. It was a long trip, but at least I didn't have to hike to the bus loop any more. I just had to get to the top of my street and wait—and it could be a long wait—for the 36C and a twenty-five-minute ride as it lurched along Ellesmere, stopping every thirty feet. Then I could either transfer to a bus that went right into the RT station at the Scarborough Town Centre—RT stands for Rapid Transit, a misnomer, think monorail from *The Simpsons* but without the crash—or make the ten-minute walk from Ellesmere to McCowan Station. We were still deep in the heart of Scarborough, and the loud, rickety RT ride to the subway at Kennedy was a twenty-minute ordeal, broken up by the incredible graffiti that lined the tracks on both sides. I don't know how much the City paid for a dated, above-ground train that sounded and moved like an unoiled tank, but it was too much. At Kennedy, which in those years was a place to avoid after dark because of especially stabby violence, you'd go down and catch the subway, and twenty-five minutes later you'd be hitting Sherbourne Station, and still have to catch a bus south. All in all it took about ninety minutes. And for me, it was worth every last one.

On half-price Tuesdays, I'd pay $2.50 at the Carlton Cinema to see foreign and independent movies, or I'd walk to Kensington Market, which at the time felt like a crazy maze of streets, though I now know it's really two north-south streets bisected by two east-west, and not at all confusing. There were so many smells wafting around the market: fish, weed, and overripe fruit, mingling with car exhaust and the smell of cement. Decades later, it hasn't really changed. I was so attracted to its vibrancy and the kooky hippie energy, which, as a young teen, struck me as terribly cool. Unfortunately, in existence are pictures of me in long, flowing skirts and overly blousy blouses, a lock of hair wrapped in multicoloured threads (a thing I'd mostly forgotten ever doing), the whole look topped with round, bluish sunglasses—really gilding the lily. I'd spend countless weekend hours walking between the intensely incensed clothing shops, stopping to try on ponchos or stock up on loose blouses and cashmere at Courage My Love, which, minus the ponchos and blouses, is something I still do. If I got hungry I'd zigzag over to Jumbo Empanadas for a pastry stuffed with beef, olives, raisins, and a hardboiled egg, which was so cheap even I could afford it at fifteen. After I'd exhausted myself with all the excitements of those few streets, I'd make my way to catch the Spadina bus at a pace I hoped exuded confidence, despite getting constantly turned around. But I knew once the signs changed from hand-painted and astrologically heavy to brightly lit Chinese letters, I'd fallen out of "the market" and into Chinatown. Which is all I ever wanted to do, to keep falling into the city.

---

* Name changed

4: KID STUFF

THE FIRST TIME I COULD'VE GOTTEN drunk but didn't, I was eleven. We were at Greg Harper's* house playing a make-believe game of *Star Wars*. Greg was a lanky ginger into sci-fi and British comedy and he was mildly funny so he coasted on that. He played the comedian so well that you almost forgot his nerdish leanings. The premise of our game was flimsy: Greg and Alan were Han and Luke, and Kristy was Leia because she had sprouted boobs and was really pretty, which of course meant all the girls whispered about what a slut she was while maintaining phony friendships with her.

There was nothing to suggest at that time that Kristy had ever even kissed a boy, though even if she had, it wouldn't have made our slut-shaming any less awful. The way we interacted as eleven-year-old girls was a good introduction to female group dynamics, and I was definitely not just a casual observer. As an adult, I've noticed these childish patterns on a loop and can still shock myself with how callously dismissive I can be of women—men too, but I tend to be more generous with men's shortcomings. I'm an admittedly bad feminist; I know that I have this horrendous, learned double standard. It's just that I have a strong negative reaction to what I see as a wishy-washy need to please and I find that trait more often in women than in men. I wish I could be more patient, *as a woman is expected to be.* If I allowed myself to clearly and fully remember the awful things I whispered and gleefully took in back then about "Titsy" Edmunds (not our best work—it didn't even rhyme) I know I would be horrified. What I do remember well is the feeling of belonging and the power of gossip: alliances constantly shifting, hopping back and forth between the two most popular girls, the hypocrisy of these relationships a baseline for how women exist in group friendships, especially as children. Two "friends" are always finding comfort in talking shit about their other "friend," who may be prettier, or better dressed, or more popular with the boys, or none of those things. (But a judgment that a girl is "prettier" is often at the heart of it. The patriarchy's culturally agreed-on baseline for prettiness in those days defaulted to skinny-yet-curvy white girls—thank christ that's starting to change.) Kristy's social status was confusing, both relying on and hindered by the power of new breasts, but it didn't matter—she always got to play Leia, and I always got stuck with C-3PO.

After our game ended (once the Death Star had been destroyed, presumably) Greg casually sauntered into the basement with a six-pack of beer, like it was something he did all the time, and my first reaction was, "No! Drinking is bad and we aren't supposed to do it!" My rebellious nature was still a couple years from maturation, but my fight-y nature wasn't, and I argued with and shamed the boys, going so far as to dump at least one lukewarm beer down the toilet. It was Miller High Life, and it was 1987, when Miller High Life was pre-ironic, yet even with its third-banana (behind Pabst and Labatt 50) iconic hipster status just a decade away, the toilet still seems like an appropriate place for it. It got me thinking, though. If Greg and Alan were refusing to speak to me for weeks over this small thing, dumping a beer down the toilet, they must've been pretty mad about it. And if they were so mad, drinking had to be awesome. It was a primitive logic.

As girls of eleven or twelve-ish, we were at the age where our parents could leave us alone for an evening and didn't have to worry about boys rapping on windows with cans of warm beer looking to "be boys"—that was still a couple of years off, despite Greg's early adopting. In grade 7, I would shoot up a fast few inches, becoming very *Skinny Legs and All*, the book by Tom Robbins that I eventually read for its title and loved for its everything. When I see eleven-year-old girls today, sashaying around in crop tops and jean shorts cut so high that I'm discomfited, I wonder if I'm remembering "eleven" wrong. But I think it's a pretty different "not-quite-a-girl-not-quite-a-woman" world now—something about the Internet.

I mean, obviously the unattainable beauty standards for women are rooted in the patriarchy, but now that most western kids can fall through Google's looking glass and have total access to everything, girls are too quickly, within a pack mentality, making themselves into miniature versions of their sexy popstar heroes. I don't want to be all old-man-shakes-fist-at-cloud, but though we still learned our roles—to be the prettiest, the sexiest, yet somehow demure—it just wasn't as fast a slide into clothing as sexual display when I was a kid. We didn't even grasp what was happening, even if, biologically, the approving looks from boys were a jolt we knew we liked. We are raised to compete with other women, but within a societal expectation of "sisterhood"—a challenging paradox that ends up supporting the patriarchal status quo.

Perhaps it was because I intuitively rejected the social cues I was picking up as a girl, but for whatever reason I had more fun playing with boys. They wanted to build forts and climb trees and play Capture the Flag. They were my people—a friendship preference I haven't been able to shake. I've been on a constant search for equality-based female friendship, but it's eluded me, especially as I age and my requirements become ever more specific. Where are the forty-something stepmoms who are fundamentally it-getty and can afford occasional elaborate dinners? Are they at bars? Is there a Tinder for cool stepmoms? Not that I don't have close female friends, but I've always felt more at ease with boy-besties. And yes, I realize how "not like other girls" garbage this sounds.

Dwayne, my first boy-pal, lived at 10 Scarbelle Lane, the cul-de-sac that sprouted off the top of Scarboro Avenue (Scarboro, no "u-g-h"—how many times did I say that as a kid?). We bonded immediately. Not in a crush sort of way—I had no special feelings for him "down there." ("Down there" was something I had discovered at nine or ten thanks to my love of shimmying up and then sliding down the poles that supported the swings in the school playground—a precursor to my mother's as yet undiscovered "shoulder massager.") Dwayne had a ramp for jumping his BMX bike. Either my parents wouldn't buy me a BMX or I decided it veered too strongly into representing myself as *not* a girl (for all my tomboy leanings, I definitely wanted to be the kind of girl that boys liked). But that didn't stop me from racing Dwayne's bike up and down the street and sometimes finding the courage to go up the ramp, though never committing quite enough to really catch any air. One afternoon, I'd gotten up a lot of speed and was screeching toward him when, out of nowhere, he jammed a stick in the front wheel spokes. I flew over the handlebars and scraped myself up pretty badly. I was so upset and shocked, I grabbed my non-BMX bike, which I'd lazily dropped on Dwayne's lawn, and limped home so he wouldn't see me cry. I was so embarrassed and pissed off. Was this what boys did to each other? Stood there while you hobbled off muffling your tears? Laughed at skinned knees with little stones and pits of asphalt buried so deep it would take my mother hours to clean?

This was a first peek into a lifelong struggle with my joy at the company of men and my occasional wish for just a little more compassion (a quality so often attributed to women) from them. This is partly why I'm so happy to see gender lines starting to blur: for starters, women not being afraid of their confidence or assertiveness, and men embracing, well, other men in a non-sexual way. Men are trained not to cry. Women are trained not to demand things. These are ridiculous standards. I hardly ever cry, and I am constantly demanding things, yet I still catch myself falling prey to a standard societal expectation of what it means to "be a man." I am always trying to upend gender roles, even deeply ingrained ones, like the ludicrous idea that "having balls" means being tough. To paraphrase comedian Sheng Wang (who apparently came up with this despite the Internet insisting it was Betty White, much to her chagrin): "It makes no sense. Balls are delicate little sacks that can't take a hit. But vaginas? Vaginas can take a pounding."

Eventually Dwayne apologized, after, I suspect, his mother made him, but it was never the same between us. I didn't trust him any more and I just stopped going around to his house and his BMX ramp. Two years later, by the time we were taking the bus to different high schools, it was like we'd never met.

That awful bike spill was around the time I started crushing on Greg—*Star Wars*, beer-toting Greg—who somehow, between grades 7 and 8, became (to me) the most handsome thing ever, even more handsome than crowd favourites Rob and Julius. But Greg liked Christine (they all liked Christine), a cute-as-a-button fashionista (seriously, this kid knew what was up) who was the unofficial group leader at school, and was constantly rich with choice re: boys to like. Mine was an awful, all-consuming crush—a theme for crushes all my life. I'd find any excuse to be around him, and his likes were suddenly my likes. We did legitimately have one thing in common, though: *Inspector Gadget*. Despite the torture of not having my feelings for him reciprocated, I was grateful to have someone to discuss that morning's episode with. There was no fake-liking the brilliance of Penny always cleaning up after the bungling Inspector. I thought it was gold, and I'd wake up extra early to eat breakfast before it was on, because there was no eating in front of the TV in my house—ever. For some reason my parents never counted this morning cartoon indulgence against my half hour of evening television (an hour on Sundays).

Every morning my dad would make orange juice from frozen concentrate, and every morning I'd want to drink it right away, before all the ice crystals had melted. He'd butter toast, slice grapefruit, and my mom would stir up some instant oatmeal, while my much younger brother, Jonathan, would ride around the kitchen on a plastic cow on wheels with an air pump that made it moo—the only place in the house, aside from the bathroom, that wasn't carpeted—getting underfoot. If I could manage to scarf all that breakfast down, only then could I watch *Inspector Gadget*.

My parents' parenting of me always felt like a combination of the tight grip of paranoia and an irresistible urge to just let me do as I pleased, so they seemed incredibly grateful my brother was so much less defiant. Although, once I cut off the air pump on that awful cow in a fit of annoyance, with the intention of rendering it silent forever, he figured out he could just blow into the hole to make it moo, so that was pretty defiant.

I VERY CLEARLY REMEMBER THE FIRST TIME I did get drunk, at thirteen, just as the school year was kicking off my final year before high school, as trees were turning from bright green to deep gold and red, a visual ode to Boy George and Jamaican flags. We'd planned the night for weeks, knowing that eventually my parents would be out some Friday night to attend the ballet or the symphony. That night finally came, and I huddled in the living room with my three closest friends, Kathleen, Christine, and Caroline. My parents didn't even ask why we seemed giddier than usual, though I doubt they even noticed—the four of us together always ended up in fits of giggles and whispers.

The moment we heard the garage door shut behind my parents, we raced to the liquor cabinet, which was, because of the lack of reverence my parents had for liquor, more like an ordinary cupboard beside the fridge than a cabinet. (Naturally, I'd prefer a more dedicated display if I were to keep liquor in the house. I don't—with three spots all with great cocktails mere steps away, there's simply no need.) My parents didn't drink much while I was growing up, although I eventually learned my dad kept a bottle of sherry in his desk drawer, which sparked in me a lifelong love of the stuff. I imagine he'd sit there punching numbers into his adding machine—a pre-computer, large-scale calculator whose gears you could hear grinding away even from the kitchen, a floor away—and sipping sherry, just a little bit.

I dragged a plush chair from the kitchen table to reach the cupboard. Everything inside looked weird and foreign, and as I gingerly pulled out bottles and passed them down, anticipation grew. I hopped off the chair and we struggled to open the stuck-on caps. Eventually, through sheer force of will, we twisted them off, immediately noticing that what was inside the bottles smelled even more foreign than they looked. Up until that point, while I'd had a thousand sips of my dad's beer foam, I'd never smelled anything like gin. I put it to my nose, and was almost immediately knocked back by its aggressive astringency. It smelled like something I imagined would be better suited for polishing silverware than sipping in cocktails. At thirteen I couldn't imagine why anyone would ever want to drink something that smelled like it would tear a hole in your gut. Now, of course, I can't imagine a more mundane life than one without gin-and-tonics.

After sniffing a few of the spirits and not really knowing the differences between them—they all smelled like they'd kill you—we narrowed it down to the options with "chocolate" or "fruit" on the labels, eventually settling on crème de menthe and some Swiss chocolate almond liqueur. Both smelled sweet and delicious, so I bravely sipped them. But the flavours were distracting to my mouth, the tweaks of alcohol *off*. Still, that didn't stop me—or Kathleen, Christine, and Caroline—from gulping directly from the bottles. In that moment, we were convinced that if we used glasses my parents would know we'd been using them for liquor. It never occurred to us that we could wash and put them away before my mother and father got home.

We passed the bottles around for a while, getting louder and more giggly as the night went on. On first pass we couldn't have had much more than the equivalent of one proper adult drink. But man, either we were wasted, or we just believed we should be *so hard* that we became so. We spent the evening stair-diving—a not entirely smart thing to do sober, let alone drunk, but then we weren't entirely smart. We scurried to the top of a carpeted stairwell (which, at that time, in the suburbs, meant any staircase) and I positioned myself, banana-style—an arched missile perched on the top step—legs flailing behind with my pals gamely holding on to them. I was face first, splayed out on a pathetic-looking towel I'd plucked from the linen closet, posi-tive that if I used a fluffy white one my mother, a woman with "display" tea towels, would surely know what we'd been up to. We counted down—"Three! Two! One! Geronimo!"—they released my legs, and I zoomed down the stairs at lightning speed, somehow not chipping a tooth. Screaming with laugh-ter, we took turns, and as experience and liqueur emboldened us, simply releasing legs was exaggerated to the point of actively shoving each other down the fourteen steps, rewarding our survival with sips of crème de menthe between rounds.

We drank enough sickly sweet liqueur that, in conjunction with the stair-diving, it was all just too much for my stomach, and at some point during the night it rejected its contents. Somehow I managed to puke into my metal garbage can in the middle of the night and sneak it to the toilet in the morning without my mom noticing anything was amiss. And no one else was busted—everyone's parents had picked up their daughters around 10:30 and either didn't smell the booze or didn't bring it up. The perfect crime.

After that night I don't think I touched alcohol much until high school. I went to a huge school with a great academic program, which is why my mother insisted I go there instead of the high school my elementary school streamed into, and where all of my friends, except for Greg, were going. Like me, he was going to Woburn Collegiate, a 2,000-student school a bus ride away from my house, and while I was excited that we'd be going to the same school, once we arrived there, I realized that something had happened—rather, something *hadn't* happened to him—during that strange summer full of paralyzing fears of the unknown between primary and high school. By the time I noticed what hadn't happened to Greg, our lockers were in the same corridor and I towered over him, skinny legs and all. Surrounded by new boys, most of them tall and unknown, Miller High Life–drinking Greg Harper no longer had my attention.

---

* Name changed

NO IDEA WHY WE USE PUSSY AS SLANG FOR WEAK; BALLS ARE WEAK.

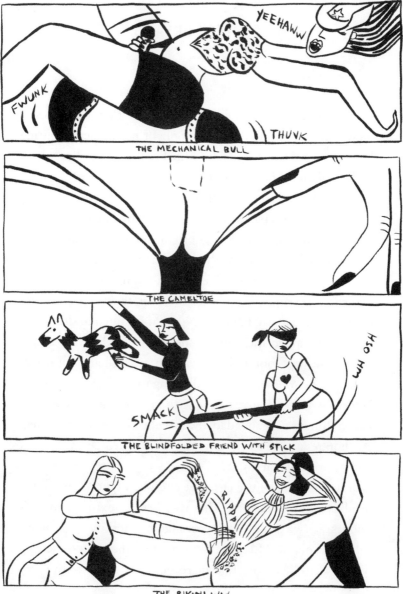

5: TEEN DREAMS

ONE OF THE FIRST PEOPLE I bonded with that first semester at Woburn Collegiate, by virtue only of having neighbouring lockers, was Dee-Dee, a girl who lived near me but who I hadn't met until high school. She stood out—always wearing those baby-doll dresses that were so particular to the early 1990s, and always paired with Doc Martens. She wore red lipstick every day of grade 9; it got to the point where she almost didn't look like herself without it. She was into smoking as religion and drew attention from all walks of boy—from nerds to jocks and everything in between, they all had crushes on her. And in a way, I did too. Not that I wanted to sleep with her, but I wanted the options she seemed to have for everything. She was cool and pretty in that long-hair, upturned-nose way I envied, as it was still going to be a few more years before my face would catch up with my prominent nose—my proud Roman nose, my dad always called it, no doubt to help ameliorate my insecurity. In grade 9, I was acutely aware of it and its presence on my face.

It wasn't long before Dee-Dee and I had synced our morning bus rides to school. This was before texting and cellphones, so we'd have to prearrange by landline—or, as we called it, "phone." Eventually we got into the habit of getting on the 8:10 35C, the Ellesmere bus that came only every thirty minutes. If you missed it, you were guaranteed to be late to wherever you needed to be. Our stops were just two apart from one another, with mine first, and as the bus pulled up to hers I'd see Dee-Dee stub out her smoke and carefully place it back in the pack, a necessary economy that kept her smelling like a dock worker, which she countered with Exclamation!, a sweet and almost putrid perfume readily available at Shoppers Drug Marts everywhere. We began spending all of our time together, and on weekends we'd go to the mall to line our pockets with nicked lipsticks. This eventually greatly displeased my mother, as, sometime in late grade 9, she had to come and pick me up from that fluorescent-lit, shitty, too-small room that exists in the back corner of drug stores everywhere where aggressive mouth-breathers just into their twenties play out all their "why wouldn't you date me?" revenge fantasies on the cool girls who pocket Bonne Bell lipsticks, with the express goal of drawing tears. I refused to oblige him, instead smirking my way through his rage blackout . . . I know, I know, I was in the wrong, but he was just such a dick, and to give proper respect to his bullying tactics, I never stole anything ever again, although I suppose the long speech my mom gave me that night didn't hurt either.

Sometimes Dee-Dee and I would head downtown to wander around the second-hand clothing stores of Kensington Market. I'd walk over to Dee-Dee's house, right across the street from the bus stop, and we'd wait for the bus together. If it was evening, she and I would always share whatever gruesome concoction we'd lifted from our parents' booze bottles and mixed up, singing Depeche Mode songs a cappella and picking up the half-cigarettes strangers discarded as they got on the bus, figuring those "gifts" made it worth waiting for the next bus, and feeling sufficiently warmed by booze that time ceased to show its usual face.

When I met Dee-Dee, I quickly decided that she and I should be best friends, hoping, I'm sure, that since boys crushed on her, perhaps their less-handsome best friends would maybe want to make out with me. I never exposed my nervousness around guys; I wouldn't dare let them see me stumble. It was easier to just crack sarcastic jokes and keep it stone-faced, so if they weren't into me I didn't have to assume it was because I wasn't pretty enough. Dee was different. She had an easy laugh and a natural coolness that, along with her looks, made her an appealing prize.

It was hard to understand, given her plethora of options, how or why she ended up dating the rodentious Chris Barker, to whom I took an instant and reciprocated dislike. He was objectively unhandsome, too skinny by half, with a slick of stringy, pale-red hair and an always askew baseball cap. His darting, nervous eyes were jammed too far into his head, but he had a car, and he carried himself with the air of a mid-level drug dealer instead of the low-level one he actually was. It was mostly his tough-guy attitude and stupidity that put me off, but also that he was suddenly around all the time, interrupting my friendship with Dee-Dee. And she blithely let it happen, suddenly, and for the first time in our friendship, not considering my needs for her attention. It was all Chris, all the time, and there was no room for me. He quickly sniffed out my disdain toward him and used his position as my best friend's boyfriend to make me feel pushed aside. Fortunately, his relationship with Dee-Dee was short-lived, and so was my jealousy, which I had conveniently wrapped up in a package of "he's just not good enough for Dee" rather than fully acknowledging my petty feelings.

Eventually Dee upgraded to Justin White*, a pro-trench-coat, handsome loner, who, by the powerful force of sibling nepotism bestowed upon him by an older brother, was connected to what I deemed to be the coolest, hottest boys in school. They were all a bit older than us, and even now when I think of them I imagine that they've maintained a youthful, handsome cool untainted by doughy alcoholic faces or the adoption of the conservative lives we railed against as teenagers. I had my favourites in this group, and over the years I either fucked or dated a handful of them, but in that first year of high school I was content just to be pulled, by my connection to Dee-Dee, into their world, which from the outside epitomized alternative cool. They listened to shit I'd never heard of like PiL and Joy Division, Stereolab and My Bloody Valentine. They read books like *A Prayer for Owen Meany* (which I still reread often and maintain is an incredibly well-crafted novel full of out-loud laughs) and *The Unbearable Lightness of Being*. But they weren't nerds; they all had slightly different styles, and all seemed to understand intrinsically how to maximize their natural handsomeness through hair and clothing. They really were a sight, the six or seven of them roaming the halls, splintering off into classes or the caf on a spare. It cemented an idea of male coolness in me from which I've never really recovered, and which was far more appealing than fitting into the constricting shell of female coolness that was too connected to beauty standards. I wanted to be them and I wanted to fuck them.

My parents loved to blame Dee for all my new sins—"You never would have started smoking if you hadn't met that Dee-Dee." It was always "that Dee-Dee." But Dee was just an easy target because she smoked and drank and didn't take school all that seriously. It was easier for my parents to assume Dee-Dee was a bad influence than accept that maybe I had some of these negative traits myself, but the truth is, I was looking for a "Dee-Dee," and if it hadn't been her it would have been someone else. It's even possible I was just as bad an influence on her as my parents believed she was on me.

Looking back, I'm not sure my smoking had anything to do with my new friend—at that time, it seemed like a shortcut to cool, and all the boys I liked were doing it. It was also just a hop, skip, and a jump to hiding beers in the valley behind the school. After last bell Dee and I would slurp them back, pretending that the piss-warm canned ale actually tasted good. Then, buzzed, we'd stumble along Ellesmere, fucking around (sometimes Dee-Dee would literally stop to fuck Justin behind a concrete hydro pole while I waited around), smoking, and eventually catching the bus to be home in time for "I just finished play rehearsal" to still sound like a reasonable excuse. I'd quickly streak into the house with claims of "needing to pee," which would always be met with "you mean use the washroom." At that age, I was smoking so much I couldn't smell the stench of Marlboros that clung to my hair and clothes, and I actually believed that a good hand-scrubbing would remove it. My parents would ask me why I reeked of cigarettes, and I'd just say, "I was with Dee-Dee," effortlessly tossing her under the bus without a second thought, but then naively wondering why my mother and father didn't like her. I'm certain this was a game Dee played with her own mother, blaming me whenever possible and helpful to her excuses.

School was aggressively boring, so by the time grade 10 came around, Dee and I had let our after-school beers bleed into day-drinking. We started by expanding on our nighttime habit of skimming from our parents' liquor cabinets and topping up the bottles with water, then mixing up a muddy "cocktail" that would slosh around in used pop bottles in our backpacks through our morning classes—if we hadn't already indulged on the bus ride to school. The taste was unpleasant, but it did the trick. Eventually, when we had drowned all of the liquors, we would head to the liquor store, conveniently located just off school grounds, for a mickey of peach schnapps (obviously) at lunchtime, which in those days was almost too easy a purchase for teens to make. We were always bumming cigs and money for booze, with zero shame about it. It got to the point that the nerds we'd regularly hit up would start ducking into classrooms when they saw us coming. These were the loner dudes from the Gifted program who lacked the social skills to fit into friend groups. We otherwise wouldn't talk to them, but I think they honestly thought at first they might have a shot with Dee, and they allowed us to use them as funding for our illicit liquid lunches far too long.

Back then, the laws were much laxer than they are today; legal age in Ontario was nineteen, but we could usually buy booze even without fake IDs. Once, at sixteen, my short-shorts and I walked out of a beer store with a *keg*. And the guys working there were so unconcerned with all the clues pointing to me obviously being underage that they even helped me put it in a *cab*. Never underestimate the power of short-shorts; we might as well game the system anywhere we can. God, I'm a terrible feminist.

Scarborough is rife with forests, valleys, bluffs, and hydro fields—all ideal places to gather lots of lit-up children—and our fun-of-choice for most of high school involved hanging around campfires. This activity, we quickly learned, also worked as an easy, believable answer for nosy parents who were wondering why we reeked of smoke—although I find it hard to fathom now that they fully bought that we were just sitting around a campfire, holding hands and singing songs. I don't remember how the blazes got started, but without exception they were extinguished the same way every time: by the piss of several teenage boys.

My favourite outdoor party "aperitif" during this time was a neon-purple, spiked grape soda called Barbarian, which was available only in big plastic bottles, like they *knew* it was going to a park in a backpack. Its alcohol content hovered just below 7 percent, but it was clearly designed to appeal to kids. It didn't stay on the market long, but while it did . . . I drank all of it.

I was never smart about drinking as a kid. It was always too easy for me to sneak out of the house hung with cigarettes, weed, and booze, like a hobo Christmas tree. Consequently, I made many ill-considered choices around liquor: like the time I downed a twenty-sixer of vodka on someone's front lawn, all in one go, before going in to the party and promptly falling over. I had to call my mom to pick me up, and on the way home she had to pull the car over every three blocks so I could throw up on the side of the road. But to her credit, she was genuinely glad I'd called her since that was what I was supposed to do if I got in a bad situation, and the bottom of a bottle of vodka surely qualified. This perhaps explains my lifelong (adult) lack of interest in vodka, to the point that I wrote an essay in 2010 titled "Vodka is Stupid," which did NOT endear me to the Slavic peoples of the restaurant industry.

There was also the time I made it to the end of Century Club, the only girl in our group to finish. I was so proud, and somehow I managed to not throw up, undoubtedly to my liver's detriment. Century Club, as the name implies, involves a one-ounce shot of beer every minute, for one hundred minutes. When you do the math, it's more than eight beers. In an hour and a half. It is fully ridiculous and probably irreparably damages your brain, and for sure kids have died, or at least have ended up in the hospital, trying to "win" at it.

Drinking was always a race, always a competition, and I wanted to win at everything, including getting drunk first. How incredibly counterproductive. I'd put back most of a bottle of Barbarian in a ridiculously short amount of time and, before you knew it, some momentarily *lucky* guy would be getting a sloppy blow job, very quickly followed up by a lapful of violet puke.

But back then, those sloppy blow jobs and make-out sessions, if not the most romantic, were formative, and woke up a frightening sexuality, which expanded in me like a universe as my experience grew. My first kiss, on the other hand, had been an incredibly anticlimactic moment after junior prom. I was on a date with a guy from music class who I really liked, but the kiss was super-boring, and I found out the next day it had all been a ploy to make his ex-girlfriend jealous.

The only reason I was bummed it hadn't worked out was because of how desperately I wanted to lose my virginity. I never thought of it as some precious gift I should "give" to the right guy; it was a burden to me, chains I wanted unlocked, and that finally happened on a trip to New Orleans when I was sixteen. Four girls and I drove down in a Honda Civic, and as my black friend Tracey got stared at, at diner after diner and for no other obvious reason than because she was with four white girls, I quickly received an education on America's overt racism. I found it appalling and confusing, while Tracey appeared to take it all in practised stride.

Other than the racism, New Orleans was a fun trip. I spent hours at Preservation Hall soaking up jazz and found a nearby bar for chugging cheap beer (when I wasn't knocking over full pitchers). I was mostly by myself since pretty much all I wanted to do was listen to live jazz, and my friends wanted to do other stuff, stuff I thought was less fun. It was there that a handsome dude with stringy blond hair caught my eye, and I decided he would do. We ended up making out on the sidewalk in front of our hotel, and as they stepped over us, my friends all tried to get my attention. At sixteen, I was the baby. They were all eighteen, and I guess, through the out-of-focus lens of Hurricane Slushies, they felt some sort of responsibility for me. But I just ignored them and jumped in a cab with what's-his-name.

I have no idea how old this guy was, but he was easily well into his twenties. I told him I was a virgin, and I thought he'd find that appealing, but I saw concern flash across his face. He quickly got over it, though, and in about as unromantic a turn as possible, we did it in the bathroom of his hotel room as his roommate slept in the bedroom. Even as he gave me cab fare to get back to my hotel across town, I felt nothing of the shame I knew I was probably supposed to feel. In fact, I was fucking elated to have it over with, and with gleeful joy spilled out the details to my friends over coffee the next morning, while they looked at me quizzically, wondering why I was so happy about something they clearly thought was so obviously seedy. I didn't see it as seedy, even then, and I hated that they were trying to impose on me the patriarchal structures I didn't even realize I was desperately trying to escape. They definitely judged me, and I felt judged, but I rejected it and spent the rest of the trip trying to shake it off while at the same time wondering if they were right or not. Eventually I chose to just forget about it, and eventually I grew out of those friendships.

I can't stand how vilified teenage girls and women are for their sexuality, while boys and men can fall dick-first into hands, mouths, vaginas, and assholes at a dizzying pace, never having to justify their libidos or their strong will to toss away their virginity. This double standard gurgles its first bubbles in our youth, but the lessons we learn stay with us, and even the best feminists occasionally have to check language and think-ing, remembering not to brand women "sluts" for enjoying sex. Sex is fucking awesome.

In spite of my lack of attachment to my virginity and my eagerness to lose it, my self-esteem as a teenager was tied in macramé knots over what boys thought of me. Which, given my gangliness and penchant for snark, wasn't much. This probably explains why I repeatedly slept with Dee-Dee's boy-friend. It started over vodka and cigarettes and late-night swims. Dee's mom was stricter than my parents, and I had access to a car and could get away with coming home after 10:00 on a school night, so I'd often hang out at Justin's place, watching TV, smoking on the porch, and dipping into the pool, all the while hoping to run into his older brother Charlie, on whom my crush was devastating. But when Justin drunk-enly made a pass one night—seemingly out of the blue and because he was a pretty shitty boyfriend—my insecurity did a happy jig and accepted, with open arms and legs, and we began a bumpy affair. ("Affair" may be too elegant a word for what were mostly just occasional drunken romps on the Whites' basement couch. What that couch has seen.) I never wanted to be Justin's girlfriend, but I really took pleasure in the secret dalliance—a hard thing to admit, given what an awful thing it was to do to Dee. But the morality of friendship didn't stop me, and certainly my own sense of right and wrong wasn't going to—after all, it had long been culturally ingrained in me to befriend girls intimately while competing with them viciously. At the time I had no idea I was doing something that so fully reflected the contradictions of a patriarchal structure and supported the idea that male attention trumped female friendship. But I can't philosophize my actions away; it was a shitty thing to do, and I felt terrible about it, but I just couldn't stop myself. The attention was too validating. Of course, it wasn't to last forever.

Sometime eight or nine months in, I was waiting for the bus and Justin drove by, saw me, and stopped. He didn't even get out of the car, just rolled down the window, and said, "I told her. She knows." I asked him why he would do something so stupid. We hadn't even fucked in weeks. He offered no good explanation other than that he felt guilty and wanted to make it work with her, which I have always thought of as the coward's way out. If the cheater feels guilty and wants to make it work, eat that guilt. Hold on to it and take its pain. What good are you doing by telling the truth in this scenario? Just stop cheating and spare your partner the pain of knowing you repeatedly acted like an asshole.

I also, of course, had a vested interest in Dee never knowing the truth: I still wanted to be friends with her, despite what a lousy friend I'd been. My need for Justin's sexual attention just outweighed my loyalty to her, even though I believed I genuinely loved her and knew I genuinely did not love Justin.

As soon as he said that he had told her, my stomach dropped and I panicked, but of course, in 1993 I couldn't text or call Dee to blubber apologies, so I'd just have to see her at school the next day, which was one of the most terrifying moments of my young life. I was gearing up for a really unpleasant showdown in the hallway where our lockers stood side by side, but it was worse than a big, yelly fight, so much worse. I caught a glimpse of Dee in my locker mirror and decided to just keep loading up my books instead of scurrying off. I figured that we'd have to see each other eventually, so I might as well get it over with. But Dee didn't even look at me. It was like I didn't exist. I begged her to talk to me but she stared past me until I gave up. She just shut me out, forever, and I never really forgave myself for what I'd done. Somehow, I guess due to her embarrassment at having been cheated on, it never really got out, so although it ruined our friendship, it didn't shatter outward and make my life hell, like it could have. Naturally, she forgave Justin. I think they might still be together.

Occasionally, before the cheating spilled out and affected the dynamic, our group—helmed by Dee and Justin, with occasional guest visits from our friend Liza and Justin's older brother Hot Charlie—would make the genius decision to go to a bar for lunch. We'd run over to one of the nearby spots, have a Long Island Iced Tea or two, balanced with a basket of curly fries and a 5 percent tip, and be back at school in time for "Mod West" (Modern Western Civilization), which was made even more interesting with the haze of booze still glowing through us. It wasn't long before the Kelsey's and the other nearby spots caught on to our shitty tip game and one by one started carding us, obviously aware we were just some high school kids. If we'd had the foresight to tip a little better, they probably would've kept serving us, but foresight wasn't our strong suit. As a group we held this righteous feeling of entitlement that somehow led us to think our behaviour in these bars and restaurants—the poor tipping and lack of respect—was perfectly fine. Now that same feeling is locked away in a shame box, buried in my memories of a distant, teenage self.

Dee and Justin always had a car (equal parts great and awful, for obvious reasons—driving a car is good, but driving a car drunk is bad), and the first time four or five of us rolled into Hurricane's on Ellesmere was also the last. This lunch hour is etched in my memory as my first real "bar" experience. The place smelled like old fryer oil—at the time I just chalked it up to "dive-bar smell." Despite the fact that we were wearing backpacks full of binders and were clearly underage, the waitress at Hurricane's decided to serve us. This would prove to be a poor choice. She was probably only in her forties, but my memory has twisted her into a grey-haired, gum-snapping waitress, the kind characters in David Lynch movies who call you "honey" are based on.

I picked up the tent card on our table and pored over all the old-timey-sounding cocktails like "Martini," "Rusty Nail," and "Manhattan." I rolled the names around in my head, really mulling them over, because I had no idea what the ingredients tasted like. At the time, Molson Special Dry was our beer of choice, mainly because it was stronger than most beers and had the word "special" in it. But that day, I was determined to have a cocktail. "Manhattan. That sounds so sophisticated. I am sophisticated, so that's what I should drink. Everyone else can have their pitcher of beer," might have been my thought process, but it's more likely that the word "sweet" is what grabbed my attention, even if I had no clue what vermouth was. As I ordered it with feigned confidence, I had no idea what to expect in this cocktail, although I have to assume that even if it had been the most expertly prepared Manhattan of ALL TIME (it wasn't, it was a tepid, intolerably strong mess), I still would not, at the edge of fifteen, have appreciated it. So, naturally, I decided to shoot it. It tasted terrible, but I felt its calming, blurring effects immediately. Liquor really is quicker.

After everyone finished their pints and the curly fries had been gobbled up, we went out for a cigarette. As I began lighting one outside the doors of Hurricane's, Justin and Charlie headed for the car instead, and it took me a second to figure out that we were skipping the bill and I had better move it if I didn't want to get left behind.

Kids are just the worst.

IN 1993, WHEN I WAS SIXTEEN, full of attitude and beer and bummed cigarettes, I decided the basement room I'd hung my Doors posters and Klimt prints in just didn't give me the late-night in-and-out privileges I felt I deserved, so I cut the window screen out with a box-cutter without a second thought, for ease of both getting out and letting in after my parents had gone to bed. It stayed like that for many years, unbeknownst to my parents, who were pissed when they discovered it sometime in my mid-twenties.

And when that wide-open window wasn't enough, I came to the crazy conclusion that I'd simply have to move out. Through friends, I found a shoebox-sized room, on Citadel Drive, in a pretty sweet house shared with three other girls (two of whom had been on the New Orleans trip), all two years my senior. The place was much closer to downtown Toronto but still firmly, doubtlessly Scarborough. I paid for it with student welfare because, frankly, it never even occurred to me to get a job; I could barely get to school each day. And my schedule at Alternative Scarborough Education, my grade 11 school of choice, wasn't exactly taxing. I mostly showed up just to smoke and pretend to work on the week's assignments. It was the kind of place where teachers were "Tom" and "Vicky" instead of "Mr. Bradley" and "Miss Du Maurier." Though I loved it, I still managed to get kicked out (the freedom offered was too much for me and I wouldn't show up for my tests), and for grade 12 I was booted back to the regular school, full of the regular people. I've never hidden well my youthful, ridiculous disdain for the *regular*; looking back, it seems unlikely that I would have bothered trying.

As I settled into my new home—my first priority was "decorating" my room, i.e. covering the drawers of the provided dresser with Budweiser labels and cut-up packs of Marlboro Reds (which, looking back, it horrifies me to admit, is way more "frat boy's first bedroom" than the rebellious design choice teen-me believed it to be)—it suddenly became abundantly clear that takeout pizza was to be a once-a-week luxury at best. I realized that I was going to have to figure out how to feed myself. Like, every day.

My parents were absolutely dreadful cooks. My dad's go-to was a rectangular block of frozen cod, which somehow retained its shape even after an hour in the toaster oven, its creamy sauce of whatever-was-around soup slowly absorbed into the fish block, bloating it. My mom didn't fare much better; her specialty was overcooked everything. Because their food offerings were so bland, I had a strong motivation when I was growing up to figure out the basics so that I could cook the family meal a few nights each week for fun-slash-relief. But now, living on my own, I had no choice. I already knew how to bake well and had started figuring out simple things, like from-scratch mac and cheese and hummus with baked pita chips, and I understood how to cook vegetables, thanks to a vegetarian boy I dated. My favourite thing to whip up in the kitchen of 123 Citadel was ground beef stir-fried with green peppers and onions, sided with mashed potatoes, with all ingredients bought at the local No Frills, so not of the highest quality. I could, and probably did, eat this dish most days. Another go-to meal was packaged "meat" tortellini with a yogurt sauce, a taste I can still call to mind, the sharpness of shaved, raw garlic mellowed by full-fat yogurt and a musty hit of paprika, a squeeze of bright lemon bringing it all together. It tasted like real food at the time, even if you couldn't pay me to eat store-bought filled pasta now.

I never worried much about breakfast, a terrible habit that has stuck with me; I have to force myself to choke down a protein fruit smoothie—hardly even food—in the morning, or I wouldn't eat until deep afternoon. Back then, lunch was usually Harvey's, where I'd bite out a wee hole in every onion ring and fill it with malt vinegar (equal parts delicious and disgusting, but even today my mouth waters at the memory), or free chips and salsa at the Chi-Chi's with purchased, and endless, Cokes, all paid for in quarters.

I will never be as fearless about anything in my life as I was about drugs as a teen. I'm sure it wasn't as bad as my fuzzy memories suggest, but there were definitely occasional week-day acid parties. I knew enough to never touch heroin, but I'm terrifically grateful it wasn't part of our scene. If Charlie, Justin's older brother who had probably never cared about the whole mess with Dee, and with whom I'd insisted on growing closer to as Justin and Dee-Dee drifted away, had wanted me to try it, it would have been a huge challenge to say no. Charlie had a frightening power over me, a power driven by my extreme attraction to him and his extreme abuse of that. He loomed over our group (now defined less by my former friendship with Dee-Dee and more by my own late–high school attachments to the boys in this group, through being in a band, and hanging out all the time) with swaggering confidence, even if his performance was liberally borrowed from a ridiculous mash-up of Charles Bukowski and a *Heathers*-era Christian Slater—a terrible Jekyll/Hyde with no obvious Jekyll. His shtick worked because he was a master of the one-on-one. Sitting on his porch, strumming guitars and humming along; smoking cigarettes in between episodes of *Roseanne*—he made me feel like I was special, because when he was with just me, and only me, he was *different*, a kinder version of his other self. He'd crinkle up both eyes like a double wink in an adorable way, and at a party, he could, with a glance, make me feel like we were in the room alone together. It was a practised, studied manipulation that I jealously watched him work on too many girls to count, almost all of them waitresses.

His parents were those "cool" parents who didn't care if you smoked, as long as you used the ashtray. His mom was into reiki and shiatsu before those were even things. They had a pool and a sauna and had basically built a home designed to appeal to teens. And who knows why, but despite having what some might call a dream childhood, Charlie just wasn't a very nice dude.

Once, after too many jello shots, I lay slumped over the bar in the basement of 123 Citadel, passed out. (Yes, somehow I'd moved into a house with a 1970s-style "wet bar" in the basement.) Charlie casually leaned over and ashed his cigarette on my hair, which I was able to see but unable to comment on, given my state. The other boys only stopped him after he dripped lighter fluid near my face and continued tapping his cigarette, enjoying his little bit of power like a kid with a magnifying glass and a trail of ants on a sunny day. Another time he tied me up with a vacuum-cleaner cord and left me in a closet for what felt like hours, but was maybe thirty minutes. He was "just joking." I was terrified and humiliated. Yet still, I adored him. It took years of his stepping too far over the line and then comforting me with drunken kisses and *permitting* me the occasional blow job for me to understand that I was allowing this abuse to happen and that only I could stop it. And he wasn't even my boyfriend, just some shitty, handsome sociopath who held the gaze of a group of kids. That experience really helped me to understand how easily women go back to abusive men, how difficult it can be to see what a monster someone really is, especially through the gauzy lens of "love." At the time, not one of my girlfriends laid any blame on Charlie; they all seemed to think anything that happened to me was my fault for tolerating his shitty behaviour. Given how we as a society react to women who come forward about abusive men, it seems little has changed in twenty years.

I made it a year at the house on Citadel before the weekday parties stopped being fun and it all just felt like a sad place full of last night's smoke and used condoms. When

I finally realized how good I'd had it with my parents, I moved back home. They were happy to have me back, though god knows why, I was endlessly selfish. They didn't really ask me too many questions and pretty much let me come and go as I pleased, on the one condition that I get a job the following summer.

* Name changed

Vodka is Stupid

The problem with vodka is that it's dumb. As a restaurateur, I'd love to not even offer it at all, especially since at The Black Hoof not serving the world's most popular spirit would certainly go along with the theme of doing things a little bit differently. But offer it, I do, although usually with a diatribe attached or a gentle nudge toward the much more interesting gin. Unfortunately, most people don't like diatribes implying that their drink of choice is dumb. It makes them feel like I'm saying they're dumb. And since my job is without a doubt in customer service I stock the affordable and perfectly acceptable Canadian Iceberg. For what it lacks in snazzy marketing and bottle design, it makes up for in tasting . . . like nothing.

That is the goal of vodka: to taste like nothing. And that is why it is dumb.

We've been assaulted by the marketing of high-end brands like Belvedere and Grey Goose into believing they are items of luxury. But they are only luxury items because they are expensive. Very expensive. Companies like Grey Goose need to justify that expense, and here's how they do it:

"Grey Goose vodka is crafted from the finest French wheat, with water naturally filtered over champagne limestone and carefully distilled according to the uncompromising traditions of France's Cognac region. Each batch is made to the exacting standards of François Thibault, Maître De Chai, ensuring its distinct freshness, clarity and unparalleled smoothness. Unlike any other vodka in the world."

Ouch. First of all, who is François Thibault? Well, his official title is "Maître de Chai," which means cellar master and is usually associated with the ageing of wine. Now this all seems a little suspect considering vodka isn't aged. Seems he's more in charge of "making things fancy by having a fancy title," but that doesn't have the same ring to it. And how does anything in the process, other than the words "natural," "traditions," and "standards," justify a $40 price tag? It simply doesn't.

It's outrageous to charge $40 for a bottle of plain spirit that has not been given any flavour or character by the addition of herbs and spices, like gin, or aged in oak barrels for complexity and softness, like scotch. Vodka's only claim to fame is that it tastes like LESS of something. I mean, really, that's what the brand marketing is trying to tell you. The less flavour the product has, the better it is. And smooth? That's usually just glycerin, a harmless additive used to give some liquors a fuller, smoother mouth feel.

Vodka is made with vegetables or grains, distilled, diluted with water, and bottled. I would guess the manufacturing of the bottles costs more than the contents. It is not special or time consuming, has nothing to do with terroir, and doesn't wear the character of its maker in subtleties of flavour.

Despite its basic-ness, it has captured the attention of the world's drinkers. It has certainly stepped outside its Polish roots (although Russia has been an excellent godfather). At the beginning of the 20th century vodka comprised almost 90% of all liquor consumed in Russia. Of course, this was after the government dropped its policy of promoting consumption of state-produced vodka which caused the price to plummet and made the warming spirit available to the masses at an irresistible price. It's almost as cheap as water, vodka's namesake— vodka is derived from "voda," Slavic for water.

North American imbibers didn't pay much attention until the late '60s, but a campaign from Smirnoff that vodka "leaves you breathless" made a huge impact on the market and by 1975 vodka sales in America surpassed those of the hometown favourite, bourbon. It seems people were so happy to believe the lie that vodka doesn't leave that tell-tale boozy smell on your breath that they didn't mind giving up flavour. Having made many, many vodka martinis for friends and customers, I can assure you that the scent it leaves on one's breath is distinctly and obviously alcohol.

So the success of vodka is based on a 40-year-old marketing campaign that it leaves you breathless, and mixes well as it doesn't interfere with other flavours. Really, how could it? And it's cheap enough to produce to have been the drink of choice in wartime Russia.

But what's good about it? Nothing, really.

A vodka martini ought to be renamed "I like being drunk" because that is its only purpose. Whereas the pleasure of sipping a well-made Manhattan is its own fun, the slight buzzy inhibitions of alcohol just a pleasing side effect. Why wouldn't you want your drink to taste like anything?

But it's not fair to compare a silly, boring drink like a vodka martini to a flavour bomb like the Manhattan. Even worse is the dirty vodka martini. If your desperation for flavour has you drinking olive brine, just drink gin. Please. Gin is vodka's smarter, classier, more worldly older sister. Vodka wants to go clubbing and hook up with Johnny Redbull, that hot guy she met last week (who's not actually that hot and wears too much cologne). Gin wants to have dinner, a little wine and really talk about stuff, like politics and indie rock.

So if your drink of choice is gin or rye or anything but vodka, you are doing the right thing by choosing a spirit based on its taste. If you're a vodka sort, don't worry too much, you are right in line with the masses. Just imagine how proud your grandchildren will be of you for toeing the vodka party line.

6: MAGIC SHADOWS

SO GET A JOB I DID, or rather, my new best friend (I had created an opening by screwing up my friendship with Dee-Dee) Tracey did. Well, actually, she got three jobs and very kindly offered a final interview to me, as I had no idea what the hell I had to do to get myself employed. It turned out that showing up was enough for the now long gone Toby's at Bay and Bloor, a low-rent "bar and grill" nestled among the glittery Tiffany and Chanel storefronts that lined Bloor Street. Toby's didn't cater to the well-heeled ladies who strolled along the strip, languidly pulling out gold cards—eyebrows arched, smiles disinterested—to charge quilted leather bags in which to hold more gold cards, no, the Toby's crowd was more mall employees from the nearby Manulife Centre at lunch, A.A. meetings at dinner, and university kids with shitty IDs late at night. Toby's was known for its burgers, despite the fact that the burgers were pre-made, overcooked messes. Even at eighteen, I knew how a burger should taste.

My new job as a server wasn't necessarily hard work. I mean, it was physically gruelling and a completely new language in every sense, but I eventually learned to carry four plates in one hand and two baskets of fries in the other, and actually got sort of proficient at it. Proficient enough that the management thought it was a good idea to let me tend bar alone on Sundays in the upstairs bar. I could not believe my luck. Just like that I was behind the bar, surrounded by all sorts of new, exciting things. I had no idea what I was doing and no proper training, so I just sort of figured it out by asking a lot of questions. What's Frangelico? What's Metaxa? How do you pronounce "menthe"? (Because I was pretty sure it was *maunth*.) Can you really carry a tray with that much stuff on it? How the hell can you remember fourteen different drink orders without writing them down? How do you remember how to make every drink EVER? What do you do when the draught runs out? HOW DO THE LIMES SIT ON THE GLASSES AT JUST THE RIGHT ANGLE?? (I had a lot of questions.)

For some reason—likely due to Lindsay, the older, hard-living daytime bartender's enthusiasm for them—Alabama Slammers were something of a signature drink at Toby's Upstairs Bar. The bottles all had those awful security tops that measure out a perfect ounce, so for something like an Alabama Slammer—whose ingredients are ¾ ounce sloe gin (which was what, exactly? I had no idea. I just knew it was bright violet and tasted delicious), ¾ ounce amaretto (possibly the most delectable flavour of all time, and it actually contains ZERO nuts, but try telling that to someone with a nut allergy), and ¾ ounce Southern Comfort (which even eighteen-year-old me knew was pretty gross)—you'd have to remove the tops, measure everything out, and write it down in a log we kept for every time a bottle needed its security measure removed to "properly" make a drink. Between smokes, Lindsay showed me how to "build" the ingredients over ice in a highball glass, top with (from concentrate) orange juice, and garnish with an orange wheel stabbed with a lollipop-red maraschino cherry.

There would have been no stirring to ensure the drink was mixed (in fact, Lindsay taught me to pinch the straw as it went in the drink so when it took a breath at the bottom of the glass it would suck up the booze that had gone in first, ensuring that when the customer sipped they'd think it was "extra strong"—this apparently translated to a fiscal windfall in better tips). The oranges used for garnish were shadows of their former selves, a citrus mistreatment that would eventually move me to flout the Toby's rule of reusing yesterday's depressing fruit.

Being behind the bar dovetailed nicely with my high school drama dreams. I had played spotlight tag with the best of them, and loved sneaking up to the rafters for a lukewarm beer, privileges afforded me by my interest in starring in as many school productions as possible (it was two). I loved every second of being on stage. The bar felt a little like that, like you were putting on a show, except you wrote and directed it, picked the music, and even did the lighting design, and all you had to do was get people the drinks they wanted, collect some money, and make small talk with strangers. I was just so excited to be making cocktails (and pulling many, many pints) that neither of those things seemed like too high a price to pay for a stage and a bunch of bottles to play with, and I couldn't get enough. It probably, in an abstract way, traced the faint outlines of what future bar and restaurant ownership might look like. Certainly management seemed like something I could do myself, as the bosses all appeared to be pretty incompetent, even to teen me.

So I threw myself into it and learned every shot known to every college kid, and signed up for a bartending course that went over the basics: shaken versus stirred, which glasses were called what, how to throw out a drunk. I got very good at low-level bartending very quickly, and was given two more bar shifts. Given that I had never made money before, I was thrilled to be earning cash hand over fist, and since I was back living at home with my parents I could pretty much spend it as I pleased, which largely meant obscene amounts of beer, gin-and-tonics, red wine and jaegers for all at the various alternative dance nights that dotted the city. Most nights upstairs at Toby's were busy with students and dudes who were into students (and into bartenders). Plus, there was plenty of after-hours fun. The guy I was sleeping with was literally a friend with benefits and would often stop by just as I was finishing up. We'd hang out drinking and fooling around until the cleaners finished down-stairs and made their way upstairs, sweeping us out.

I was barely eighteen, and incredibly, unknowingly naive; the very definition of naive, I suppose. Eventually, I began having bar "regulars," one of whom was a guy who would reliably come in every Sunday at 4:00. He was unendingly chatty, but pleasant enough, and he tipped well (not well enough, it would turn out). I'd engage him as I prepped for the night: adding water to the bar mix, a disgusting, acrid, over-sweet, neon-green powder meant to evoke fresh lime juice, which it failed to do in every sense; and cutting the dry, with-ered sides off last night's lemon wedges and spritzing them with soda to bring them back to "life." Even though I was supposed to, I couldn't bear to keep the limp, dried-up oranges. I was a perfectionist even then—in a place that cer-tainly didn't demand it—and always threw them out, hiding them under some napkins, and cutting up fresh ones, breaking the rules. One Sunday, as I was skewering maraschino cherries, I ran out, and had to go downstairs to get another giant jar. I must have moved too quickly around the bar, because the affable *gentleman* I had been making small talk with for months didn't have enough time to put his *dick* back in his *pants*. I looked away, hiding my reaction, which was a mix of shock and betrayal and a held-back laugh. Despite the ABSURDITY of it, I was pissed off. He probably thought he was being sneaky—a fair assumption, considering he could've been stroking away, uninterrupted, for *months of Sundays*.

I ran down the back stairs and blurted out what had happened to the kindly female manager and insisted we call the cops. I then went back upstairs, played it very calm, and just kept chatting with the guy as though nothing had happened while my manager (who'd followed me back upstairs) kept an eye out from across the room. The police showed up pretty quickly, and I just looked at the guy, eyebrows raised, very pleased with myself for calling him out. I then had to go to the station and make a statement. It turned out that he had a long rap sheet of similar infractions, and this one was the last straw. He ended up going to jail for six months, and I got walked to my car for a long time after that out of fear of some sort of retribution. It wasn't motivated by any explicit fear that he'd come after me, it was more my manager's way of demonstrating some sort of protection, because what else could she do?

As women, we exist in a world where 50 percent of the people in it are naturally stronger than us. If you're a woman you either have a date rape story or know women who do. Catcalls on the street, threats of violence in real life or online, and way too high odds of being sexually assaulted are the water we swim in. Young women are told to "be careful and watch out, there are bad men out there who might want to hurt you" while young men are told "Have fun! Wear a condom!" And until we break this ugly cycle and start raising our girls to be confident and our boys to respect women, leading by example and parenting better, it will continue to be the water we swim in.

Eventually I was fired from Toby's for failing to show up for a shift. I was for real stranded at a cottage, but I'm sure they were looking for reasons—see: "after-hours fun," plus I often ate my weight in cheese sauce. My next job was, let's just say, a lateral move. My on-again, off-again dream boyfriend, Jack, who I'd lusted after since grade 9 and had finally lightly snagged at nineteen, was going to film school at Ryerson University and ran what he called a "script meeting" every Sunday at a grimy pub near the campus, in the heart of what's considered downtown. We weren't superorganized, other than that we always started the meeting at 8:00 p.m. Sometimes there'd be six of us, mostly just a smattering of friends and Jack's classmates, and sometimes the numbers would swell to fifteen. We took it very seriously, this workshopping scripts thing, but it was really just for fun and we'd always do some ad-libbing, while trying to be better *writers*. Pints would be drunk and we'd make sure to tip well, as a few of us were in the industry and understood that our group wasn't exactly a server's dream table. I'd learned a lot since my days leaving garbage tips at the lunch spots near my high school, mostly by working in restaurants—a thing EVERYONE should do for at least six months because it changes your perspective.

After a few months, and around the time I was fired from Toby's, I inquired after a job at the grimy pub with the friendly Australian bartender. Turned out someone had recently quit and there was an opening at the upstairs bar, which was a student hangout (so far, it appeared my destiny was to be in "upstairs bars" where students hung out). It seemed like a perfect fit for me. I interviewed with the owner, a lovely man far north of seventy-five who had a mind-blowing collection of jazz 45s. The next week, I was pouring measured pints.

I liked the job; it was a fun place, and other than having Peggy Lee's "Fever" on constant rotation (a drunk-old-man favourite—trust me, you'd get tired of it fast), I had few complaints. I especially liked the strange banter-based flirtation I had brewing with the owner's son, Danny, despite his being married and more than twice my age. I turned him into Bogart and imagined myself Bacall. Perhaps I had an unhealthy attachment to fantasy, but my Basquiat-inspired film school boyfriend (inspired in the sartorial sense only, although when he denied taking culture and style cues from Jean-Michel I'm pretty sure I laughed in his face) had just dumped me for good, and I ate up the attention the owner's son was giving me.

It started innocently enough. Danny was into music and would find a way to ask me about what I was listening to as I set up the bar in the mornings. He'd always be around for "meetings" as I finished my shift, and he'd keep my cigarette lit and my glass of vodka full (what did I know? I was *nineteen* and still years away from discovering vodka's true, boring self—double vodka on the rocks, two limes, seemed terribly grown-up, the specificity of it suggesting adulthood, a desire to have something a certain way, and the confidence to ask for it). We'd sit out on the patio and talk for hours, and I could tell he was interested romantically, which made me feel sophisticated instead of creeped out, a not entirely unfamiliar feeling. And he never seemed to care how obvious we were being. One night, we were hanging around at closing and he told the bartender to go home, that he'd lock up. As I was about to make a winning shot in eight-ball, he came up behind me and kissed my neck. I let it happen, it was what I wanted. We got pretty hot and heavy on the pool table, balls everywhere, but saved fucking for when we were in a hotel, weeks later.

Looking back, I'm embarrassed I was so easily conned, and by a skeevy criminal lawyer no less. I actually believed we were in love. I romanticized the hotels and the out-of-town getaways and painted it all in 1940s gold dust. We were film noir stars, and having grown up on a steady diet of *Magic Shadows* and *Saturday Night at the Movies*, I found the script easy to follow and got caught up in the *glamour* of it all. I started gravitating to pencil skirts, printed silk shirts, and wide-brimmed hats instead of my usual jeans and Converse. He had me hooked, and for our entire relationship I thought the late-night trips to grotty underground casinos in Chinatown were exciting, rather than what they actually were: part of a web of addiction that included gambling, cocaine, and, evidently, inappropriately young girls. Because for all my worldly protestations to the contrary, at nineteen, I was still, emotionally, very much a girl.

And when Danny died unexpectedly after a week in the hospital, some nine months into our dalliance, that's exactly how I handled it, with a girl's grasp of the world and how things work. To this day I'm not entirely sure what killed him, although his lifestyle was not, in any way, healthful. Nonetheless, I was devastated, and in my contorted reality, his family's loss was absolutely secondary to my extreme, exaggerated hurt.

It was a horrible idea to go to the funeral, but of course I went, and it was an even worse idea to stumble into the shiva, hoping his wife somehow didn't know I was "the" girl—"that" girl. I felt a strange mixture of discomfort and entitlement being in such close contact with his wife. Of course Danny had painted her to be an awful person, and of course I'd believed every word. It made it much easier to swallow the guilt that would sometimes gurgle up in my throat, taking me back to how I'd felt around Dee-Dee, and making me wonder if maybe I was just plain bad. Becoming physically weakened by it all (because, of course, *my* pain) and finding no available chairs, I settled on the floor, only to find out later what an egregious offence that was at a shiva where I, technically, was not one of the people mourning. It was probably no worse than carrying on with a married man and then having the gall to attend the shiva, but still. That selfish lack of tact was not even a thought in my head at the time. I was "heartbroken."

I left the pub shortly after that, although not before I met Tyler, my starter husband-to-be, across the bar. I'd seen him a few times over a couple of weeks. He would come in around midnight after his shift at a nearby pub and always sat at the bar, although I had definitely noticed that he'd taken a table the one time he'd come in that I wasn't bartending, presumably to have me serving him. He laughed at my wisecracks and had such a kind and calm vibe about him, I was drawn to his warmth. It didn't hurt that he was extremely handsome . . . seriously, dude looked like Chris Noth. Finally I grew tired of waiting for him to ask me out and I suggested that instead of coming to see me at *my* bar he pick me up sometime after my shift and we go to *another* bar. I was so excited for our date, and I even wore heels to work, knowing I'd regret it but choosing not to care about a little foot pain. Besides, I was super-stoked to actually be able to wear heels; when I'd worn them with both recent exes Jack and Danny I towered over them, which made me uncomfortable, but shouldn't have.

Tyler and I went everywhere that first night, running around downtown like kids, skipping to a soundtrack of "Lust for Life" on repeat, stopping in way too many bars for way too many rye-and-gingers and finding time to make out in between, the city lights a twinkling backdrop to a giddy, rye-fuelled romance. He was so much fun, and I instantly felt so safe around him that I pretty much immediately started spending four or five nights a week at his apartment, which wasn't so much an apartment as a room in a house in the east end. Our first six months were fun and easy, and filled with a lot of sex. It was nice to be with someone who was totally focused on me, and I thought I loved it; it felt like, somehow, I'd found home. But I was only twenty-one, and just really needed somebody to absorb all my bullshit.

I'd been waitressing and bartending part-time at this incredibly busy cocktail bar on College Street. It's hard to imagine now, but through the 1990s, College Street between Bathurst and Grace was literally one of the coolest places in the world; even a non-Canadian magazine said so, so it must have been true! It hummed with life, and the bars were all interesting, independent spots. There was the place to hang with friends and play pool, its blue-and-white-striped awning a beacon for young, beautiful, hip twenty-somethings; the jazz spot; the really low-key dive bar with the great patio; the actual pool hall that played awesome music (GBV and Built to Spill were in constant rotation); and a couple of mediocre Italian restaurants (it was, after all, Little Italy).

There was also Souz Dal, the dimly lit, gorgeous date spot that served martinis—1990s martinis: overly juicy messes that bore no relationship to a proper martini (gin, dry vermouth, bitters, and a twist, no more, no less—although you could debate the addition of bitters with bar nerds all night. I choose not to). This was the time of Cosmopolitans—abbreviated to "Cosmos" by girls in sequined tanks, boot-cut jeans, and high heels everywhere—and chocolate martinis, and other ghastly things of that nature. And Souz Dal was Toronto's destination for all that and more. It really was an incredibly beautiful spot, opened and built by seven art students who eventually sold it to my boss, because they were *seven* art students. They'd painstakingly crafted every detail of the place, including three domes carved out of the ceiling and hung with hand-forged metal hoops that held a bunch of candles; they were a giant pain in the ass to light but cast shifting, mesmerizing shadows over the walls. Tables were painted wood, and chairs were welded metal with velvet cushions, somehow untacky, and it was all anchored by a small copper-and-steel bar. The patio out back had a criss-cross of fire escape stairs overhead and a church-style candleholder filled with Jesus candles, technically called prayer candles, lending a very secret-lair feel.

Being the bartender at Souz Dal was the first cool job I had. Despite it being a decidedly 1990s cocktail list, it was extensive, and it was a lot to memorize. I took it on like it was a very important project and in just a few days learned every drink, how to shake two cocktails at once, and the importance of speed and organization. It was there that I learned, more through doing the opposite of my boss, how important it is to "work clean." I kept my station very organized and well stocked, because on a busy night there was no time to spear more pineapples. The money was pretty great, too, especially compared to the seventy-five bucks I'd be lucky to take home following an afternoon shift at the pub. Souz was often so busy I'd have to load up my tray with cocktails and carry it over my head to get to the front tables, and if that proved impossible I'd scoot out the back and down the alley with my overloaded tray and quickly come back in the front door.

My boss didn't say much to me, and he wasn't exactly Mr. Personality, but he was easy enough to work with, although on the weekend shifts, with just the two of us, I soon ended up doing most of the work for half the money, which he doled out once a week. It was hard to keep track of the tips that way, which made me feel taken advantage of. This experience strongly influenced my future monetary decisions as a restaurant owner. There would be no "house tip-out," and if I were going to be taking a share of tips, I would work just as hard as my staff. Harder, even.

A couple of months into full-time bartending there, Tyler and I decided to marry (well, I decided, and he agreed) after an alarmingly short courtship fuelled mostly by one too many boilermakers, lots of sex, and laughing. One morning we woke up and I looked over at him and just blurted out, "We should get married," and instead of finding this alarming, he accepted it as a great idea. But of course not everyone concurred. My mother, in particular, found our six months of togetherness to be wholly inadequate. She managed to keep her concerns to herself, but I could see it all over her face whenever Tyler was at the house in Scarborough. She was too polite a woman to be straight-up rude, but I could tell she didn't like my prospective husband, or the fact that I might *actually* marry him, which I did.

At that moment, happy and—I thought—in love, I was positive that this was an excellent decision, despite the quiet murmurs of my parents. I desperately wanted to move downtown and get away from the White brothers and the everyday drop-in, party vibe of their Scarborough home that anchored our whole friend group—Tyler offered that escape, if only for the very obvious benefit of shared living expenses. But it wasn't a financial decision, I genuinely believed I really loved him and, I thought, the only way to prove that was to marry him. I also saw it as a fresh start. I hadn't yet begun to see myself as just pulling him along on a ride with me. My leadership skills were like a gale wind, even as a young woman, and I know now that Tyler just wasn't solid enough to withstand that kind of bossy. I needed someone with a strong sense of self and an equally strong personality, but of course, back then, that wasn't at all clear to me, so I just stepped onto the roller coaster, totally sure everything would be fine, laughing all the way. That is not to say Tyler didn't have many wonderful qualities. He was hilarious—or, at the very least, found my jokes funny—an artist, super-handy, and a great cook, and we always had fun. He was also particularly kind and would do little thoughtful things, like bring me snacks at Souz Dal when I worked twelve-hour shifts, and defer to my wants when it came to picking the movie, and just generally treat me like a princess, including midnight nachos when I'd be hormonally craving midnight nachos. I could tell he was proud to hold my hand when we walked along College Street, and he never did anything but treat me well, but he was a bit broken. His parents' divorce had been hard on him, and he had actively sided with his mother while maintaining a polite relationship with his father.

After our wedding, we went through the motions of building a life together easily and quickly, joyfully decorating the rented Grace Street home I still live in (although now own) with thrift shop finds, and repainting every room in unnecessary colours (seriously, a forest green living room—what was I thinking?). Tyler already had a cat, Mistress, a beautiful tabby with a lovely disposition, but we got a second one together, with an emphasis on really bringing home the "family" theme. Pod was three-legged and absolutely perfect, grey and white with big grey-green eyes and the kind of face that would have made him Internet-famous had he not been born too soon. He didn't use a litter box, only peed outside (the dog of cats!), and he couldn't scratch furniture because he'd fall over, short one leg and all—he was full of personality and just adorable. But what I loved most about him was his single-minded pursuit of his needs; unlike Mistress, who'd sense my period cramps and thoughtfully massage my swollen belly with her feet, Pod would only cuddle at his whim, and had no concern at all for anything outside what he wanted in each moment—an enviable way to live.

Though Tyler and I quickly became very familial in our attachment, the truth was that we were better friends than lovers, and that friendship is what kept us together for six years despite how much we'd argue about the stupidest things. For example, I really wanted him to read a book I loved and it made me crazy that he just wouldn't do it. I don't know why I wanted him to read it so badly. Maybe I thought "if he loves that book then I didn't actually make a bad decision," and maybe his stubborn refusal to just read the damn thing was his way of having agency in our relationship, where the power tipped heavily in my favour, but mostly because I took it and he let me.

Pretty quickly after we were married, the intense new-relationship sex we'd been having petered out. Despite my trying really hard to keep some semblance of a sex life, we'd go long stretches of all desert, no oasis, which definitely made me cranky. In turn, that crankiness was exacerbated by constantly feeling like I had to play both sides of a discussion; Tyler was so agreeable that it left me frustrated and irritable. I just wanted DISCOURSE. We didn't fit together, but we'd become so codependent, we didn't even realize it. Even when the sex completely dried up, we still cuddled, which was confusing and made me think we really did love each other and were a family and would of course work out our differences. I really had no idea how unhappy I was, but unhappiness always finds its way out. Sometimes my frustration at some little thing Tyler had done would lead me into yelling fits that shocked me. I could be extraordinarily cruel, and would occasionally say things so regrettable that the words would bounce around for days, reminding me how cutting I could be, racking me with guilt. But still, we stubbornly refused to break up—I just didn't want to fail at something I'd done on a whim, so I blindly rejected any sneaking suspicions the relationship was not good enough. I wanted my parents' clucks and grumbles—which, at some point, they began to share with me—to be wrong. So I stayed and tried to make a friendship into a marriage.

While still full-time at Souz Dal, and freshly married, I was easily distracted from depressing thoughts like "oh shit this marriage was a really bad idea" by newly blooming thoughts of opening a bar of our own. Because what better idea was there for two unhappy people than to have a baby, in this case, shaped very much like a bar? In lieu of a lavish wedding, my parents had generously offered to help us either buy a house or start a business. Seeing my boss do the bare minimum and still make money made me think that, with some effort, I could run a really special bar. And by this point, I was so frustrated at some of the practices at Souz, as I had become just savvy enough to fully understand how unfair the work-to-pay ratio was, that I started to really believe I could do a much better job with a similar concept. And Cobalt—the idea, anyway—was born.

7: NAIVE GIRL BUILDS BAR, KICKS OUT HUSBAND

TYLER WOULD PICK ME UP FROM WORK at Souz Dal almost every night, and before we'd make the short walk home, I'd stir or shake us a couple of cocktails, sometimes Manhattans or Stingers, and sometimes my own twists on the fruity drinks that made up most of the menu. I didn't even fully realize it, but I was slowly making my first cocktail list. If I'd had a particularly stressful night, I'd lead the conversation with some iteration of "Goddammit, I could do the job so much better than my boss," and we'd discuss, in minute detail, all the things we'd do if we had our own bar: what the drinks would be called, how much they would cost, what kind of music we'd play, what neighbourhood we'd want to be in, what we might name it. "Maybe we'd have a fireplace!" We wouldn't. We kicked the idea of bar ownership around, scraped through it over many drinks, a constant distraction from how much the first six months of marriage weren't exactly reflecting what I had imagined the first part of a marriage was maybe supposed to be. I mean, we had put a house together and we both went off to our jobs every day, me at Souz Dal and Tyler at a nearby pub, but the near-constant fucking that should have been consuming us, based on what I'd gleaned from cheap books and movies of the week, wasn't exactly a raging fire. I had no intention of giving up, though, and I let myself get swallowed up by the fantasy of opening our own place instead, a fantasy that had become vivid and engulfing.

One Friday, stuck in traffic, I noticed a giant "For Rent" sign at the old Lola's Lounge, on the north side of College just east of Bathurst, and saw it as a figurative as well as a literal sign. I rushed home to tell Tyler, and called the number given and left a message, trying not to sound too twenty-one.

We saw the space the next day, with the owner's son, and decided immediately this was the perfect spot. After a few phone calls back and forth, the owner of 426 College Street, Mrs. Erdos, agreed to meet us—a perfectly logical next step in signing a lease, but since everything about this was so new to us we approached this meeting with kid-in-candy-store levels of excitement. The spring weather played along, clear blue skies and a light wind whipping across Adelaide. Tyler and I walked up the steps of the appointed Japanese restaurant with feigned confidence, draped in our finest ill-fitting business wear. We were there to meet both Mrs. Erdos, our genteel, perfectly coiffed, potential new landlady, and her smarmy, money-specific son, who'd first shown us the space and who easily fooled with his hippie vibe, worn like a costume, complete with requisite long hair shoved behind his very keen ears. Nothing got by him. Mrs. Erdos seemed nice enough, and responded to my giddy excitement and "confidence" with an interest I read as genuine, maternal even.

Everything about this meeting struck me as *very important*, and I was putting so much focus on just getting the space that nothing else mattered, even stuff that should have, like the inflated rent. But while my negotiation skills have grown in exponential leaps from navigating many leases over the years, my approach hasn't: focus in and get what you want, step by excruciating step. And all I wanted was to be told yes, at any cost.

As we picked at the last of the very basic sushi platter, talk turned to our plans for the College Street space. I explained that we wanted to do a cocktail bar, and both Mrs. Erdos and her son had advice. "You should put in a bunch of taps," offered the son, his mother proudly smiling approval, as if this were the best bar idea of all time. We nodded along and, despite our early-twenties instinctual lack of interest in unsolicited helpful hints, it seemed important to be as gracious as possible. I picked up the tab and remember thinking that was a super-classy thing to do, a surefire way to guarantee she'd choose us over the many (so she said) applicants. I believed in my charm, and it never entered my mind that this, like all things, would come down to simple economics. If we could pay, we could play.

I have come to learn that, generally, the specific goals of the landlord and tenant are the same: they both want to rent the space with equal fervour. But back then, it felt like a contest, and my eagerness to win blinded me to the details of the rental contract. I now know to negotiate for a minimum of two rent-free months, to help balance the pain of dumping money into a space that will likely never be yours. This is also a strong argument for land ownership. I now make sure that I absolutely understand what "additional rent" means, in no uncertain terms—with numbers. And I have learned through many hard lessons to curb my enthusiasm—a foreign concept to bright-eyed, bushy-tailed, twenty-one-year-old me. Because of this unbridled enthusiasm, Tyler and I probably ended up paying a "wow-that-girl-really-wants-this-place" tax. I mean, I can't prove it, but this negotiation was in no way the Erdos family's first rodeo and in every way was ours. We very likely paid for our naiveté in actual money, because anyone with even a hair more experience would have negotiated a better lease. Or, at the very least, hired a lawyer.

On top of it, it never even occurred to me to incorporate the business, which is the most basic first step ever. This small oversight would eventually prove to be not so small and very stupid. Incorporating a business protects you from personal liability. If you don't incorporate and then you proceed to fuck up your business and you happen to own anything at all, you could lose all or some of whatever those things happen to be.

We waited for five anxious days to hear back from Mrs. Erdos, our confidence eroding by the day. We just wanted to know it was happening, to lock it down in writing. Then, after many meetings and credit checks (and an extremely helpful parental co-sign), for the first year the space was ours! Even though my parents weren't super-thrilled with my choice in husband, they had promised to help me start a business and fundamentally just wanted me to be happy—the one thing they insisted on was that I put everything in my name. And I was happy. In fact, I was over the moon with manic excitement.

Tyler and I celebrated like we'd won the lottery, with cava on the patio at the spot where you drink cava on the patio. We spent hundreds of dollars, instead of saving them, assured, under the drunken enchantment of *possibilities*, that we were heading down a path that was clear of debris and lined with money trees; seeing the freedom of ownership far more clearly than the responsibilities; acting like the not-quite-adults we were. It was so easy to ignore how little like lovers we had become because there was always something fun to do. We got along as pals, decidedly unsexy, great roommates.

We settled on the name Cobalt because it was my favourite colour at the time, and I liked the simplicity of one, clean-sounding word. Not "The Cobalt," not "Cobalt Bar," just "Cobalt." We told all of our friends with the same sense of smug, excited reverence that thirty-something yuppies in the park probably have with other first-time parents: "Holden Atticus Henderson . . . we're just literary people!" We were treating naming the bar like it was an important work step, and we didn't fully realize how much actual work was ahead of us.

ONLY A FEW WEEKS AFTER OUR SUSHI LUNCH with the Erdos matriarch and son, the place was actually, technically, ours. It was really happening. Layers of neglect lived on the façade, and the tall doors were in desperate need of sanding and staining, but I was already mentally peeling back the layers—peeling them back for real a few days later revealed stamped tin under eighty years' worth of paint and wood.

The key slid in easily and I shook with gleeful anticipation as I walked into *my bar* for the very first time, somehow feeling that I truly deserved this. Adult ideas like "white privilege" and fortune of birth, coupled with great parental trust and generosity, weren't even close to forming. I now know that my stepson, clever as he is at twenty-two, has much to learn. Youth really is wasted on the young, if I knew then what I know now, etc., etc., ad infinitum.

Light filtered through hastily papered-over windows, giving everything an ugly beige hue; rays pushing through dust clouds settled on pockmarked tables and worn, painted tiles. But what hit me first was the smell, which I somehow hadn't noticed the first time we'd gone to check out the space: stale beer, damp newspapers, and neglect, with high notes of rotting citrus left sliced open on the bar, as though the bartenders had been raptured in the middle of service. A pile of clunky metal chairs lay stacked in the back, counterparts to the patterned Formica tables that were straight out of the 1950s kitchen, missing only an aproned housewife lifting a steaming casserole out of the oven. The chairs were mostly sliced-up disasters, the chunky filling oozing out of hundreds of unsuccessful chair-surgeries, peeled-up, dirty duct tape only making it worse. I immediately started mentally reupholstering them in burgundy fabric. Reupholstery wasn't a thing I'd ever done, but I imagined it would be simple, and something I could learn to do. It turned out that it wasn't exactly simple. Fabric had to be cut on the bias, stretched taut, and then pleated around the corners and staple-gunned to the seat. Not simple, but not out of the realm of the possible.

Quarter-full bottles of shitty domestic beer lay scattered about on tables, many doubling as makeshift ashtrays, surrounded by peeled and balled-up labels. They were a reminder that just a few years prior, in its previous incarnation, this place had been a favourite haunt for me: Lola's Lounge. I was happy to see that the owner, in his hasty midnight run, had left the very cool painting of "Lola" still guarding the entrance with honey-haired-Sixties insouciance. It was the only thing I was grateful still remained, and eventually it would end up on Cobalt's tiny back patio. That patio, which was never licensed, somehow existed incident-free for our last two years of business after Tyler finally followed through on years-long promises to construct it. This was a theme in our troubled marriage: me wanting a thing (sex, a book read, a patio) and never really getting it, and yet unable to see, for far too long, how mismatched we were as a couple. Because kids—not having them; being them.

As we stood taking it all in, poking into closets and opening old fridges, the massive amount of work ahead started to sink in. It would take days of junk removal and serious scrubbing just to get it to a building site that didn't reek of garbage and rodent decay. I had no idea what to do or where to start and no idea what had made me think we could just figure it out. It was a major renovation that required at least a basic understanding of construction, which we didn't really have. Tyler's mom had an ex-con ex-boyfriend who did, though, and although I found his casual misogyny and pumped-up machismo intolerable to be around, he was a source of endless help and direction. I think he felt really indebted to my mother-in-law, who had never judged him for his shady past, and as a result he went above and beyond to help with the reno as a retroactive favour to her. He wasn't a bad guy, probably, although I had no real interest in verifying his *goodness*; he just wasn't someone I wanted to spend too much time with. I'd quietly cringe every time he called me "sweetie," conflicted by my instinct to inform him emphatically not to call me "sweetie" versus our desperate need for his assistance. But there was absolutely no way we could have done any of it without his expertise. All I had was a very unformed idea of how I wanted the bar to look, based on a hyper-romantic fantasy of what a bar should look like, a fantasy whose outlines I'd been idly colouring in the whole time I worked at Souz. I could see it in my head, I just had no real idea of the practical steps needed to make the place match my vision.

I was obsessed with the idea of some semi-private seating and wanted it to feel like you were stepping into a doorless confessional, with an arched entryway, "like a church, like a church!" I kept saying. The cubby-hole seating, even with its small step up, was still very much part of the room, and even though Souz Dal didn't have that exact thing, per se, somehow, the arch forged a relationship; it felt similar and *inspired* by. I couldn't believe it when Tyler managed to frame in perfect archways, and when an old pal's mother, an artist, showed me this awesome paint-and-garbage-bag trick that made the walls look like deep red leather. It was exactly as I'd imagined it.

The learning process was fast and furious, every day a new technique, a new way to drill, saw, hammer. I learned that you can wet drywall and then form it to fit a curve, and it will hold the curve as it dries; that there's wood that's thin enough to bend, that shakes with the wobble of Jell-O; and that if you buy Ikea lighting it's going to *look like* Ikea lighting. I learned that I hate entranceway tiles immediately *after* we installed entranceway tiles. I learned that I could paint for many, many hours without tiring, always doing just one more coat. I learned lessons in economy versus judicious spending; that trying to repurpose crappy tables with meticulously cut up shards of stained glass was probably not the best idea, but boy did I love those tables—so much work went into each one. My in-laws settled in with me for days to help glue down glass, then grout and polish each table. The polishing was a real bitch. We'd spend hours making sure there was no trace of grout left on the shiny, jewel-like surfaces. The success for us was in not having to buy new tables within our extremely limited budget, and having something unique, albeit horrifying to my current tastes.

But it worked. The room was becoming more inviting, comfortable, and maybe even a little sophisticated. I was, frankly, blown away by what we were doing. Every day inched us closer to a finished bar, and we had lots of friends and former co-workers offering to pitch in. It felt like a party a lot of the time, despite the squabbling with Tyler, most often to do with his mom's ex-boyfriend contractor. The contractor wanted to do everything in a very traditional way, and he was a bit of a bully, so I'd have to really push Tyler to say no to him. It was complicated by the fact that I didn't actually know what I was talking about when it came to construction. But I knew how I wanted every detail to look, so after much harping, I convinced Tyler to remove the bar lighting we'd spent money to put up and install three beautiful glass pendants instead. As Tyler was installing them, one fell and broke. I looked up at him, standing there on the bar, and just rolled my eyes and swore, "Un-fucking-believable," or something to that effect. I had no compassion for how obviously bad he felt and just left muttering that I was heading across town to the antique store where I knew there were still a few more pendants. By the time I came back I'd calmed down, but it was such a stupid thing to be mad about. I just could never stop myself with Tyler.

There was a little lounge area tucked beside the bar with low-slung seating in the form of the most perfect and incredibly comfortable deco pale-green corded velvet theatre seats, with beautiful wood sides, which were screwed into the floor. These were arranged around a kidney-shaped, low table. It was always the first spot to get snatched up by larger groups.

In the '90s, "antique" or second-hand stores were mostly musty basements filled with your grandma's trashed knickknacks plus her silver and crystal. Dark times. Eventually, in the early 2000s, second-hand stores morphed into "salvage shops" that specialized in barn board, repurposed wine crates and industrial copper lighting. My favourite piece in the bar was a deco gumwood mantel, unearthed in the basement of a regular antique-store haunt. This stood opposite the bar, perfect for resting drinks and leaning. We outfitted the mantel/bar with an adorable ceramic lamp and a large bouquet of white lilies.

Despite my inexperience, the importance of good lighting was always ingrained in me, so Cobalt was very nicely lit. Everything was on dimmers, including the newly hung vintage drop lights over the bar and the basement stairwell lighting. Flickering candles sat in patterned glass holders everywhere. And adding to the magic was a stationary disco ball that bounced little rays of dusty light over the entire back room and made it feel like you were inside a bottle of sparkly nail polish.

There was a raised dais in the front section of the bar that curved in the shape of a guitar (not, it's important to add, *intentionally*), the curve echoed by a drop-ceiling that hid vents and other ugly things best kept hidden (at least until the great Duct and Piping Exposure of the turn of the century that infected restaurants and bars everywhere). The tables and chairs up on the dais, by the front window, were painted pale green and looked great against the natural cork floor. It was interesting to see which regulars preferred this section over the more intimate tables in the back. Across the pale-blue, mottled ceramic tiles of the entry—incredibly resistant to the assault of winter's unending salty slush yet ill-considered simply for the sin of being hideously ugly—sat an amazing antique stove, strictly decorative, dug out of three inches of poured concrete in the creepy basement. Its creamy, patinated top made the perfect place to stash business cards and a ridiculous guest book. Should you somehow be thinking business cards and a guest book are a cute idea, know that, at twenty-two, so did I.

The bar sat on a slight angle to the left, which really helped break up the room. We distinguished the bar area with a floating "wood" floor (not quite real wood, but *from* wood; it's just a cheap way to achieve the look of hardwood, especially effective in low bar lighting) that looked great for a few years until the ravages of too many spilled cocktails ate away at its seal, and its charm.

Bottles lined the wall behind the bar, backlit by hundreds of Christmas lights (a technique I still employ) that gave the impressive whisky collection a lovely amber glow. The bottled beer fridge was left over, another gift from our predecessor, angel Lola. It had been a horrific shade of purple, but after we recovered it with a metallic Formica, it looked great. And the draught flowed out of the of-the-moment refurbished keg fridges that could be found in almost every bar in the city instead of proper walk-in keg fridges, thanks to their ease of installation and affordability.

The bar stools were the only furnishings not recovered or second-hand, bought from a restaurant supply store. They were sturdy, comfortable, and utilitarian. They weren't ugly, necessarily—think something you'd find in an elevated pub chain—but not a thing I would ever buy again. They still live on, slightly out of place in a basement hipster bar on Dundas West, and every time I go there the curve of the "merlot" stained backrests and shine of the chrome legs instantly transport me back to my mid-twenties. (The stain options came in an array of colours, from basic walnut to emerald green, but I chose "Merlot," no doubt for its name—after all, I was still, at twenty-two, years away from dismissing merlot, the wine, as unnecessary, and later, eventually coming around to begrudgingly accept that it is sometimes capable of charming, even me.) Just a glance at those bar stools, crammed around a different bar, will pull me in quickly: an imagination time-machine back to my Cobalt days. In the same way, a Stone Roses song's jangly guitar will shove me back into my VW with the sunroof open, speeding around Scarborough, long before bar ownership, seventeen and fancy-free.

After taking over the lease in July, we opened only five months later, which felt like a real accomplishment given our lack of experience and newfound learned-on-the-fly abilities.

The last few weeks of the build hurtled forward at lightning speed. We had picked December 1 as our opening date sometime in September and promised ourselves we'd stick to it. It loomed over us with matter-of-factness, and by the time it arrived, I was bouncing off the walls with nervous excitement. I couldn't wait to show our friends and family what we'd done, but more important, in a sartorial sense, I was desperately grateful to put on a sparkly top, high heels, and velvet pants (beautiful Bill Blass 1970s-cut slacks, with a gold metal label, inherited from my mother) after months of living in dirty jeans and T-shirts that were mostly drywall dust.

I took my time getting ready, relishing putting on a bit of makeup, fully participating in the "belle of the ball" narrative I felt I'd earned. Tyler was already at Cobalt as I'd taken a bit longer to get ready, but I still made it with half an hour to spare, having prepped all my bar stuff hours earlier. Reliably, even though the party started at 8:00, my parents showed up at 7:35. They'd always give themselves way more time than was necessary to get anywhere, like, they'd leave Scarborough for downtown—a half-hour to forty-minute trip at most—with a cushion of an hour, "just in case." My mom was so proud with how the bar had all come together, it felt like she was finally starting to forgive me for what a rotten teenager I had been. We had lately settled into a nice pattern of regular talks on the phone, but some part of me still felt like she didn't fully trust me. Much to her credit, though, even if I was complaining ruthlessly about my crumbling marriage, she just listened and never judged or let me know exactly what she was really thinking, which was probably some version of "oh dear god please break up." Watching her and my dad see Cobalt for the first time that night and be visibly amazed by it made me feel so good, like I had finally pleased them. My mom hadn't seen it in weeks, and in the last month it had transformed. And my dad just looked so happy. Their pride was affecting. And I felt, for the first time in my life, the beginnings of the freedom and independence offered by self-employment. I knew it was going to be a lot of work, but I was ready—for the drinks-making and the learning and the training staff, all of it. I had flicked a switch permanently, and I knew I could and would never not be my own boss again.

Our friends and family started trickling in between 8:00 and 9:00. I was so nervous that people wouldn't come, but by 10:00 the party was in full swing, well-wishes in the form of flowers and Champagne piling up on the bar, cocktails sloshing around their wide-rimmed glasses with more ferocity as the hours ticked by and fourth drinks were slurped back. It was an almost perfect night, with the exception of a ridiculous argument with my best friend, Tracey, who'd asked me to be honest about what I thought of her new boyfriend while we were both a bit drunk round midnight. I chose to take her request at face value, a poor choice, as it was the beginning of the end of a friendship that I had so believed in, despite our differences, which were based mostly in our differing perspectives on just how much of a brat I was. But that bump—I didn't then recognize its significance—couldn't dampen my high spirits. I poured myself more Champagne, caught Tyler's eye, and tipped it back, positive this was up there with the "best nights of my life."

I would spend the year teaching Tyler to bartend, but in the beginning, I ran the bar and Tyler did table service, a necessary reversal of traditional gender roles in bars that I enjoyed—it was just a little thing, but any way I could challenge how things were usually done made me happy. It took a bit of time for Cobalt to be an everyday success, but the weekends picked up fast; within six weeks we were over capacity most Fridays and Saturdays. In addition to serving the cocktails of the moment— Crantinis, Cosmopolitans, and Mango Margaritas—we also served properly made classics: perfectly cold gin martinis, Sidecars shaken with fresh lemon juice, and a really delicious Manhattan. I was naturally good at making cocktails that tasted balanced, and, as my palate evolved and as the trends started to shift away from sweet/fruity drinks and back in time to pre-Prohibition-era cocktails, I got better and better at it. But as good as I was at it, it was always a means to an end, a way to get what I wanted: to be my own boss. That's not to say I didn't want to be the very best at it—I did—but having met people who are really passionate about drinks and drink-making, it's hard for me to see myself as ever having been "passionate" about bartending. It was fun and it played to my skill-set, but I always saw beyond that particular horizon; I just didn't know what, exactly, I saw.

Other than upgrading the vermouth many years later when the LCBO, Ontario's government-run and only liquor store, finally caught up with the world and brought in Antica Formula, and eventually making my own bitters, the Manhattan has remained the same. I mean, it's a Manhattan, it has a recipe; mine is just slightly tweaked. But I can't not highlight the abundance of other ridiculous drinks on the menu; the Luke Skywalker (vodka, Baileys, Kahlua, and cream, basically a Mudslide) is just one egregious example among many. (I also can't not highlight their cheesy names, like the Fizzy D'Amour—Fizzy of Love. What does that even mean? It was cava and a dash of passion fruit liqueur, and it was, frankly, delicious.) Cobalt had a huge cocktail menu, badly in need of editing, and all copies have been burned. But silly drinks and inexperience notwithstanding, it was a solid first effort.

At that time there weren't a lot of places in Toronto serving proper cocktails, made with dense ice, careful measures, and a little pride. You pretty much had to go to a hotel bar to get a martini that tasted right, the best of which was the Roof at the Park Hyatt (née Park Plaza), and if you were lucky, Joe Gomes, a classic, unsung hero of Toronto's bar scene, would stir it for you. (Joe remained at the Hyatt, working full shifts, all charm, into his eighties—he only just recently retired.) Tyler and I wanted to bring a bit of that suave hotel bar sophistication to College Street, but marketed to young people who'd feel out of place at a fancy hotel bar and out of pocket at the cost of a martini at one. We kept our prices really low but still made the drinks with care, measuring everything, tasting for coldness, dilution, and balance. And that was back when nobody was slipping a straw into a drink to quality check; we had to do it subtly so customers wouldn't think we were trying to rip them off. So funny, as it's now so ubiquitous, in fact, that I worry when I'm at a bar and don't see bartenders tasting.

I really thought what Tyler and I were doing at Cobalt was something new, but there were a lot of lessons to be learned, and all the hard way, of course. Like the time I decided to preserve my own cherries without fully understanding what "preserve" meant. I thought I could just jam cherries into giant jars, cover them with booze, cherry juice, and sugar, and leave them on a shelf in the basement, indefinitely. For a while, it worked out great: we had delicious liquor-plumped house-made cherries. But then one night, when I was working by myself, I got my first lesson in fermentation: a loud, awful POP followed by shattered glass cut through the strains of Luna's "Bewitched." I ran downstairs, leaving the regulars at the bar to watch over things. Shards of glass were everywhere and cherry juice seeped into the unfinished cement floor of the storeroom and was making its way under the dry storage doorway into the public hallway. I mopped up what I could and then spent half an hour after service scrubbing down the floor and picking up cherries from under shelves. So I had to teach myself how to can, relying on a combination of *The Joy of Cooking* and trial and error. At first I made small batches, using purchased cherry juice, but as I became more confident I started experimenting, and that was the beginning of the iteration of cherries that I eventually perfected. The first thing was to stop using purchased juice and to make the juice from fresh cherries—after a couple of tries I landed on the right ratio: roughly a fifth of the cherries meant to be processed would be blended and strained for juice. The cherries were really tasty but would lose their vibrant red colour, so I researched how to keep them looking as good as they tasted, and apparently the answer is vitamin C. I found a recipe that gave the ratio for acidulating canned foods for colour preservation—basically the equivalent of one crushed vitamin tablet per quart mason jar—and this is where my cherry recipe really turned a corner. This recipe contained a tip that would take the flavour from good to amazing—grinding the pits. The seeds inside the pits of stone fruit contain the primary flavouring agent in Amaretto and we perceive their intense nuttiness as almond flavour. And—fun fact!—they also contain trace amounts of cyanide, but you'd have to eat like fifty seeds to suffer any ill effects.

At the time, I also thought it was okay to mix fresh citrus juice with sugar and water and use that as a bar mix instead of doing it the right way: adding juice and sugar separately and getting dilution from ice alone. It was a better approach than the from-concentrate-only mix I'd learned to make at Souz Dal, but I didn't understand that I'd only slightly improved it with the substitution of fresh juice. Why the hell was I even using a speed mix in the first place? I was comfortably sitting in the zone of baby steps, too inexperienced to radically rock the boat.

But it was so much fun. I rode my bike the quick five-minute commute from our place on Grace Street most afternoons to be at Cobalt with enough time to clean and organize for the night. I was so intent on making it work that scrubbing toilets never seemed like a chore (at least not in the beginning). The sheen of being a boss was thickly glossed on. I loved having no one to answer to, and the new power of that was as intoxicating as the access to all the margaritas I could stomach. Tyler always referred to them as "medicinal margaritas," and when I was bloated and cranky with PMS he'd make me one and say, "Take your medicine." It was a very effective panacea for all sorts of sadness, not the least of which was how little my marriage resembled my idealist version of what marriage was supposed to be. I'd grown up with parents who truly loved each other and I'd heard them doing it plenty of times at the cottage, where the rooms were close and the walls thin. Now, I found myself drowning thoughts of disharmony, mostly in margaritas. And it was easy to keep in a fundamental sadness, to protect it with the real and superficial happiness of a successful business, and lock it away with the false idea that my friendship with Tyler was the same as a loving marriage.

Tyler and I would split up the weekday shifts. He'd work

Sunday and Tuesday, I'd work Monday and Wednesday, and we'd both work Thursday, Friday, and Saturday. So it wasn't that we didn't see each other, but, in the first year, we didn't have time off work together much. Eventually, as we hired staff, we'd make sure to not work Thursdays and we'd go out for dinner, often at the nearby Gamelle, a pretty little jewel box of a French restaurant that had a painstakingly painted tin ceiling, a great wine list, and classic French food done with care. We'd sit in the front window and hold hands. People often told me how happy we seemed together, and I almost believed it.

RUNNING COBALT CAME VERY NATURALLY TO ME, and I never felt as though I had no idea what I was doing. I relied a lot on my Souz Dal experience, which involved making sure the place ran well and was kept clean. Cobalt wasn't a real leap; I was just adding beer orders and citrus runs and figuring out payroll. Don't let anyone ever tell you running a bar is hard. Running a restaurant is hard. Compared to restaurants, bars are a walk in the park—especially if they're busy.

Back then, in the late 1990s, food and drink didn't get nearly the media attention it does now. Restaurants got reviewed, but being pre-social-media kept the hype limited, and bars were all but ignored. So when *The Globe and Mail*, Canada's national paper, wanted to feature Cobalt on the cover of the Arts section, with a picture—probably because half the Arts section and all the Style section journalists regularly got wasted there, but still—I was flabbergasted and thrilled. My hair was lighter then and I had it done for the photo in a style that was very Sarah Jessica Parker circa 1999, and that's being generous.

I was proud enough of the little bit of media attention to have the piece framed and I leaned it in the window of the bar. It took at least a year for me to realize how silly this was. As it turned out, I didn't have to worry about media preservation, because my mother was all over that project in a serious way, keeping even the smallest mentions of Cobalt or me in a lovingly tended binder.

After the *Globe* piece ran, within a few months we could count on busy, busy nights Thursday through Saturday. I'd head toward the bar for a 9:00 p.m. start and see people bursting out the doors, not to smoke but to cool down (no matter how much we cranked the air conditioner, when it got packed, it got hot). Walking into the pulsing room and getting right to work was such a rush, and it never got old. I loved bartending, the technique and speed of it more than the small talk, but I could fake that. And I did. I could be both incredibly charming and incredibly terse, sometimes at the same time, which either charmed customers or put them off forever—my brand of snark isn't for everyone. Lots of things about this world have jaded me or become old hat over the years, but not the feeling of pride I get when I walk into one of my spots and it's booming.

It wasn't long before Cobalt developed a loyal crowd of regulars, all of whom had their different habits. One of my favourite groups—mostly guys, but sometimes their girlfriends would join in on their bar-hopping—came in almost every Saturday after midnight and ordered somewhere close to a case of beer and rounds of shots, with occasional mixed drinks thrown in. They were fun, polite, and rowdy in the right way; they laughed and were loud, but never broke shit on purpose, and if they did happen to shatter a pint glass, they always apologized and drunkenly tried to pick up the pieces, while I'd shoo them off. They all became lawyers and bankers, and were essentially bros, but nice, benign bros, more in it for the jet skis and high-fiving than the misogyny—the Brandon Walshes of bros. And of course they tipped really well—they must have if I remember them so fondly. I still email one of them at least three times a year with legal questions and pay him in foie gras.

One of the ways we brought people in was with DJs, mostly indie rock and Britpop, but some electronic and dance as well. In the 1990s this was a big thing, especially in small bars, and I can't remember busy spots that didn't have Technics 1200 turntables set up behind the bar or in a corner. We had a couple of really fun collective DJ nights. Like "Easy Tiger," which was headed up by two dudes whose musical tastes mostly lined up with mine, but extra heavy on the Britpop and the Oasis-inspired haircuts that were *de rigueur* for DJs spinning mostly Britpop. And "Committee" was a rotating band of tuned-in pals (some of whom I'd gone to high school with) who played basically whatever they felt like. Both crews were standouts: they knew how to pack a room and were just fun to work with.

At some point, maybe two years into bar ownership, I realized that what they were doing wasn't all that complex, so I bought myself the dumbed-down version, a double-deck CD DJ system, and figured out how it worked and how to smoothly transition from song to song—this wasn't proper mixing, and it wasn't records, but there's still an art to selecting—I acknowledged the lesser skill with my DJ name: DJ Press Play. My main jam has always been indie rock. New Order ruined me first; I fell in love with that jingle-jangle guitar and those harmonious synths. It's perfect grand-scale pop music disguised as something smaller, which means I'm a bit stumped by the current musical climate, heavy on beats and expropriation, light on melody. And although I realize this will brand me hard and deep as "white girl" (as though somehow loving indie rock doesn't already) I cannot for the life of me figure out trap music. I drunkenly yell for Pixies and Jesus and Mary Chain tunes at bars. Because NO ONE plays that shit any more, it's a spotlight for aging hipsters. (Is there some sort of support group?)

My obsession with music, unsurprisingly, took root when I was a teenager. One of my favourite things back then was to drive around Scarborough, windows down, with my current favourite album blasting on repeat. So many of my happiest teenager memories are associated with music and freedom and driving, and I've never quite recovered from the impact of falling in love with a certain genre and forever having that as my secret watermark for "cool." It's a devolved and stagnant way to judge, but I'll never get over it, especially if we're the same age. I mean, at least if you're a kid, I don't expect you to love The Stone Roses and Stereolab.

So learning to DJ felt like a very natural thing for me. I was fastidious in blending songs that didn't just make sense beatwise but were in keys that mixed well. And when that wasn't fun enough, I'd make correlations between a band and then something from the lead singer's solo catalogue, all culminating in the perfection of "Lost in the Supermarket" by the Clash, followed by their version of "Police on My Back" (written by Eddy Grant of the The Equals), followed by The Equals'

"Baby Come Back" (they both have the word "back" in them!), followed by Eddy Grant's "Electric Avenue," followed by Electric Six's "Danger High Voltage" (the Jack White sung indie dance hit), with just enough funk to follow "Electric Avenue" PLUS "Electric" then head into The White Stripes' "You're Pretty Good Looking (For a Girl)," which was a great transitional song from which I could step toward almost any indie tune, though it probably would be Joan Jett's "Doing All Right with the Boys" to balance, and on and on like that. You really only needed a basic understanding of music history to follow that one, and obviously the songs had to work well together to even bother adding the fun connections component, but it's what kept me interested, trying to string together more and more songs with real or dubious links.

For a long time, running Cobalt was really fun. I was just into my twenties, working long hours almost every day, fuelled by pride and necessity, but bartending for great tips, plus a small profit, DJing once a week, and drinking all the gin-and-tonics I could soak myself in. I felt like I'd won the fucking lottery. We even started a dinner series called "Sunday Night Supper Club," partnered with a popular, gregarious local chef. It was insane. The kitchen was a disaster, and hardly a kitchen, but we put out a really nice five-course menu every Sunday for just under a year. It was $45, so cheap it was practically free, and we didn't really make much money on it, but it was my first taste of what running a restaurant might be like.

It really did feel like a dream. The bar was making money and it was a fun, if slightly dramatic, environment. I had this ridiculous, sexist notion that Cobalt should hire only pretty young women, and the staff was all just into their twenties, around my age, which made the place equal parts crazy fun and crazy disaster, grade school all over again. I found myself very comfortable in the role of mother hen, too concerned/ involved with the minutiae of the staff's personal lives, which always seemed to be precariously perched on different spots of the metaphorical roller coaster. Gloria was constantly on the precipice of breaking up with her terrible boyfriend, Jessica was a cutter, Layla was manic and emotional, and Andrea was just a bit misguided, but good-hearted, and I saw myself in each of them. They'd come to me with their news, good and bad, and took turns ganging up on each other. One time I said something off-handed about Gloria's relationship (essentially that Gloria should leave her abusive, middling rock star boyfriend) to Andrea, and before even twenty-four hours had gone by I found myself having to apologize for my judgmental comment to a tearful Gloria, who had heard from Jessica (who had heard from Layla, who had heard from Andrea), but somehow, through broken telephone, my comment had turned into "omg, Jen said Gloria was WEAK for staying with Carl" or some such nonsense. I was only a couple of years older than most of the staff, and I was also very fond of all of them, but I wasn't mature enough not to get caught up in their catty garbage, never mind my own, and everything I learned was how not to manage, how not to be a boss. It was way too gossipy and interconnected, and by the end of the business I pretty much never wanted to see any of them again. Which was, no doubt, mutual.

Most relationships seem to be based on tolerance and a vague sense of liking the other person, but the assured mutual destruction of divorce is sometimes enough of a deterrent to keep people blindly going through the motions of mediocre love, and Tyler and I were no different. By year four of Cobalt we were basically living as roommates, not acknowledging the resentful tension, and sometimes cooking elaborate meals for friends and treating ourselves to the occasional lavish meal out to help fill in the constructed picture of a happy life together. But how could we be happy if we never fucked?

It got to the point where I couldn't take it any more, and one day I basically told Tyler that I needed to have sex, and if he and I couldn't make that happen then I'd find it elsewhere. Obviously this is a marriage-ending conversation in most circumstances, but he just seemed focused on the fact that we would remain married, even in the face of my announced infidelity. We didn't make rules or anything, and I absolutely wouldn't have cared if he had slept with other people, which I assume he did, but why we didn't just break up is beyond me.

One night, a few months into what should have been a breakup, we managed to have sex, but we were both so drunk we somehow left a pot of pasta water on high and woke up to the smell of dry metal on fire. I was furious and blamed Tyler, so instead of the sex being a positive turning point, it was a negative one, and the ugliness of the fight made it clear we should just stop trying. We drank too much and fought too much. We just weren't a good match. We finally broke up, but we couldn't afford to live apart so we spent eight months living in the same house while being "officially" broken up, and just ended up getting back together. So unhealthy.

After a number of attempts at making it work, we finally gave up trying for good in 2004. I knew I wanted a divorce, but I just couldn't find the words. Part of me probably thought this was it. I was mentally playing Peggy Lee's "Is That All There Is?" on repeat. Maybe this *was* all there was to the circus?

I was confused and stressed and unhappy, but just couldn't seem to tear off the band-aid. I knew we weren't good together, but we had developed a strong codependency based on this idea of "family," which included our roles as matriarch and patriarch of Cobalt. I honestly didn't think there was anyone else who'd put up with my shitty temperament, which was based mostly on my being extremely judgmental of Tyler rather than accepting of him. It never occurred to me that the relationship was bringing out the worst aspects of my personality, and that maybe if I were happier I'd show more of my good qualities, more often. This has led to a lifetime belief in the immutability of people; we don't change, not really, we are just low-lighted by poor relationships with lovers, family, and friends and highlighted by great ones. But still, I waffled for months, making lists of pros and cons when all I had to do was ask myself one simple question: Was I happy? Sleeping with other people and not my husband certainly seemed to strongly indicate no, but none of the local waiters actually made me want to leave Tyler—they were fun, but not before 2:00 a.m. As my marriage disintegrated into resentful friendship I would selfishly put the staff in positions where they could see I was sleeping with other guys. It was obvious when the waiter from a nearby bar came by at 1:30 a.m. and just never left, even as the staff gathered their coats. It wasn't that I'd kept that from Tyler; I had already made it clear that our dried-up sex life was untenable and I had no choice but to discreetly fuck local waiters. I just could have been more discreet. I think they felt I was taking advantage of Tyler, but it was so much more complicated than that, or it seemed that way to me. Tyler and I were ill-matched, but codependent, and our relationship wasn't built on a strong enough foundation to withstand the pressures of being married co-bosses and constantly around each other.

I had my slap-in-the-face "Aha!" moment in the form of an illicit make-out session with a guy I had a little crush on. He was a friend of a friend and we'd always had good banter, but one night, at our mutual friend's house for dinner, we snuck out to the balcony for a smoke and I just kissed him. It was fun, and didn't end up going anywhere, but how much I liked it was the wake-up call I needed. I barely slept, so high from sparks I hadn't felt in ages, from the idea of even having a crush on someone—it was enough to keep me tossing and turning all night, and I knew I'd have to end things with Tyler permanently.

It was a coward's way out—"Oooooh, I like a boy and I kissed him, so now that I can focus solely on that I can finally let go of the dead-weight, driftwood marriage that's been over for years!" Not very empowered, but I've decided it's fine, because I was still under thirty. All is forgiven.

The talk was brutal. I told Tyler I couldn't take the unhappiness any more. I told him I had made out with someone else, and that it wasn't just a sex thing, that I actually liked him, and that I was sorry, which was only half true. I told him I still loved him, which, at the time, felt mostly true. Despite our romantic love being a distant memory, I still cared about him, just in an incredibly selfish way: I wanted the protection and security offered by a marriage and had held on to that for way too long. We went round and round in circles, cried a lot. It felt final this time. I wanted it to be final so I *finally* asked him to move out, which he very graciously did.

We imagined we could still somehow run a business together, because we were *geniuses*. At first it was fine, we behaved very respectfully toward each other and tried to just erase the past and repurpose our current situation as two people who'd only ever been friends, but after almost a year of this arrangement, Tyler's eventual girlfriend wasn't super-keen on all the postmodernism. She, probably correctly, was very uncomfortable with how close Tyler and I were. We were both equally uninterested in resuming any sort of romance, but we were too involved, day to day, for any new girlfriend to feel comfortable, and she expressed her discomfort in progressively scarier ways. By the time she just about overdosed, we were starting to clue in that some real emotional distance wouldn't be such a bad thing.

Our relationship grew more and more estranged, yet still, we stubbornly refused to close the bar, which by this time was a sinking ship, although I remained blissfully unaware of just how "sink-y." I had, by this time, checked out in a real way.

cobalt

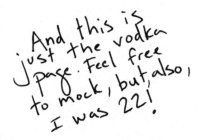

6.75

vodka cocktails (2 1/4 oz.)

vodka, orange, grapefruit, lemon, lime	vitamin c
vodka, coconut rum, pineapple	malibu stacey
vodka, apple and sour apple liqueur, apple juice	the spy
vodka, sour apple liqueur, amaretto, lemon, lime	crabapple
vodka, crème de cacao	chocolate
vodka, crème de cacao, frangelico, cranberry	cherry blossom
vodka, crème de cacao, cream, bailey's	chocolate truffle
vodka, crème de cacao, crème de menthe	after eight
vodka, crème de cacao, banana liqueur	chocolate chimp
vodka, crème de cacao, raspberry	louis XIV (14th)
vodka, crème de cacao, galliano	harlot
vodka, amaretto, frangelico	frosty nuts
vodka, crème de cacao, goldschläger	platinum blonde
vodka, drambuie, b&b, scotch	santana

8: ROLAND

I HAD FALLEN IN LOVE. Not some rebound distraction, the real shit. And it was such a nice change of scenery from the awful fuck-dates I'd been going on that I wilfully looked away as my business crumbled.

With my new, chosen freedom, I'd done a few typical things, aside from dragging home boys at 2:30 in the morning: I accidentally lost a bit of weight and on-purpose got a haircut, figured out how to put on makeup, and bought a few pairs of jeans that highlighted my ass. I also enrolled in a baking class at the local cooking school. It was extremely rudimentary: basic muffins and quick breads that worked up to the final class which focused, very anticlimactically, on a very un-delicious Black Forest cake. Mostly because they weren't going to use real cream for that many layers, and the cherries were those gloopy canned ones that trigger childhood memories of eating them by the spoonful; the ones that almost taste good, but actually contain only traces of real cherry. How not good it was didn't stop me from leaving it on my new romantic interest's doorstep, as a baked love note. (He was pretty pleased with the gesture, and he didn't not eat it.)

My habit was to pop into Cocktail Molotov after class on my way home, mostly for its proximity to my house but also for the bartenders, who were all very friendly and played great music. Dundas Street West, where Molotov was, lived up to the moniker I'd given it—Dirty Dundas—even though it was just a short walk south from the well-maintained, flower-planter/Christmas-light-heavy College Street. The vast divide between the vibe of College—which was quickly tipping into not cool any more, despite having once been decidedly so—versus the up-and-coming gentrification of rough-and-tumble Dundas West was emphasized by the upkeep, or rather lack thereof, the sidewalks received (now fixed) and the infrequent street-cleanings (now nightly occurrences).

One Wednesday in early January 2005, after one of my first baking classes, I walked into Molotov and there were a few people at the bar. I particularly noticed the pair of black men sitting in the middle. They stuck out, for terrible reasons like their age and race. Despite the multiculturalism of Toronto and our neighbourhood, places like bars that play indie rock were, and sorta still are, mostly white. It's a problem, also, when it comes to relationships and sex. The idea that people have a type has always infuriated me, as it usually is code for some noncommittal blanket that covers up basic racism: *What do you mean you don't date Asians? Oh, they aren't your type. Okay, ya, that makes perfect sense.* We're always bragging about a utopic, integrated, post-racial society that doesn't actually exist here. I mean, there are far worse places to live, but I don't care for the hypocrisy.

I sat a few stools down from the more extraordinarily handsome of the two and took a few sidelong glances while trying not to stare. Only to say that what I was immediately attracted to was how he looked, his eyes, his cheekbones, his air and confidence, and his lean body. Is that discriminatory against fat, ugly men? Attraction is a strange thing, and we are liars if we try to take looks out of it, but looks and race are different things, and we must acknowledge that our looks preferences are so often based in underlying and subconscious (or gross and very conscious) racial prejudices.

I had a couple of whiskies, and at some point in the evening the bartender introduced me to Roland, the handsome man, who I realized I'd seen around but had never met. I guess she figured that because we both owned bars (he more by marriage than of his own volition) we might have something to talk about. We chatted, and shortly after, Roland leaned over to his friend and said, "Who she looking at?" His friend pointed out the obvious and Roland said, "Okay, get the hell outta here."

His voice and Haitian accent were intoxicating, and we talked about our shared love of design. He was an expert, and Cocktail Molotov had previously been his design store, where he retailed Eames chairs among other stuff as well as designed and built a beautiful collection of modernist lamps. But, even better, he was an artist. A painter.

I was hooked.

My memory would eventually summon up the time I had wandered into his design store, also called Cocktail Molotov. This was a few years prior, and I'd gone in ready to buy, ignoring the fact that all the beautiful furnishings and trinkets were way out of my budget. I shuffled around the store, picking things up, sitting in Eames rockers, and eventually noticed a man fiddling with something intently, his glasses perched on the bottommost point of his nose. No hello. No eye contact. No nothing. After a long few seconds of awkward silence I passive-aggressively cleared my throat. He looked up at me over his glasses, obviously annoyed, and said, "What you want?" I rolled my eyes, turned on my heel, and left in a huff, completely oblivious to his insane sex appeal.

But at the bar, loosened by whisky, I was anything but oblivious, and it wasn't long before we were making out like teenagers. Unusual behaviour for both of us, considering we each had a fairly recent separation behind us. I'd only been living alone since September and this was January, and Roland had separated the previous June, so we probably weren't looking to make any public declarations. But even as it got later and the bar filled up with the dudes from Broken Social Scene and their pals, we remained obliviously locked in a kiss. And then more kissing.

I even let my hand slide down to his crotch and linger over a good-sized hard-on, whispering, "That's a nice dick." I desperately wanted to take him to bed, but didn't want to rush it, because I really liked him, and the patriarchy says to take it slow when you like a dude so he won't think you're a slut (it's baked in and we all eat the brownies). After a few more whiskies, he asked me if I wanted to come upstairs, where he still conveniently lived, to see his furniture. "Is it attached?" I returned.

As he showed me around his place I removed various articles of clothing but kept my bra and high-heeled boots on.

He was hooked.

We talked and kissed for hours, but somehow, we didn't fuck. I woke with a start at 5:00 in the morning to full-on small-spooning. We'd apparently cuddled all night, the intimacy of which freaked the fuck out of me. Penis-vagina sex would have been fine, but SPOONING? I started getting dressed, ready to bolt, but Roland insisted on walking me home, just around the corner. (Shockingly, we had lived seconds apart and owned bars on the same street, but had never met until we were both single.) I thought it was sweet that he offered, and I let him. We kissed goodbye on my front steps as the sun peeked over the roof of the church across the street, and I closed the door behind me, ecstatic, scared, and knowing I was done for.

And we hadn't even fucked.

LIVING ON MY OWN GAVE ME A HUGE SENSE OF RELIEF and freedom. It was so nice to be able to just fool around with dudes and have a place to go back to, instead of my usual, all-class make-out sessions in a hidden area of the bar you couldn't see from the street. Yet, the house was still littered with signs of a dead marriage: old sneakers belonging to Tyler scattered by the door, a baseball bat leaning up against a bookshelf, and two toothbrushes in the cup on the bathroom sink. I hadn't even thought to take down our wedding picture from the mantel, assuming that since I was completely over Tyler and our marriage the photo was just part of the decor and something that didn't matter. I never thought it would freak out the potential boyfriends I brought home. And maybe it did, or maybe they just weren't that into me— but I didn't like that story as much. It was so much easier to just leave the pictures up and assume I was perfect, and if they didn't stick around they just didn't want to get tangled up in a woman's impending divorce and her possible unresolved feelings about that.

To be honest, I didn't really enjoy dating beyond the

initial sexual experience. I found the elevated emotions, heightened by a recent breakup and infused with happy sex hormones, annoying, especially since all I really wanted to do was fuck. But even the fucking wasn't all that satisfying. If it wasn't a man-child (you know the type, works for a tech start-up and is somehow adept at finger-banging while being terrible at every other aspect of interaction, likes quality beer but is really getting into Old Fashioneds, and will constantly try to make a case for Farrelly Bros movies being "actually quite misunderstood," and also digs comics, A LOT, it was some dumb waiter (like literally, as dumb as an actual dumb-waiter)—basically whoever was handy, and no one I actually wanted to be with, no one who was worth seeing in daylight.

This was all compounded by being a woman who'd managed to be the one in a million born with just one breast. Not in the middle like some third, lonely eye, but short one, missing one, incomplete. It's called Poland's syndrome and it mostly affects men, for whom a missing nip and pec is far less of a big deal (lucky me!), but at least I managed to avoid the usual accompanying webbed fingers, so that's . . . something.

As a teenager, this was a source of much conflict and resentment. I blamed my mother, myself (but never my dad, he was faultless in my eyes). It was unfair, I didn't deserve this. I'd pray to wake up cured one day, like it was some sort of affliction rather than the random birth defect it was—my mother certainly wasn't to blame. I'd bargain and pray that it would be passed on to someone more deserving. But it wasn't something I would come to terms with as a girl or a teenager, the shame too strong for a soft ego. And as a teen, the excruciating pain of a huge libido and a strong desire to be naked countered by a fear of exposing my body to boys who were too young to be kind or too stupid to hide their shock was almost unbearable.

All of this stayed with me through my adult dating life: I would never take off my shirt the first time I had sex with someone new, and always found creative reasons to keep my bra on the next few times, until I'd have no choice but to explain, and I was good enough at fucking that the smart, kind guys would get past it. Despite having an implant surgically placed at sixteen, my breasts didn't match, and I was short a nipple and up one scar. It was such a contradiction with who I was, who I still am—someone who wants to go braless and run around naked. A few friends knew the truth, which probably means everybody did. I didn't really care about that, so long as they never rubbed my face in it, which, remarkably, no one did. But I rubbed my own face in it, angry that I couldn't wear certain things, angry that I had to learn how to pick the right tops and dresses, something that, despite my much better attitude about a life with "just one breast," still frustrates me now. I had to learn to find myself beautiful. And I couldn't do it alone.

ROLAND AND I HADN'T EXCHANGED NUMBERS the first night we met, but he called me the next Monday at Cobalt. It was just after opening and no customers had arrived yet. When I answered he said, "Is that Jen? This is Roland, you remember me?" I told him I'd met a ton of men with Haitian accents in the past week so I'd have to think about it. Silence. I later found out he almost hung up then and there. But I giggled and told him of course I remembered him. He tried to make a lunch date for 11:00 a.m. the next day, which struck me as insane considering I'd be lucky to get out of Cobalt by 3:00 a.m. We compromised at 2:00. WHO MAKES A LUNCH DATE AS A FIRST DATE?

On Tuesday I showed up a few minutes late and was immediately uncomfortable. I sank into my cropped silver-fox coat, uncharacteristically squirming in the plastic chair that already felt like it would collapse under me. We were at a local café where he was a regular and I was disliked for sending back hard-poached eggs one time. (Seriously, people who like hard-poached eggs are basically the enemies of good food. WHY WOULD YOU NOT WANT A PERFECT, SOFT-POACHED EGG? It's CRAZY.) I felt like the staff were staring and whispering, because they were. I asked him if he noticed the obvious discussions the servers were having re: us, together, and what was up with that, were we dating? etc., etc. He said, "This is bullshit, so rude," so we decided not to order and went down the street to a spot that had wine, and proceeded to have an incredibly easy, interesting conversation that was so engrossing we only noticed the employees trying to subtly close up around us three hours later when chairs started going up. I was so embarrassed. We'd gotten so lost in each other that I'd ignored the cardinal rule of being a savvy industry customer, and we quickly gathered our stuff and left.

In front of his building I kissed Roland, and as I walked away he called out, "Don't make me chase you." I laughed, knowing he wouldn't have to.

And still, we hadn't fucked.

We made plans to meet the following Wednesday after my next baking class, around 10:00 p.m., at Cocktail Molotov. I was on time, a little fluttery and dressed for a date. I slid onto one of the stools closest to the door, had a drink, and waited. A few minutes went by before Roland came over, from a table just out of my view at the back of the bar. He took my hand and offered me a drink, his charm just as I'd remembered it. I lifted my glass, pointedly looking at it—I already *had* a drink. He seemed distracted. He said he was just wrapping up with some old friends, would I mind waiting just a few minutes? I didn't mind, it would give me a chance to get some wine in me and calm my nervous stomach.

But five minutes quickly turned into fifteen, and I was starting to feel a bit uneasy. I have this really weird thing where if I'm nervous leading up to a date I'll have to shit like five times, which I've always trusted to indicate a serious enthrallment, or, at the very least, attraction. "I like you SO MUCH I shit my pants!" So I was in need of the toilet, but I ignored the feeling because I didn't want to walk by Roland's table and have him think I was spying, which, in retrospect, seems insane. Instead, I stubbornly held it in until the feeling passed, with the help of a couple glasses of wine. I assumed he had his reasons for not asking me to join his table in the first place, I mean, we'd only just met. But on the other hand, we had *made plans*.

Roland eventually popped over, clearly flustered, to see how I was doing. More hand-holding, more apologies, more assurances he would be joining me very shortly. I probably managed to just hold back an eye roll, but figured, what the hell, free wine. I was un-rich enough for that alone to be enticing. Another half hour went by.

He was now darting back and forth between me and what I imagined were *important* guests. When it had been almost an hour, my pride finally felt more than a little pinched and I resolved to leave. Seconds later he came over and sat down, and I tried to hide my annoyance. I told him he had just caught me. Who knows why I stayed, but he is a very charming, handsome man, and I was really into the promise of sleeping with him.

As we settled into a conversation and I decided to let his lapse in judgment pass, a couple of tipsy girls walked past on their way out. The one with the megawatt boobs gave me some hard-core side-eye but Roland just focused on me. Immediately, a couple of red flags popped up and it occurred to me that I might be on a date with a total player, which, in the moment, I decided was fine. He was hot; who cared if this was going to be tempo-rary? It's not like I wanted to jump into a relationship.

After a while, he suggested sitting at a table, which I Nancy Drew-ed happened to be the same table the girls had just vacated, since it was the only one out of my line of vision. There was a guy and another woman at the adjacent table, and Roland knew them. I gathered they had all been chatting just moments before. The woman was quite flirtatious with Roland, insisting on speaking in French even though the other guy and I weren't fluent. When Roland went to the washroom, I noticed a wallet on the banquette right beside me, in the seat that was very likely still warm from holding Booby McBoobs. I asked if it was anyone's then opened it, and when the dude saw the pic, he said it was Roland's "girlfriend's" wallet. I felt humiliated, and was grateful the dim light buried the flush that rose on my cheeks. But I didn't say anything. I just took all my focus and shoved it at the dude, an architect, who was clearly interested, perhaps to the point of exaggerating Roland's relationship with boobs-girl. As it turned out, she was strictly a fling that hadn't heeded Roland's request to not come by that night as he had a date with a girl he really liked—me. None of which I knew. I just believed the dude, and he was cute enough that I figured I'd cut my losses and obvious-flirt with him.

After about twenty minutes of this (a third of the time Roland kept me waiting, I might add), Roland stood up, clasped his hands, and said "Goodnight, *les enfants*" and went upstairs to his apartment, which suggested that maybe he wasn't some hardened player after all—a player would have finished the game. I went to the bar and had a brief huddle with the bartender, who I was friendly with. I asked her directly if Roland was just dicking me around, and she said he really liked me and tonight was just a comedy of errors, and Booby Boobersons wasn't, in fact, his girlfriend; he just had a lot of interested parties and was handling it poorly. Because I didn't even have a cellphone then, she called Roland for me. He told me to come upstairs whenever I wanted. I lingered over my wine for a while—fair's fair—then eventually went up to find him relaxing in his bed. He patted the spot next to him, and nodded toward the space beside him. We cuddled, kissed, talked, and slept for a bit.

And still didn't fuck.

Finally, the following Thursday, we were to go on a proper date, dinner. Roland suggested his favourite restaurant, Lee Garden. I instantly dreaded the idea of fluorescent lighting and no wine—well, no wine I'd want to drink—and put my foot down. I felt I had been extremely accommodating thus far, going on afternoon "dates," getting practically stood up.

There was no way we were having our first real date in a plastic-tabled Chinatown institution. I insisted on Le Paradis, an affordable and bustling yet intimate French bistro, way out of our neighbourhood, where we'd be unlikely to run into anyone we knew since we weren't into being public about a thing neither of us was sure was going to be an actual thing. We were also very aware of how hot and fresh the gossip that we were dating would be, and at least one of us had an ex who would maybe react poorly to the news of us as a couple, so for the first months we were pretty cautious.

We had a long, talkative dinner. We held hands, gazed at each other, and drank lots of gamay. We talked about nature versus nurture, and he joked that I was Hitlerian in my approach, but even so I found our discourse exciting, not antagonizing. I revelled in all the things we were trying to say at once, our conversation jumping around from politics to exes to business, but always settling on an exposition of who we were. We understood immediately that we both valued truth, in its rawest, rarest form.

We left the restaurant and walked a bit, snowflakes settling briefly on my fur jacket. He put his arm around me and we kissed under the streetlight. By the time the cab dropped us at my place, I knew.

We finally fucked.

And it was perfect.

THE FIRST TIME ROLAND AND I WENT TO NEW YORK, more than ten years ago and four months into our relationship, one of our afternoon pit stops was SoHo's one-time cutting-edge Café Habana (now open in Dubai, which really dulls the edge off), the perfect mix of Caribbean vibe and food with hipster touches, a very difficult thing to achieve with any authenticity (a silly word that we should just leave off the table altogether instead of judging whether it applies in describing a Caribbean place run by a white dude). But to my memory it was one of the first really successful cultural mash-up restaurants that now poke out of gentrifying neighbourhoods like whack-a-moles, thanks in no small part to taco places like Chicago's Big Star and, more recently, Mission Chinese in San Francisco and New York. The place became a piece of the "we fell in love in New York" story. We ate the grilled corn, tolerated the rest of the food, drank Cuba Libras, and soaked in the scene, highlighted by the friendly, just beautiful enough without being terrifying, mostly mixed-race servers.

It marked us, that trip. It was in our "just fine" hotel room, all we could afford and still highly recommended to our under-thirty friends, that I finally showered in front of Roland. It meant so much to show him my body, to finally reveal myself without the protection of a bra or dim lighting. I purposefully left the curtain open, knowing I had to just jump. And despite having been through it before with other boyfriends, it was not at all like riding a bike. It never got easier, and this already felt way more truly, madly, deeply than any past relationships. He looked on from across the room, eventually coming into the tub. We were both overwhelmed with a flood of happy, love feelings; I probably cried through our kisses. It's hard enough to get naked in front of a new lover with just the normal societal pressures grinding down on women—poking at our muffin tops and demanding thigh gaps. Try doing it short one breast. But in that moment Roland looked at me with the most sincere love and lust, and I knew he found me beautiful. Despite having thus far relied mostly on a well-built ego for my feelings of self-worth and attractiveness, his look actually made me feel, for the first time, like a fucking goddess. And it was at that moment that I fell in love with him. I respected him so much, I reasoned that if he found me beautiful, maybe it was true. Which doesn't sound very feminist, but it was the thing that helped the most.

He thought he'd take me around Manhattan, and I let him keep getting hopelessly lost for a day before showing off my finely tuned directional skills (plus . . . it's a fucking grid with numbered streets!) and leading the way to secret bars and tasty food. I loved taking him to my favourite cocktail spots: Angel's Share, hidden at the back of a restaurant, and the reservations-only trailblazer Milk and Honey.

And we did his stuff, too, most notably the Museum of Modern Art, where he quietly demonstrated his vast, unending knowledge of modernist and postmodern art. He easily identified every single painting at an impressive distance. I mean Every. Single. One. I was pretty blown away, as my knowledge of art up to that major turning point was mostly based on "Do I like this?" "Do I want it in my house?" Which, as it turns out, is exactly how to care about art.

On our way home, I was twelve hours into an ear infection that was getting more stabby-painful by the minute, and as we waited to board the plane, Roland cupped my ear and stroked my hair, looked concerned, and basically did whatever he could to alleviate my pain—and he's being doing it ever since, which is why I married him as soon as both of our divorces came through. It's a strange thing, reconciling the idea of marriage with a strong feminist sensibility, and I can't justify it other than to say it felt important to me at the time, and it was a hell of a party. Now, with our relationship based on years of experience with each other, being married means nothing. We are a unit, existing as individuals and as a couple. We live a beautiful life, and he will always be the only man I'll ever love.

THROUGHOUT THIS BLISSFUL TIME, cartoon hearts pulsing around my head, stars in my eyes, I gave even less attention to the business than I had been.

I showed up for my shifts at Cobalt, but beyond that, I was pretty checked out. I was too busy with my new life, building a happy foundation with Roland. I hadn't ever overly scrutinized the books, a mistake I would never repeat. Tyler was totally in charge of the money and bookkeeping side of things, which was fine with me as I have always equally hated paperwork and numbers.

One Thursday I went to the bank to buy change for the weekend, and the teller kept insisting she couldn't access the $4,000 or so in the account, that it was frozen. I stared at her for a few seconds, stunned, and then, entirely while trying not to, I burst into tears, so confused by what was going on.

I had often asked Tyler if everything was okay, if we were on top of our bills. He'd always said yes. And I had no reason to doubt him. The whole business was in my name, and when the government froze the account, the $300,000 in unpaid taxes fell on me. Hard.

9: BIG IDEAS, BIG REALS

I WAS DEVASTATED BY MY NEW SITUATION of prospective poverty. I knew I'd have to face reality, and my boyfriend, and the horrifying idea of "what now?"

I left the bank wiping my tears but gathering my pride, and walked straight to Roland's place. We'd been together more than a year, long enough that I felt comfortable showing up a mess, both physically and otherwise.

He was painting in his makeshift studio on the patio of Cocktail Molotov, and when I told him what had happened at the bank, he just hugged me and said all the right things. And when I'd finally calmed down and stopped crying, he told me to close Cobalt right away. At first I balked at this. This was a business I'd built from the ground up and that I had been running for eight years. How could I just close it? What would I do? Go work in a bar? Answer to some asshole manager? All of these thoughts came rushing at me like a tsunami. It was like I couldn't see that there wasn't any other way out. I didn't have the $300,000, and the government certainly wasn't just going to forgive the debt and tell me to start over and "THIS TIME DON'T FORGET TO PAY US, SWEETIE." I was fucked and I knew it, but I couldn't get my head around just closing for good. Cobalt was all I'd known for a good portion of my life as a working woman, it was my baby, I had built it and nurtured it for eight years, I couldn't imagine life without my bar, and the thought of getting a "regular" job was incredibly unappealing. I felt cornered.

Roland sat me down and explained I could probably declare bankruptcy, that it was likely my only option. I shot back that there MUST be other options, bankruptcy couldn't possibly be the ONLY option. But, very calmly, Roland just kept saying that I had no choice here, and as the words started to land and make sense, I realized he was right. I was, for the first time in my life, in a "no way out" position. I hated the lack of control, the failure, and the idea of destroying my good credit, possibly forever. Yet, by the time I left the patio to go upstairs and make dinner, I had already started to formulate a plan to close Cobalt immediately.

I don't think any of our friends or regulars were too surprised we were shutting down—it had been an eight-year run, something to be proud of (minus the giant debt), and everyone knew we were divorcing. What better way to close a party bar than with one last party? The theme would be "Everything Must Go," and we would have all our favourite DJs from over the years spinning. At first it felt sad to be planning a closing party, but by the end of the month, having wriggled out of our lease, I was incredibly relieved. So much so that I spent most of the final service dancing on the bar, the weight of an impossibly indebted business lifted away.

We paid off all the small suppliers by selling the chattels, like fridges, tables and chairs, and glassware. I had no intention of not paying all the beer and liquor companies who had done so much to support us with things as small as thirty-day terms and as big as beer fridges—and yes, of course I'm aware of the quid-pro-quo-ness of this sort of "help," and the obligation that came with that beer fridge to keep it stocked with only one beer. But there was no way I could crawl out of a $300,000 tax hole. It was bleak. And Roland was right, my only choice was bankruptcy, because of course I hadn't incorporated the business. With zero experience, how was I to know that incorporating the bar protected me from personal liability, and if I'd done it I could have avoided forever marring my credit score? But here I was, marked by another indelible lesson, learned the hard way. Always, always incorporate.

Bankruptcy is a horrible experience from start to finish. And it never ends: that thing they tell you about having poor credit for seven years after? Not even close. It's been years since seven years came and went. I own four, going on five successful businesses, a home, and a car, and I *still* can't get a loan without my husband's co-sign. Bankruptcy really should be the last option, because it fucks your credit score forever. (Note: I FINALLY recovered my almost-perfect credit score in early 2016, almost exactly ten years later.)

All bankruptcy operations seem to be buried deep in the suburbs. Mine was no exception, an undistinguished office with drab furnishings, garish lighting, and unsympathetic men in awful suits who offered me nothing, least of all empathy. They are vermin, trained to make people feel small, irresponsible, and corrupt. It's a completely humiliating exercise, and I think they enjoy it. Roland wanted to come with me but I decided to go on my own; I didn't want to put him through what I was pretty sure would be an unpleasant experience. And I was right. I showed up for my 11:00 a.m. appointment five minutes early and they made me wait almost forty minutes to see my assigned trustee. He was stuffed into a cheap suit, and he barely looked at me as he explained how this would all work. I didn't own anything, so bankruptcy really seemed like the right solution. The only creditor was the government, and it was just so much money I knew I could never pay it off. I really tried to explain to Cheap Suit what had happened, how I'd found myself there, but he gave zero fucks. They charged me $2,000, which seemed like a miracle compared to $300,000, so I signed the paperwork and slunk out. Being condescended to and made to feel like a flake by a conservative old dude only compounded my own feelings of having severely fucked up. And my father certainly wasn't impressed.

AFTER CLOSING COBALT and dealing with all the bankruptcy stuff, I knew I'd have to start working again right away. Somehow Roland and I had been managing on very little bits of money, maybe $500 a week, which included my rent, a scant $1,500 per month for a three-bedroom house. I'd taken on a roommate because I didn't want to leave my much-loved Grace Street home, and even though the total rent was a great deal, and the roommate covered half, I still had expenses of around $1,000 per month. Roland was almost completely supporting me.

Yet, despite our lack of disposable income, we had a very happy life. We had our house wine, some $8 Italian bottle that was the least-bad $8 wine I could find, and we loved it. I'd cook dinner every day—nothing fancy: stews, pastas, roast chicken, and the occasional grilled rib-eye, which we'd slice up and share. I'd bake pies, hoping Roland's youngest son, Jamal, would, at the very least, start to find me less evil. He was twelve when I showed up, an awkward age no matter what, never mind an ugly divorce between his parents. Roland's older children, twins from a young "get out of Haiti" marriage (and, truly, another story for another day), had always welcomed me, and Jamal's older brother Ishmael was at an age where he wasn't around much, but Jamal and I had to make it work because we spent half the week together, Thursday to Sunday. It took some time, but we eventually became very close. I think of him as my kid, and I couldn't possibly love him more.

Roland and I found happiness in each other, and I honestly felt I could just go on like that, in the blissed-out joy of trips to the market, slow-prepped meals, and picnics at home. Roland used to love to set up pillows and a blanket on the living room floor. We'd listen to music, order Chinese, fool around, and just enjoy being in love—all on those blankets on the floor. It was the first time for both of us, falling in love, and despite my previous marriage not turning out the way I'd hoped it would, I was grateful for the experience; without the maturity that I'd gained, I wouldn't have been emotionally prepared to deal with a man twenty years my senior, or his kids.

Roland never made me feel bad about not working, which wasn't for lack of my trying to get a job. I wanted to make my own money, and the appeal of being a housewife, which had felt so freeing and so good, was fast wearing off. I needed something other than preparing beautiful dinners to occupy my time. I was getting restless, but I couldn't find work. I applied for jobs anywhere and everywhere; I applied with friends in the industry, shitty places, good places, absolutely everywhere except fast-food places. No one would hire me. People I'd known for years, restaurants I'd been patronizing—I could not get a job anywhere. Eventually I realized that people weren't interested in employing someone who'd been their own boss for eight years, and I'd have to try a different approach. I replaced "owner" with "manager" on my resumé and started applying places where I didn't know a soul. Within a couple of weeks, I finally got an interview with The Cocktail Club.

All I really knew about this place was that it was a bar catering company with a good reputation, doing everything from film festival parties to weddings, but specializing in big events like Pride and large-scale fundraisers. I was hired on as a bartender, and I was excited. I'd been looking for work for so long that finally finding it was a huge relief. I rode my bike home that evening after the interview to tell Roland the good news, practically giddy. We went out to our favourite local spot, the long-gone Niagara Street Café, and celebrated over wine and much hand-holding.

The giddiness faded fast. Bartending at The Cocktail Club was gruelling work and, at times, an absolute shit-show. The set-ups took hours and they were insane, there was almost never enough help, and they often involved lugging twenty-pound bags of ice up many flights of stairs, dozens of times. Eventually, at my own restaurants years later, we would do alcohol batching for speed, especially during busy services. But at The Cocktail Club everything (including juice) was pre-mixed in giant buckets and funnelled into those awful white plastic speed-pour jugs. The one manager I usually worked with struck me as an incompetent frat bro, one of those dudes who loved his "powerful" position and always looked like he was doing something while getting literally nothing done. Everyone else came from nightclub backgrounds and seemed dumb. Out of fifty or so people, there was one guy who was funny, so once I found him, I hung on. We'd trade jokes and sneak occasional shots to help pass the time on twelve-hour shifts. On one particularly horrendous job, for a Pride event, I worked from 9:00 in the morning until past midnight with not enough shade in a scorching-hot parking lot on Church Street. Three days of that. Just me and one other person doing set-up and take-down. No real breaks. And even the supposedly fun film festival parties sucked. I didn't care about seeing stars, but serving the demanding, awful people who do care about that sort of thing was completely un-fun.

It's safe to say that I hated it, and the money wasn't good enough to balance out the hate. After four months the bosses offered me a management position, but I realized that it was time to make a change. I had to find something at least marginally better. So I turned the job down and gave my notice.

I landed an interview for bartending at a private club, one of the first in Toronto that aimed to be exclusive yet cool, failing on both counts. The appeal of the place for me was strictly economic: it seemed like I'd make good money there, with its young, bourgeois pretensions so obviously displayed. During the interview the smarmy manager, in a moment of prescient irony, stumped me with a question about what the main ingredients in a Bordelaise sauce are (Bordelaise contains bone marrow, and one of the anchors of the Hoof menu is roasted bone marrow). But I got the job.

On my first shift, they put me on the bar for a private party with zero training, aside from a cursory lesson in how their POS (point of sale) system worked. I was a good bartender, so I was able to handle the moneyed, bourgey types who mobbed the bar pretty much by myself, but people had long wait times if they wanted anything other than beer and wine. There should have been two of us working, but most bartenders don't think that way—they want to keep all the money for themselves—and bartenders who become managers (who aren't that good at managing) staff that way to keep operating costs down, stupidly failing to realize that the business can bring in more money when properly staffed. A properly staffed bar is a really good sign to know immediately if a place is well run.

That day I ended up selling $1,600 in mostly drinks, which, for a four-hour shift, is pretty good. But it easily could've been $2,000 with an additional bartender. As my finishing time loomed closer, other employees started to set up for the night shift. They were all very blasé and didn't seem to care too much about the details, wiping tables half-heartedly and setting them with crooked forks. It had all the markings of a place with serious leadership problems.

By the time I was gathering my stuff to leave, the general manager who'd hired me finally checked in, wanting to discuss availability. I said I was available to work anytime and then asked him about my tip-out. He informed me that since it had been a "training" shift I wouldn't be paid anything, nor would I be receiving any tips. So, I asked, who was going to get the large amount of tip money I'd brought in, likely close to $300? I didn't wait for his response. I walked out the door and never went back.

I understand the purpose of a training shift. And I understand why you might, as a server, have to do a couple for free. But what I worked that day wasn't a training shift; that was a company taking advantage of me, tossing me behind a bar on my own to make them money, and then handling it poorly. To not even give me a little hush money was a strange, bad call.

So far, working for other people wasn't going that well.

THROUGHOUT THE FINANCIALLY UNCERTAIN TURMOIL of 2007 and 2008 I'd been dreaming and plotting. I desperately wanted to open a restaurant. I didn't have much of a budget for dining out or travel so most of my inspiration and planning came from staying plugged in to restaurant culture through obsessing over food mags and tooling around on the Internet. I was building it in my head, imagining how cool it would be to have a place with a dedicated (and good) cocktail menu as well as an excellent wine list, where the food wasn't just "appetizer" "main" "dessert." I wanted to bring the casual but excellent dining that was happening in Europe and New York to Toronto, and I wasn't even considering what a risk and challenge it would be. Even after Cobalt, thoughts of failure never entered my mind—I've always managed to charge through life with the confidence of a mediocre white man. In spite of whatever injustices I felt heaped upon me by my gender, my middle-class white privilege was a protective salve and I 100 percent believed I could open a great restaurant, even if I only really had bar experience (I didn't count the "Sunday Night Supper Club" at Cobalt as real restaurant experience).

I'd spend hours thinking about every detail: how the room would look, what colour the walls would be, and what the bar top would be made of. Cocktail Molotov was my model, so it was easy to just mentally remodel it. At the time, Roland and his ex-wife were in the process of selling the building, the last of the financial ties that bound them, and I knew that the space would become available. So I fearlessly imagined it mine and made many crude drawings of where things would go.

My concept for the restaurant was very straightforward—and different from the traditional ideals restaurants had been upholding in Toronto for decades. I hated how, generally speaking, if you wanted to eat great food in Toronto in the 1990s and early 2000s you'd have to be prepared for an incredibly stuffy dining experience, so I wanted to upend that and create a space that ultimately felt very casual, but still served great food and drink and offered excellent yet not stiff service. I knew if we kept the prices as low as possible there would be a market for this type of dining. There was a generation of boomers' kids looking for more fun, less tie-wearing, with, if not a big disposable income, then at least enough to spend a hundred bucks for two (which takes you pretty far at the Hoof, even almost ten years later). I wanted to play the music of my youth and its modern-day equivalent, indie rock, and I wanted to play it loud, not ear-splitting, but loud. Most important, I wanted to wear jeans and Converse to work. I mulled over how to erase formality while preserving service and hospitality, and I realized the best way to do this was by staying true to the ideas of cool I'd locked into as a teenager. As pretentious as it sounds, I wanted to open the kind of restaurant where I'd want to dine, which didn't quite exist in Toronto.

I knew there was a worldwide, slow turn toward charcuterie, a centuries-old preservation technique that, in the days before refrigeration existed, involved salting and dry-curing meat in cool, dark caves. In the early to mid-2000s charcuterie exploded, becoming a thing young cooks wanted to learn. It lends a certain cachet; even newer restaurants are still dedicating space for charcuterie, which has transcended its "top dining trend" status and settled into its rightful place as staple.

The idea of trends in eating has always been a sticky topic for me. I understand food writers need stuff to write about, and I get the whole "kale as zeitgeist" thing and all the attention heaped on to what's essentially a curlicue of cabbage by web "content creators" desperate to pile on to whatever the Next Big Food Trend is. It just gets so dull. I liked kale before it was one of the popular kids (following the Brussels sprouts domination of the mid-Oughts). And I still like kale, as the media shoves it off the stage to make way for whole-roasted cauliflower. Which is probably over by now.

In truth, I never thought what I was doing was cresting on a trend; I just wanted to create a space that felt true to my idea of a comfortable, casual restaurant. The problem with being moments ahead of the trends is that you end up getting called horrible names like "tastemaker" or "over." And I never wanted to be boxed into a thing I had a strong hand in guiding in Canada, just because it became ubiquitous. They say imitation is the highest form of flattery; I say it's a good thing I have a million more ideas and will never have to remain stuck in any sort of moment.

Whole-animal eating, which had been championed for years by Fergus Henderson, chef at St. John in London, was also something I was thinking about. I could feel that the liberal moralizing about it at the fringes was about to tip into a full-on trend. Which was, frankly, about time. Using the whole animal should be everyone's reasonable starting point. It should be a given, not a trend or a style of cooking. If the animal has given up its life for us to eat, the least we can do is not waste any part—it's only polite, to paraphrase Fergus. When the Hoof first opened, it got pigeonholed a bit as that place that serves "weird food." But now, after years of growth, as more and more places have adopted the philosophy made famous by the aforementioned, inimitable Fergus Henderson, heart and sweetbreads and, of course, bones have followed pork belly's lead and have soared in price. People have finally started incorporating these so-called "odd bits" into their home cooking (and yes, I'm aware that Italian, Chinese, and all sorts of other cultures have been doing this forever). Maybe we can finally move on from the idea that this is "dare food" for white people. Maybe it's just food now. But that's how trends work, they either peter off and die a slow death or they become part of the zeitgeist, the new normal.

At first I thought the best thing would be to keep it really simple: find someone who could make the charcuterie and then base the menu around that, plus some cheese and maybe a few other little things. The focus would be a snacky sort of eating, with lots of cocktails, wine, and great beers to choose from. The more I talked to friends and Roland about it, the more excited I got.

Despite my lack of means, relative lack of experience in restaurant management, and no place to put the restaurant in my mind, it was all I talked about. I just believed I could do it, without fully realizing what an all-consuming big deal it was to run a restaurant versus a bar, and definitely without realizing what a male-dominated industry I was stepping into, and how much of a challenge it would be to overcome that, even with unending determination and a strong vision.

It was starting to look like there was a real possibility that I could take over the rent at 928 Dundas West, the space where Cocktail Molotov sat, mostly languishing, making just enough money to convince Roland's ex-wife not to let it go. After a few more months it was undeniable that the business was dying, and hours and hours of negotiations between Roland and his ex-wife finally came to an end when they agreed, through lawyers, to sell the building to acquaintances of ours. I had built my restaurant mentally in that space, and I was worried it was never going to happen, so Roland and I convinced the buyers to agree to lease me the storefront as a condition of sale.

When the keys were in my hands, I felt an enormous sense of relief. After months and months of dreaming up my perfect restaurant, I could finally, actually do it. At last, I had a space to go along with my concept and enthusiasm, and one with a licensed patio, washrooms, and a perfectly serviceable bar. I already had two names in mind, one of which was Elodie; evocative of something very pretty and feminine, it was the overwhelming friend-favourite. But I listened to my gut instead, and The Black Hoof was born.

ROLAND HAD AGREED TO FINANCE THE HOOF with a good portion of the money made from the sale of the building, which was extraordinarily generous of him and a huge chance to take. But I didn't even see it as a risk because I felt so sure that I was going to open the most exciting restaurant Toronto had ever seen. I don't think he necessarily believed me, but he believed *in* me. Roland showed so much faith in me—not some tangible idea of faith, but dollar-style faith, money-where-your-mouth-is faith.

Though I've since learned the value of "under-promise, over-deliver," at the time I was going around actually saying "I'm going to open the best restaurant the city has seen in years." Roland would smile and say, "Yes, yes, honey, I'm sure you will," even though he secretly thought I was being hubristic, or, more accurately, "crazy." Given everything that had happened with Cobalt, he wanted me to manage my expectations, not something I've ever been able to do outside of watching comedy on network television.

I had a very clear idea of what I wanted The Black Hoof to be. It had to have a simple design, one that would age well, and one that we could execute ourselves for $60,000, a lot of money but gobbled peanuts when opening a restaurant.

The paperwork that is usually a giant pain in the ass was all very straightforward, mostly because the liquor licence was a transfer instead of a new application. (I hire someone to take care of all my licence stuff now. It isn't expensive enough to not be worth it, and to have someone else, an expert, worrying about filing endless forms properly is priceless.)

As soon as we had access to the building, Roland and I started the demo. It was August 2008 and the goal was to be open by October. I sat on the cold tile floor of the empty room and drew a sketch. Very rudimentary, but it's still how I *design* spaces. I can always imagine how something will look once it's painted, relit, furnished, etc. Once I have a general idea of where I want everything, I can start dropping in the ideas in my head, and then I just work toward that. Obviously, little things change course along the way, but the Hoof ended up looking, and still looks, very much how I imagined it that day in August.

We tossed whatever we didn't want onto the sun-baked sidewalk of Dundas West, seemingly attracting the notice of only the older Portuguese men who spent hours sipping beer at New Açor, the bar two doors down and a fixture of the block. Eventually neighbourhood twenty-somethings picked up the boxes of branded pint glasses and the miscellaneous items we just didn't have a use for.

Back then, artists could still afford to live in Little Portugal, the name I stubbornly hold on to even as greedy real estate agents keep insisting it's "Trinity-Bellwoods"—a sneaky but effective trick picked up from the ever-booming New York market. It's what I hear the kids calling the stretch between Bathurst and Dovercourt along Dundas West, and I GET that, in an ironic twist, I'm a chief factor in the gentrification, but I still kind of hate it. I'd fallen in love with Dirty Dundas and was not looking forward to the mainstream restaurants that would follow in the Hoof's steps.

At that time, though, gentrification was not what I was fretting about; I just wanted to open the restaurant. So I kept the basic structure the same as Cocktail Molotov, both for practicality and in the interests of keeping costs down. I cannot emphasize enough how smart it is to try and get a licensed place that already has washrooms and is only in need of the most basic cosmetic changes, especially for your first restaurant project. I now know I can build a restaurant from nothing fairly cheaply, but back then? It was just so much easier to have a starting point, plus I had the advantage of Roland's intimate knowledge of the building. He knew every plumbing hiccup, all the electrical, and what to do to solve problems as they came up.

Every morning we'd get up, have a quick coffee, and head around the corner to "the space," as we called it. It's a habit that's stuck—it's always "the space" when it's being built and "the restaurant" once it's open.

We had beautiful Eames stool bases left over from Cocktail Molotov; we just ordered new seats for them from Modernica. I chose a minty sage green, which is actually called "celery" in the catalogue, something that makes no sense to me since the colour is so clearly seafoam. That was one of our biggest expenses, but worth every penny. They are timeless classics, and I'm so proud they aren't knock-offs. I have an aversion to knock-off furniture and treat it as I do imitation art. So, in the interests of integrity, no knock-offs. It's something I can't shake, though I do recognize it as completely, ridiculously bourgeois.

As the bar seats slowly made their way from Modernica's California warehouse, Roland and I focused on the build. Floors had to be turned from shitty ceramic tile to wood, no easy feat. We had to drill a subfloor through the grout, a bit of an easier drill than through the tile, but we couldn't see the grout once the subfloor was laid out, and couldn't just guess at grout-lines, so it all had to be meticulously marked. Still, it was better than the alternative—the time-consuming, gruelling work of ripping out the tiles. After the subfloor was in, we installed what we could afford, and what we could afford was plywood. It's a super-cheap way to go and looks great, but it has to be cared for. We re-coat with a few layers of urethane every few years, and it still isn't enough to keep it from wearing, but it will serve you very well for at least five years and costs almost nothing.

Lighting is the most important component of any good design. I don't care what anyone says to the contrary. It hides a multitude of sins, and if you do it right, people look more attractive. You want dim overhead lighting, but you have to balance it with something underneath, so that faces don't get wonkily lit and leave you with a roomful of people looking like the wrong side of *Seinfeld*'s "two-face." In a restaurant, candles on the tables serve this purpose perfectly, and no matter how cliché, it always feels like something is missing when places choose to forgo them, or, god forbid, use those awful fake-flicker, battery-operated ones. We use refillable oil cartridges. They last exactly as long as we're open, and they cost a bit more than tea lights but skipping the mess of wax and constantly chasing burned-down candles makes the extra expense absolutely worth it.

I always wanted to hang diner-style lights over the bar, but two different shapes, one the classic round and one with the slight nipple on the bottom. It's a familiar look, but mixing the canopies gives it interest. The soft dispersal of the light on a dimmer is a beacon; it makes everything look all glowy. And I still like the way these lights look, many years later. You really can't go wrong with classics.

Roland's previous light-building experience has never stopped coming in handy, and he installed a giant globe in the dining room, which is only barely separated from the bar area. The room is just a rectangle, and too small to really divide into zones, but the lighting helps. Roland still had great connections to this lighting parts company in the States, and we were able to get everything we needed at wholesale prices. We were not wasting any money. It was all

Roland's, and I wanted to be sure not a penny was ill-spent.

Once the lighting was in, the place was really starting to look like something. We sat on the newly varnished plywood floor and I lay down and just stared at the globe in the back room. Such a simple thing, but after dark it achieved just the right effect, offering enough light that you could almost read the wine list, and not so much that it was garish. I must have lain there for hours, admiring our work. The major stuff was done. The marble bar was installed; I got the cheapest option, which had no edges and just sat on top of the wooden bar that had seen so many whiskies pass over it in Cocktail Molotov, mine included. I regret not spending the extra money for the edge every time I look at it, but I can justify the oversight as a tip of the hat to the history of the space, showing all the layers, or some bullshit like that.

I was putting all of my energy into renovating what would become the Hoof, but there were other concerns I had to address, like who was going to produce all this charcuterie. I didn't know anyone who was ready to run a kitchen, let alone produce dry-cured salumi and pâté en croute. I figured it was worth a shot to put an ad on Craigslist, looking for a charcuterie chef. Every day I eagerly checked my inbox but I didn't get much, aside from a lot of lame applications. Then one day something good showed up. It was a short bio, followed by a long list of charcuterie items the applicant had been working on for the past six months in his job as sous-chef at Lucien, a French restaurant. His name was Grant van Gameren, and I immediately knew this was going to be the last resumé I looked at. The list was just so impressive and straightforward. It felt right.

Grant and I began communicating via email and very quickly started batting around vague ideas of what our potential arrangement might be—would he be an employee, a partner, how would this be structured? I wanted someone talented to build something great with and he seemed like the right fit but also the only real lead I had. I immediately latched on to the idea of Grant running the Hoof kitchen so I could concentrate on the build, since our October opening date was fast approaching.

Roland and I made plans to go eat a plate of charcuterie at Lucien. Grant was very friendly, shy, and humble. He really wanted to make sure we enjoyed what he'd made, and we did. It was great stuff: a moist beef-and-dill salami, a lavender-cured duck breast, and some very nice dry bresaola, as well as a creamy, classic chicken liver mousse and a perfectly salty capicollo. This was enough to quickly push the vague email conversations toward something more concrete. I knew Grant and I had to work together in some capacity.

I was scouring Craigslist every day for all sorts of stuff, and getting lucky with random items but couldn't find the simplest thing: plain tables and chairs. Finally, just as I was ready to give up and try to find the money in the budget for new furnishings, a friend mentioned that a place he DJed at was going under and was selling off a bunch of stuff. We ended up getting the plainest tables and bases possible for $20 each. When I upgraded the dining tables to really lovely but still plain hardwood years later, the Craigslist finds became our patio tables.

When it came to the chairs, I was searching for those bent-plywood school chairs you see everywhere now. We needed thirty-five or so, and I was struggling to find a large lot of them. But after much searching I found the place that manufactured them (thank you, Internet) and was able to pick them up for $30 apiece, just right for our rapidly depleting funds. The school chairs served us well for two years, and then I replaced them with metal Tolix Marais chairs; these are ubiquitous, but for a reason—they look great, they stack, they're lightweight, and they last forever, which justifies their price. Ours happen to stand out with their pretty shade of seafoam green and perforated seats. Eventually, in 2011, the plywood school chairs went to Grand Electric (Toronto's version of Chicago's Big Star, a haven of loud music, tacos and bourbon instead of tequila) for their opening. It was a gift from me that had long ago felt like a gift *to* me at $30 each, and it was the least I could do to help those guys stay under budget. The cheapest possible chairs ended up opening two of the city's busiest restaurants.

Meanwhile, I was taking the same approach with the "kitchen." It was small, not quite six feet by ten feet, barely big enough for one person, never mind the three that have to manage in the tiny, awkward space every night. Each day I pulled up Craigslist, looking for cheap stuff—not that there was that much we needed, or could even use, considering the cramped quarters, but we did need a long metal table for the back wall, ideally with a sink. And after some patience, I eventually found one. It was in storage at some guy's garage in Scarborough, but it was exactly the right size, and it had a small hand-washing sink, which almost none of them do, so for $225 it seemed like a steal. It just needed some love. I scrubbed it down with steel wool and Brasso until it shone, and all traces of cancerous little rust zones were rubbed away. It was a great find that still anchors the Hoof kitchen.

I bought a new line fridge for the *garde* "station." If you are reading this book to glean any insight into opening your own restaurant, if you take nothing else, heed this: ONLY BUY NEW FRIDGES. Used ones are almost never worth the little bit of money you save, and every time I ignored that rule I was buying a new compressor within a year. So just don't do it. And don't forget, fridges need to breathe. I could've saved myself way too much money by venting my under-bar fridges, which is as simple as cutting a hole in the bar and popping in a pretty, antique grate. It is a game-changer. And finally, if something's wrong with your fridge, clean the air filter, it's probably that.

With the kitchen taken care of, we just needed a dishwasher and an ice machine to be done with equipment. I have had great success with renting dishwashers. They tend to break a lot, and when you rent them, there's a guy on call all the time. I've lost count of how many times the repair guy has ducked in during a Friday night rush (golden rule: the dishwasher will always break down on the weekend, when you need it the most) and gotten the machine back on track. There is literally nothing worse during a busy service than a dishwasher break-down, and when I've had to, I've ferried bus pans piled high with dirty dishes across the street to the prep kitchen attached to Cocktail Bar, run them through the machine there, and rushed them back over. On repeat. All service.

As far as ice machines go, just make sure you get something that produces dense cubes, which is the most important start to making proper cocktails. I couldn't afford a really good one for opening, so I made do with the sad, quick-melting cubes of a lesser brand, a holdover from Cobalt; it was awfully hard to say no to free.

With respect to cooking, we didn't think we'd be doing that much, as the menu was going to be so charcuterie-heavy, but since there was an electric stove just sitting in the upstairs apartment we installed it beside the dishwasher, where it slid in with the steel prep table butting up to its left side, just in case.

The only major thing we didn't have was a hood (desperately needed for proper ventilation), although we wouldn't go without for long; in the meantime, I had to pump the front door every time the kitchen seared foie gras. So much for not really cooking.

For the menu's growth from a wee card with a few sandwiches (and seared foie) to a tour de force of delicious odd bits, I have Grant van Gameren to thank. Despite the teeny, tiny opening menu, we quickly came to realize the potential for the Hoof as a full-on restaurant. It's challenging to look back on a troubled relationship, even one that's based in business, and not see just the ugly parts—and although there's no shortage of ugly, having a cook as talented as Grant was essential to the Hoof's explosive success.

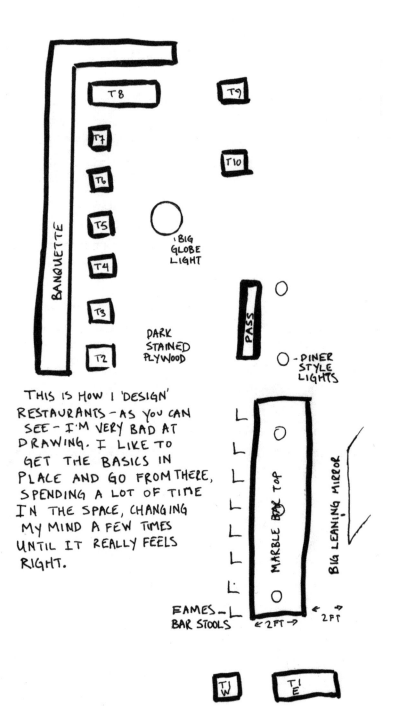

T8

T9

T7

T10

T6

T5

○ ·BIG
GLOBE
LIGHT

BANQUETTE

T4

T3

PASS ○

○ -DINER
STYLE
LIGHTS

T2

DARK
STAINED
PLYWOOD

THIS IS HOW I 'DESIGN'
RESTAURANTS — AS YOU CAN
SEE — I'M VERY BAD AT
DRAWING. I LIKE TO
GET THE BASICS IN
PLACE AND GO FROM THERE,
SPENDING A LOT OF TIME
IN THE SPACE, CHANGING
MY MIND A FEW TIMES
UNTIL IT REALLY FEELS
RIGHT.

L

L

L

L

L

L

L

L

EAMES — L
BAR STOOLS

○

○

MARBLE BOX TOP

BIG LEANING MIRROR

←2FT→

←2FT→

T
W

T
E

10: HOOF GOES BOOM

I LIKE TO CROSS THINGS OFF LISTS. Sometimes I do it so eagerly and efficiently that I haven't fully considered the ramifications of quickly getting something "off my desk" versus giving the thing thoughtful attention and proper mull time—consideration it might actually require. In 2008 I needed a chef. Grant was really good at cooking. What could possibly go wrong?

I was frantic and excited in the days leading up to the opening. I didn't have enough basic restaurant knowledge to have thought about things like what we would pour water out of (I really wanted the egalitarian approach of just pouring tap water for people the moment they were seated, rather than going through the whole "flat or sparkling?" thing), so I grabbed a couple of old olive oil bottles from my house and we used those, and it stuck. I was intuitive enough to know exactly what I wanted, but lacked some of the experience necessary to streamline things. I was all over staff for their language choices, or how they were moving in the room, or the way they delivered food, but I had no idea about seat numbers, or roll-ups, or that splashing vinegar in the hot water we use to polish cutlery would help keep it streak-free.

With the kitchen sorted (for opening, and for a couple weeks after, that was just Grant), the next step was a small front of house staff, and I got lucky with Patrice, an amazing, very professional server who was the girlfriend of a cook Grant knew. Without her assistance and expertise on floor service, I would have drowned. She taught me so much, and I'll always be grateful for her detail-oriented service; she was an essential part of the Hoof's start-up and stayed on for two years.

Patrice's help in the weeks prior to opening gave me the time to focus on making a really small, really solid cocktail menu, a total departure from the many pages (including a table of contents) that was the Cobalt menu. I wanted just six drinks that would provide something, whether you were in the mood for a tall, refreshing drink, light on booze, or a Manhattan to ruin you for all others. One drink, The Fancy Concord, on the opening menu even had vodka as a base (*gasp*!). It was 2.5 ounces of vodka, muddled with Concord grapes and tarragon, shaken over ice and then fine-strained into a glass that had been "painted"—a technique I maybe invented that involved using a pastry brush to dab a little bit of liquor on the inside and rim of the glass—in this case it was icewine, a *very Ontario* product; it was then garnished with a little bunch of champagne grapes and very lightly spritzed with house vanilla extract (at the table, obviously). It was intricate and showed off some skill, but wasn't overly complex at just five ingredients, two of them accents.

I had been to New York a couple of times between the closure of Cobalt and the opening of the Hoof and definitely took some cues from what I saw happening in bars there, a real attention to detail, including what ice to use. I used fresh herbs, fresh-squeezed juices, and I'd eventually upgrade my old Cobalt ice machine to one that made nice, big, dense cubes, *de rigueur* for proper drinks. I had so much fun with infusions, like Szechuan-peppercorn-infused rum, caraway tequila, or lavender gin—basically, if it existed in the world of spices, I tried it in every liquor, keeping all my experiments in little bottles and jars behind the bar, which was practical and also beautiful. Some infusions worked out better than others, but I would even turn fuck-ups into something I could use because I couldn't afford to waste anything. One "mistake" was an extremely bitter jasmine-tea-gin infusion that I'd left way too long. The tea had grown tannic and unpleasant, and the flavour had tainted the whole batch. In small doses, though, it made a nice bitter tincture and was the perfect antidote to the honey-sweetness of an Earl Grey–infused gin and lemon drink I was working on called Tea and Sympathy. All of this now sounds passé—the fresh ingredients, the infusing, the cutesy names—but at the time, in Toronto, it was rare to get quality cocktails anywhere, let alone at a restaurant. It was avant-garde, but also an accidentally canny business move as profit margins on liquor are way higher than on beer or wine. And our cocktails are so good and such a part of what we do, almost every table orders a round to start.

The renovation was exciting and exhausting—two months of scrubbing, painting, tiling, and installing. Roland and I worked really well together, and he trusted my taste, based on nothing but his instincts. We had a tight budget but he never made me feel like I was being irresponsible with his money. There was already a sense that this was our thing, and after having gone through such a difficult time with his ex, it was starting to feel like we were a real family, like it was us against the world.

Finally it was October and opening night, which was really an exercise in self-control and attempting to remain calm as things kept going wrong. All the kitchen rags we had ordered had been used up in the weeks leading up to opening and needed to be washed at my house; we kept having to pop over to the nearby restaurant supply store for yet another forgotten item; and at literally the last minute, 4:30, we realized that we didn't have any dessert, so I ducked out to a baker friend of Grant's who worked out of the Palais Royale on the lakeshore to pick up a couple of pies. It was a gorgeous, sunny day and unseasonably warm for early October and I was in a major hurry, Lake Shore Boulevard was wide open and too tempting, and I was going way too fast. Naturally I was pulled over. The cop said cop things while I blurted out too many words about opening a restaurant for the very first time and pies. He let me off with a reduced ticket, but it was still a waste of fifteen precious minutes. By the time I got back to the restaurant I was a mess of stress and nerves. And then my family showed up an extremely helpful forty-five minutes early, completely unaware of how much the opposite of helpful this was. My mother, who always has the best intentions, kept asking me for camera batteries, oblivious to the fact that I was tremendously stressed out and didn't have time to worry about batteries for her camera. I just kept hissing at my dad to take her for a walk until we opened at 6:00. The busboy/food-runner could not seem to remember what was on the charcuterie board, the lights kept dimming every time the dishwasher ran a cycle, we didn't polish the cutlery as we went and ended up spending an hour doing it at the end of the night, and the CDs were skipping (I had this romantic notion of only playing whole albums, which did not last long). Never mind that we basically had no idea what we were doing. So the night could be summarized as:

- family management
- taking orders
- making drinks
- trying to course out tables
- working with a new team for the very first time

It was terrifying and chaotic, and just north of disastrous, but at the same time so exciting to finally have the doors open and to be able to serve people food, and we got through it.

That first night was filled with exalted and exhausting highs, but the next six weeks, which felt more like six months, were slow and scary—like nobody-came-in-some-nights scary. Occasional Sundays and Mondays, Grant, Patrice, and I would sit at table 1 in the front window trying to look like a lot of people having a really good time (*acting*), but for who? At that time Dundas West wasn't the hipster promenade it is now. Sometimes an hour would pass and no one would even walk by save for a few hobos and pros. Fuck, I miss them, especially the prostitutes, they were a constant reminder that gentrification was still in the early-adopter stages, years away from white thirty-somethings actually adopting. What an ironic twist, my slight resentment of a thing I unwittingly ushered in.

During these early days, Grant was very kind and friendly— I think the humiliation of a mostly quiet restaurant kept him more puppy dog than pitbull. The tumbleweeds and crickets were worrying. We'd get some industry people through our door, and they always seemed to enjoy it, drinking and praising enough for ten tables, and Fridays and Saturdays were starting to have at least one solid seating, but we weren't even breaking even—something I knew for certain, as I had the insane notion that I was the best person to do the books because we couldn't even afford to pay anyone. (By "do the books" I mean recording sales and sales tax by hand in an old-timey ledger, and hand-writing and sending out the weekly cheques. Crazy. Hiring a restaurant-specific bookkeeper ten months in was the smartest decision I made that year.)

THE POWER OF A POSITIVE REVIEW, especially in that time, cannot be overstated. These were the halcyon days before Yelp, TripAdvisor, and bloggers had all but drowned out the voice of critics, which I'm of two very distinct minds about, depending on the review the critic gives my restaurants. When it's a great review, I'm all, "Critics are such an important voice and help synthesize what the masses are saying, but in lovely purple prose." Terrible review? "Fuck critics, we're in a post-criticism society."

After those first six weeks, sometime in late November 2008 we finally got our first major review, and it could not have been more exciting. It was a four-star, absolutely glowing review from Corey Mintz at *The Toronto Star*. Corey happened to be filling in for the regular critic while she popped out a baby—and I'm forever grateful to her husband, as I'm quite certain (although there's no way to definitively PROVE it) she never would have given us four stars. The Hoof was right up Corey's alley, and he just got it, all of it. He was so into the food, in fact, that he didn't even notice the cocktails, which I'd devoted so much time and attention to, and for which I gave him shit years later after he'd stopped writing food reviews and we'd become friends. I saw it as a huge blind spot to discuss only food in a restaurant review, something reviewers around the world have finally caught up to. It's not just eating, it's dining. It's the experience. But the rest of it? He got it: the casual yet attentive and detailed service; the fun, dimly lit, vibey room; the loud but not-so-loud-you-can't-talk atmosphere; and, of course, Grant's delicious, addicting food—I still dream about scallops and bone marrow, a simple, satisfying dish that was very popular in summer 2009.

That review was, without question, the turning point. Yes, *Now Magazine* had gotten there first with their ridiculous headline—"Cold Cuts Get Hot"—and terrible photo, both of which still make me cringe. But the *Star* review was the one that opened the floodgates, and everything changed very quickly after that. Lineups went from non-existent to two-plus hours during prime time on the weekend and seeped into Thursdays as well. It was an exciting room to be in. You could feel the crackle of energy bouncing between staff and patrons. It felt like absolutely everyone was talking about the Hoof, as in: "Have you been there yet?" which created this urgency for people to make a point of coming, just so they could answer "Yes." It was very much a point of pride for people to want to become regulars, to be "in the club." Restaurants have always evoked that, and despite the Hoof being almost an anti-restaurant by design, it was no different in the reactions it elicited. Our democratic approach of refusing to take reservations led to bloated prime-time wait times, which at that point nobody even seemed to mind, as there was such a sense of excitement about the place. The Cocktail Bar wasn't around at that time, so people would have to walk three blocks east, sometimes in freezing weather, to the nearest bar, a place that I offered sage advice about in an attempt at conspiratorial camaraderie: "Don't drink the house wine."

The no-reservations policy, very new to Toronto, all went okay-ish. Asking hungry diners to wait two hours at a grotty bar before being permitted a table at The Black Hoof was a huge ask. But it wasn't about an attitude or a lack of hospitality; it was only about math. There were 39 seats that could be turned four or more times on a busy night, and maybe 250-plus people who wanted to eat there on a given Friday or Saturday. We simply couldn't accommodate them all. But here's the democratic part: if you wanted to eat at the Hoof on a Saturday night, you almost always could with a little insider knowledge and some patience. The line would usually start to die down at 11:00, so if you were into late-night dining, you were set, as the kitchen was open until 1:00 a.m. Thursday through Saturday. Or if you showed up right at 6:00, you were all but guaranteed a table. It's much trickier to get a spot on your chosen night at a very busy restaurant that takes reservations. So yes, we were setting a precedent in Toronto with our no-reservations approach, but once your table or bar spots were ready, we always called you at least three times, plus a text, and eventually we created a cozy waiting area right across the street in Cocktail Bar. (This would evolve into a strong business in its own right—a very important thing when creating any sort of annex to your business. The new addition must be able to stand alone.)

I was busy enough with the duties of the explosive growth of a room so ill-equipped to handle anything explosive that I was totally neglecting my health, so much so that my drastic weight loss and lack of sleep was something I almost didn't notice. There was just too much to worry about, how could I find time to eat?

Grant didn't believe in a staff meal back then, leaving all the cooks to just work straight through the day to service, grabbing food on the fly from the kitchen when they had a moment. When I would suggest feeding the staff, I was told that it was just too busy. But I felt it was important to give everyone a little break to sit down and enjoy a meal together, so the no-staff-meals policy was one that left when Grant did.

Our staff meals are always well balanced and delicious and include a protein, carb, and veg, plus salad. Sometimes we'll have pasta, but we try to stay away from meals that are too carb-heavy, they just weigh you down during service. We take it seriously, and order food specifically for these dinners. It's mostly just the cooks, but sometimes even the front of house participates. Everyone relaxes, spends the first half furiously dicking around on their phones, and then finally someone tells a funny story and laughter erupts. It's just necessary to give people a proper break to eat and have a moment to catch their breath, every day, no exceptions. It was a major turning point for the different way I wanted to run my business once I had autonomy. A restaurant has to be run with leadership, but also must treat its employees with respect. People need to have a break and eat; this idea that somehow it's weak to sit down and eat food is from a playbook created by kitchen dinosaurs. I have a staff who respect me, maybe fear me a little bit, but who also know they are cared for and valued. At its best, it's very parental, and when you understand all that, the moniker "family meal" (a nickname for staff meal used by restaurants the world over) makes a lot of sense.

I was tending bar, including food service, for all eight bar stools and doing service bar for the thirty-one-seat restaurant, as well as taking names at the door. What I should have done was hire a bartender so I could focus on managing the room and hosting, a job often considered entry-level but which is actually one of the most important in the room. We needed people to agree to hideously long wait times, which usually meant charming them into it, selling them on it, with confidence—no job for a shy nineteen-year-old studying art history. But instead of doing the smart thing we hired a host just to deal with the crush at the door, and luckily we got someone who was great at it, Julia Gilmore, who I'm happy to say still works for the company now, but in a managerial role. I'm so fortunate to have people like her around me, and in a lovely turn of events, she met her future husband, Lee Evans, through the Hoof, and now Lee is an integral part of running the Cocktail Bar. I didn't stop working full bar services for a long time—a combination of wanting total control over the drink-making and bar service while still being able to oversee the room, as well as this feeling that if I were "just" managing somehow it wouldn't be enough, that Grant's hard "actual" work would always be more *everything* than what I was doing, which was still a ridiculous workload.

This was such wrong-headed perspective. As an industry, we always seem to assume that physical labour is somehow more difficult than creating culture, that back of house is harder than front of house. And in a straight-up physical way it is. But as an owner, I was the one taking financial risks and making decisions that I'd have to stand behind so the restaurant could shine, could be something different from the thousands of other restaurants out there. One of the key things I did was turn the lights way down and the music up, which wasn't, at the time, something Grant wanted. I'd be setting this tone that I could tell people were responding positively to because I was in the room actually serving them, while Grant was concerned that what we were doing was too outside the mainstream; he wanted a more traditional setting for his food, he wanted people to see his food, for it to shine. But I stuck to my guns because we weren't technically partners then, it was still very much my restaurant, which was probably why I was able to set the baseline so strongly. And that possibly made him feel hobbled, perhaps eliciting a negative reaction to a perceived lack of control. By the time I gave him 50 percent of my business (yes, basically gave, his buy-in was peanuts), it was almost a year in and we were busy all the time, so he had no choice but to stick with what was obviously a winning formula. Doing that takes a tremendous amount of fortitude. And even though I didn't have to argue with him early on in our relationship to make my points, it was a very stressful environment; the tension between front and back of house was palpable.

At the time we were putting in roughly the same hours. Managing all the parts of the restaurant that weren't kitchen-related was up to me, including but not limited to hiring and training all front of house staff, creating and maintaining a wine list, keeping track of expenses, running around doing errands, working full services right to close every night, calling repair people and dealing with them as required, keeping the cocktail list fresh and interesting, and on and on and on. It isn't necessarily easier work than running a kitchen, although obviously it's less physical; it's different and requires tangential focus. The chef needs to focus on one thing, making delicious food, which in and of itself is a huge challenge (or all restaurants would serve excellent food), and I have a tremendous amount of respect for the people I've known who are capable of that. But I admire them more when they understand and respect what it takes to do all the stuff that isn't related to making the food. It strikes me as a very male perspective, this idea that lifting pots and brunoise-ing vegetables and breaking down pigs is *real* work while talking to people, opening wine, and running around the floor all night isn't. It's a huge part of what can be a dividing line between front and back of house. I've never met a cook who fully understands the stress and effort that go into making a dining room run properly (unless they've worked both front and back). Obviously, the hours an average cook works are gruelling, and often there's a huge pay gap between front and back. It's an ironic reversal of what "pay gap" usually means: in the restaurant business, where men rule kitchens in every sense, they get paid much less than the women serving tables (unless of course they're the head chef, then they just get paid a little less. I'M KIDDING).

In spite of all of this, in the first year I hadn't fully digested that Grant's subtle digs (like making a joke about how I'd been "out shopping" when, of course, it was for the restaurant) and obvious lack of interest in what I was doing ("but who even cares about cocktails?") wasn't how it had to be, but it was only a glimmer of how bad it would eventually get.

I remember, in a happy moment of a perfect service sometime in year one, shaking a cocktail, grinning over at Grant, and shouting above the din, "I'll never get tired of this!" I was so naive.

The Black Hoof was a meeting place for cooks and servers, and after *The Toronto Star* and *The Globe and Mail* had lavished praise, it was pretty much always packed, even on Sundays and Mondays. All the cooks in the city wanted to hang out by the pass and talk to Grant. In an effort to attract restaurant workers I'd decided to make the unusual choice to close Tuesdays and Wednesdays and be open Sundays and Mondays, the days restaurant workers typically have off. Industry people are really who you want early-adopting your restaurant, because: a) they will spread the word quickly throughout the high-density restaurant world; b) they'll come after their shifts and give you that late-night rush; and c) perhaps most important, restaurant people, more than possibly any other group, love to drink, and they will drink a LOT. It worked like a charm. Some nights I'd look up from my station, elbow-deep in stirring cocktails and pouring pints, and see a packed room. At 11:00. On a Monday. It was surreal.

When you have quick success like what we were experiencing, especially in a city and industry that struggles over such a small pie, it's a really tough line to negotiate. I often let my ego get the better of me, like strongly encouraging patrons to have rye Manhattans when they preferred bourbon (and I will maintain to my grave that the rye version is far superior), I mean, even if most of the time I managed to persuade them to see the light through the rye, maybe I could have just served them bourbon, but that was not my style. And if a customer was rude to me, I had a hard time turning the other cheek, often resorting to a frosty demeanour or slightly rolled eyes. One particularly rude patron was picking on everything, the food, the wine list, everything. He had obviously come in with preconceived notions and was unhappy with his seat at the bar, and instead of just trying to have a good time he chose to get extremely snarky. He sent back his dry martini for having too much vermouth, when it had drops at most. I gracefully replaced it. He loudly complained to his friend that there weren't enough expensive wines on the list. When he protested that he could've just got a plate of "cold cuts" at the store rather than come and be "forced" to sit at the bar at this "loud, obnoxious, restaurant," I suggested he do just that. I told him that there wouldn't be a bill (he and his friend had only had two drinks and a charcuterie board at this point) but we were done serving him. He was shocked and said something to the effect of "Are you fucking kidding me?" I wasn't. I had tried to be nice to him, I had tried to deal with his rudeness, but at a certain point, it just wasn't worth it. And I'd do it again. I felt totally justified—after all, the diner had drawn first blood. But Grant was furious. I could feel him watching the whole thing play out. He thought I should have just dealt with this asshole's extreme rudeness. I disagreed. And if you happen to think "it's hospitality, you have to be nice, even to the dicks," fine, you're entitled to feel that way, but I didn't open my own business to operate under the tight chains of the status quo. This sort of thing happened only very rarely, and if someone was just a bit difficult or unpleasant, of course, I'd happily serve them and take their money, but when people were obnoxious assholes for no reason, I wouldn't accept it.

I felt a wave of both excitement and jealousy building in the restaurant community, and we were so busy that our egos often got in the way of handling it properly. Once, early on, a competing restaurant that had opened with a concept similar to the Hoof's in a nearby neighbourhood tweeted something like: "Can't get into the Hoof? Come on down to _____, we have plenty of room!" I thought it was tacky, but it enraged Grant. He tweeted a really sarcastic, nasty reply suggesting what an unclassy move it was to try and draw away our customers. I agreed it was an odd choice, and I was totally complicit in Grant's tweet from our shared Twitter account, but it caused a lot of friction. Apparently that restaurant's chef-owner forgave Grant the public shaming long before he and I patched things up, which I can only attribute to bros being bros.

Eventually I learned *some* peer diplomacy, as I started to see the real-world consequences for my perceived arrogance (getting called a bitch and hearing about it), while Grant just sailed on through it all. It's always felt like the city is quick to hang me for even a whiff of arrogance while they encourage and applaud ego and macho swagger in my male contemporaries.

But whatever undercurrent of envy I was sensing from the restaurant community as The Black Hoof made its mark was never overt. People were quick to suck up and make obsequious small talk, because everyone wanted to be a part of the magic that was happening at the Hoof. Cooks and bartenders were constantly asking to stage, and peers treated both Grant and me with a mixture of reverence and resentment. I was often told how "lucky" I'd gotten with the Hoof's success. One Sunday night, an older cook was drinking at the bar. He looked around at how busy it was and just straight-up said,

"Wow, you really got lucky with this place, huh?" I just smiled and said, "I don't believe in luck." But I heard that all the time—how "lucky" I was, as though it had just *happened*, an indignity that I'm sure Grant didn't have to suffer.

But that was just a few veterans who didn't like feeling pushed off the pedestal. Most industry peeps just wanted to be there, to be a part of it, at the bar, shoving in southern fried sweetbreads and swilling wine after midnight, laughing with their co-workers and going for periodic smokes. And the great reviews just kept rolling in. We placed second on *enRoute*'s "Best New Restaurants" list, and as much as I've grown to hate these markers and random judgments performed by biased journalists and unqualified bloggers, that review, in a revered publication that has a lasting impact on tourist foodies in our little country, was exciting.

We couldn't have been any busier, and it felt great.

HOOF BITTERS

- Add 500ml rye to each base.
- Leave 1-2 weeks. Strain.
- Blend bases together.*

  *Add bitter base last.

- cloves
- cardamom
- star anise
- cinnamon
- peppercorns

- ginger
- lemon &
  orange
  zest

- gentian
- wormwood

HOOF MANHATTAN

- 60ml 10yr aged rye
- 27ml antica formula
     sweet vermouth
- 2ml hoof bitters

- Stir + chill thoroughly.
- Strain into chilled coupe glass.
- Add 2 Manhattan cherries.

MANHATTAN CHERRIES

- Combine 2kg sour cherries with
  2kg sugar.
- Add 300ml each of bitter almond
  tincture, sweet vermouth, rye +
  600ml water.
- Bring to a boil + simmer for 20 min.

11: HOOF GRANT HAPPY SAD

DESPITE THE ACCOLADES AND THE MONEY rolling in hand over fist, there was never a time when I felt consistently good about my partnership with Grant. There was always an undertone of uneasiness that clouded everything like the bottom of a pickle jar. As with all horror stories, it had started out auspiciously enough—if you squinted hard, on a good day, you might even have thought we liked each other. Having Grant on board made me feel more secure at the time, but when our relationship started to show cracks—sometime shortly after making our partnership official in April 2009—it cracked quickly, like a rush-job concrete walkway poured between two semis in Little Italy, and it turned out that "secure" was the polar opposite of how I actually felt.

I should have seen the signs, because there were lots of indicators that pointed to a troubled pairing, but I chose to ignore them and forged ahead, shushing my vague concerns about Grant and our diametrically opposed personalities. We went ahead and made a handshake deal essentially saying we'd act as equal partners going forward (even though that deal wouldn't be finalized on paper until we incorporated the business). He'd only contribute $20,000 to our $70,000, and he would be permitted a very lax payment schedule that would end up being more than a year, which, honestly, wouldn't have been a crazy approach money-wise if it had all worked out.

The position you are in as a restaurateur with a vision offers a lot of freedom, but you must tie yourself to a chef, whether it's employing or partnering, so you have to try really hard to find a good cook who's maybe a good person, too, because the natural animosity that can develop between front of house and back of house can be negotiated only by reasonable people who recognize each other's value. And the problem with a lot of young cooks who are ready for chef jobs or ownership is that they really only see the value in what *they* do, in the physicality of it: in the sharpening of knives; the hours spent tending to a veal stock; the Zen of peeling a bushel of artichokes. And in the worst-case scenarios, they might even have an aggressive disdain for everything outside of what goes on the plate. Perhaps they'll even take pride in their ignorance of wine or cocktails, wearing their lack of knowledge like a badge of honour, like a burn on their forearm, prominent and ugly, but something to show off.

One day, in the weeks leading up to the opening, I was painting the bar and putting up tiles when Grant strolled in with one of his friends. He was different from the shy, pleasant guy that Roland and I had met the previous week at Lucien when he'd fed us charcuterie, desperate for us to like it. He was wearing a puffed-up bravado—*bro*-vado, a very male, very immature put-on that bros sniff each other out with.

"Bro" has become my catch-all term for any guy suffering from too much testosterone and a "bros before hos" mentality. There are many different types of bro. There's office bro, the dude who high-fives everyone and calls all his female peers "chicks," as in "Brenda from accounting's a pretty cool chick." He's always suggesting strip clubs for after-work drinks, and big-ups the "chicks" who go along with it as "so cool" and "bad-ass." There are hipster bros. These guys are harder to pick out as they look so much like regular hipsters, but don't be fooled! They have too much money to be actual hipsters, and they drive things like white Beamers. Their record collections are anchored with un-ironic box sets of Hall and Oates, but missing any of the markers that stamp a collection with proper hipster "credibility." They drink cheap beer pretending it's what they like, but mostly they don't really think "girls" are funny, and treat the "ladies" as accessories. There are dad bros. They have poker nights, drink expensive vodka, have master's degrees, and are white-centric misogynists but genuinely believe they're post-racial, enlightened feminists. And of course there are the chef bros. Chef bros are easy to identify by their overt chest-puffing plus knives and tattoos (of knives!). Grant and his bro (who he introduced to me as "his boy"—an expression appropriated from rap by performative white boys everywhere—so icky) didn't say much to me. They just walked around the space looking at everything, occasionally subtly raising their eyebrows as though I weren't there. After they left, Grant sent me an email saying that his pal thought the place "didn't really look like a charcuterie restaurant."

I've thought long and hard about how my self-esteem, something I believed in as solidly formed, cemented, was so easily picked at during this time; how effortlessly I nudged away my instincts, ignored my gut; and how automatically I tapped into my most motherly character trait: nurturing accommodation.

Grant seemed to me like he'd had a very hard life and my instinct was to mother him, a strong instinct, despite all the personality traits I have that might seem diametrically opposed to "nurturing." (But then, you obviously haven't seen me around babies.) I accommodated Grant's moods to the point of feeling like I was losing my sense of self. I'd complain to Roland, sometimes frustrated to the point of tears. I tried everything reasonable, which mostly meant repeated attempts at communication and conciliation, but nothing worked. I said black, he said white, I said up, he said down, and so on. To get anywhere, with any decision, I'd have to have the kind of winding conversation that left him feeling whatever small thing I wanted was somehow his idea, and left me feeling exhausted. Like the time we disagreed about how a server had handled something. She had correctly responded to a customer's request to bring the food all at once—it was only three items—but Grant flipped out when she put in the order, saying that's not how the kitchen does things and she would have to course it out. I understand wanting to present each dish on its own, it's a better dining experience, but in this case, the customer was in a hurry and just wanted to have it all at once, so what's the big deal? But Grant wouldn't relent and forced the server to course it out. She ended up picking up each course as she dropped the previous one off, which was a ridiculous waste of time, all so Grant could prove a point that wasn't even worth squabbling over, leaving the customer unhappy. Ironically, I'd usually be the more likely of us to put forth an attitude of "this is how we do things," but I would always try to accommodate easily dealt with requests about food. This is often a point of contention between front and back of house but ought not to be, because it's mostly a way for the (often) men in a kitchen to puff their chests and show who's boss. The server ended up in tears; I ended up trying to mediate.

The worst part about looking back on this time is how complicit I was in this negative atmosphere. I wanted an equal partnership and a pleasant environment. This was challenging enough to achieve with the external pressures of a dining public holding our casual restaurant to extremely high expectations, but it was made extra-difficult by the necessity of negotiating a minefield of negativity, ranging from sullen silence to whispered rage. The day following a particularly black service, Grant would be all smiles and jokes, as though none of it had happened. But what even was "it"? Mostly it was his interactions with servers and with me during service. I understood his snippiness with servers, although it happened far too often, but I didn't understand how he felt comfortable snapping at me as though I were his employee rather than waiting to discuss whatever had gone wrong (usually something very minor) after service. It didn't set a good example for the front of house staff to see him undermining me in that way. A tough boss runs a tight ship and leads by example, perhaps occasionally verbally reprimanding when necessary, but leadership should never have anything to do with ego. Good leaders tend to have healthy egos, but there's a big difference between showing confidence and displaying ego for its own sake.

There is an absurd, militaristic, master-servant relationship that happens in restaurant kitchens. It's a pattern that is hard to break, and one that I've seen over and over again. Men bond with bosses who treat them like dogs and then throw them a bone with a few "atta boys" and a couple of cold beers after service, like somehow their brutal behaviour ceases to matter when the gas is turned off. This kind of chef leadership style doesn't ever seem to bother the cooks at the receiving end of it, at least not long-term. The way line cooks and sous-chefs take behaviour like this all in "status quo" stride speaks clearly to the problematic way restaurant culture was grown and continues to be nurtured. The men (and they are mostly men) who trained this generation's chefs spent time in the kinds of European kitchens where the physical abuses would shock you—pots and pans being thrown at heads, hot tongs pressed onto forearms, and actual fistfights. I've heard stories about young cooks being taken into walk-in fridges and slapped, and a certain very famous chef is well known for his repetitive, hard chest pokes, exercised with all fingers pointed, bruising, whether intentional or not, being the obvious result. And if that's how the young men are treated, just imagine what happens to women entering these testosterone-and-gas-fuelled spaces, where the abuses often take on a sexual character (not that the young men are immune from an overly sexualized "hazing" style of abuse, because they aren't)—being humped from behind, bra straps snapped, dicks exposed. I think in most modern kitchens there is a slightly better base-line environment than in the European fine dining kitchens that set this abusive tone and made it all just par for a young cook's course—survive it and you are worthy of being a chef. It feels like leaps and bounds have been made now that the abuses tend to be less physical and more emotional, but that is a problematic way of looking at substituting one form of corrupted power for another, because we are still actually stuck in an appalling cycle. Whether the abuse is physical or emotional or sexual, very often the victims eventually gain power and become the abusers. It's so sad to see, and so hard to understand: YOU WENT THROUGH ALL THIS SHIT, WHY ARE YOU BEING SUCH AN ASSHOLE??? But, obviously, there is lots of science to support why victims so often become perpetrators. And often the perpetrators are given full rein to rule so unpleasantly due in part to how difficult it is for people to speak out in kitchens. There is a hierarchy in place, and part of doing an effective job is taking orders, to the point where it can be really hard to see when the line is starting to blur from normal work bossiness into completely inappropriate dickishness. *If everybody else can take it, why can't you?* And speaking up may get you branded "weak" or a "pussy" (favourite kitchen derisive language) or a "fag," all meant to underscore how kitchens are the domain of men, and real men can take the heat.

One particularly brutal fight I had with Grant started about the usual service stuff and degraded into name-calling and yelling. The last thing I said to him that night was, "God, you're such a fucking selfish asshole," and I meant it, and I barely heard him respond with "You're such a fucking bitch" as I left, too angry and distressed to even cry. That fight was only the beginning of the conflicts that would come with more frequency and fewer answers. He seemed to have a lot of pent-up anger toward me that I'd try to get to the bottom of but was never able to. He just wouldn't communicate, but he was so rude to me and to Roland (often not even bothering to respond to a morning greeting) that I was left always wondering what I'd done wrong, and when I'd ask, I'd get a mumbled

"Nothing." It's not just that Grant and I didn't get along. I strongly felt that he hated me and everything I represented. I'd walk into the restaurant and Grant and his sous would immediately stop talking, and it was obvious that they had just been discussing something I wasn't meant to hear. That was suggestive enough to make me pay more attention to the last hushed sentences the next time, which would only confirm my suspicions that they did in fact think my husband was lazy, because being an artist wasn't really "work," and that they were being encouraged to joke about how little I worked, as though spending all day at the restaurant and all night working service somehow wasn't enough. To a certain kind of cook, the chef bro (DON'T FORGET WOMEN CAN BE CHEF BROS TOO!), nothing, apart from kitchen work, is ever enough. They place no value on the thinking and creative process that goes into making a restaurant special, which is a deep irony, considering how they present their plates as art and themselves as artists.

Oh how I love the hilarious incongruity of men opining on their grandmother's pasta and influence while leading kitchens that, for all intents and purposes, loudly proclaim, "Leave the real cooking to the men and go make me a sandwich." It will never stop amusing me, and I'd laugh out loud if it didn't make me so sad. These are the kinds of kitchens that win the accolades of the world, amassing Michelin stars and sailing on to ridiculous, but sadly determinative, lists that set the tone for kitchen culture from the top down. They pay poorly, if at all; it's a well-documented fact that most of these high-end restaurants function with a base of unpaid labour working in short-term internships known as "stages"—though they are, no doubt, a valuable resource for learning how to cook, if you have the chops.

Those kitchens are also extremely unwelcoming places for young women. Despite some discussion happening around this, the culture in kitchens is still dictated mostly by macho men with no interest in real leadership, who instead define themselves by the false glory of a dictatorship that worships and cultivates master-servant relationships, and churns out cooks who think abuse is leadership and who will eventually mete it out with equal ferocity in an endless, repeating cycle. And women should be wary of these types of kitchens; they are demeaning, humiliating, and horrendous work environments, for both sexes, but as in most fields, to prove your mettle as a woman (if you don't you'll end up in pastry, "where you belong," because you most certainly won't be able to cut it in a "real" kitchen) you'll have to work twice as hard and will be allowed fewer mistakes.

Grant was constantly trying to interfere with how I ran the front of house, while I tried never to interfere with how he ran the kitchen and always gave him the benefit of the doubt. If there ever was a problem in the kitchen, Grant was quick to be defensive. He didn't handle negative feedback from customers well, and I would always back him up, agreeing that the customer probably just didn't "get" the food. One Friday night under a crush of people a potential customer got really rude with me about the wait time. I explained as politely as possible that there was nothing we could do, but I'd keep him updated should the wait be less than anticipated and promised to call him. He just kept telling me it was ridiculous to expect people to wait two hours for dinner. I said I understood it was a long wait and that maybe he should try on a quieter night, or right at 6:00 p.m. That's what seemed to spark his anger, and he went on a tirade about how precious his time was. He was a real piece of work. Grant happened to walk by to go outside for a cigarette as this was happening. I told the man there was nothing I could do and that I'd love him to try again someday, but that I needed to speak to the next people in line. He left in a huff, and I saw him talking to Grant outside. Later that night Grant tried to make me feel like I'd handled the situation poorly, which I didn't agree with, and which Grant had decided based solely on a stranger's word. It turned into a shouting match that left me going home in tears, wondering how I was going to deal with a business partner who didn't ever seem to want a united front.

The Hoof was such a busy restaurant that it was easy to ignore how unpleasant the environment was, how an emotionally abusive culture enforced through hierarchy set the tone in the back of house. This disgusted me enough that I made sure the dishwashers were treated like gold by the front of house staff, even though I was occasionally complicit in the cooks' childish behaviour, wanting to fit in for just a moment. This was a hard line to walk. That divide between front and back, which I wanted so badly to erase by paying the cooks well and generously tipping out, was being redrawn by Grant and his leadership style. And the really complicated, challenging part is that Grant's style (which he somehow performed without yelling, more in whispers and threats) was what the cooks responded to. I almost don't hold him responsible—he was only, after all, playing the role that was expected of him. So what if I found it repugnant?

Somehow Grant and I went on like this for just over two years. We even took a wreck of a building across the street and opened the Hoof Café during this incredibly busy time. The best part of that space is the beautiful back bar. I had an idea to turn old leaded-glass windows into cupboard doors while flipping through a pile of stained glass in the basement in one of my salvage spots. When the beautiful leaded-window back bar cupboards were up, Grant gave all the credit to the contractor, placing more value on the execution than the idea (to which) I took silent, seething exception. It was a perfect metaphor for how much he valued labour over ideas. He never once, ever, even after the space was done and clearly beautiful, said anything positive. Like, never. But just try to taste his food and withhold positive feedback—it would not have been well received. And that was really the crux of it all: I completely had Grant's back and he didn't have mine. It sucked.

The Hoof Café was meant to be a place where diners could sip on cocktails while they waited for their table at the Hoof, as well as a being the proper prep kitchen we so desperately needed, so why not make it a brunch spot, too? But while the Hoof Café was a huge, instant hit under the leadership of the extremely talented, if short-tempered, Geoff Hopgood, with lineups constantly snaking around the block, it was a financial nightmare. We weren't losing money, but it was an expensive place to run. It took four cooks to manage brunch, and we couldn't price anything above $14 or people would freak out. And of course, diners were drinking $3 cups of coffee, not $12 glasses of wine, so it was really hard to push people to spend more than $20 to $25 a head, even with amazing Caesars. It really was the best brunch in town. The menu was resplendent, starring things like suckling pig Eggs Benny, with biscuits and velvety, always perfect hollandaise; a smoked salmon pita pocket, garnished with salt-and-vinegar shoestring fries that I still dream about; and one of our side options was the most perfect bacon I've ever had. There was also a nighttime snack menu that was woefully underappreciated and perhaps occasionally too ambitious to be called "snacks," although I still managed to put back a lot of pierogies and fried chicken, and the pastas could make you cry. But after just over a year we shut it down so Grant could, ostensibly, have a platform for a tasting-menu-only restaurant, which, in my opinion, was really dumb. I felt cornered into agreeing to this concept, getting the sense that if I said no it would be a huge, weeks-long battle, and I was running out of energy to fight.

We should have stopped daytime service and, in general, food service, offering just snacks at night (like what we currently have). This approach is the most profitable thing ever. It's cocktails, hardly any staff, simple food, and we still get to do really cool innovative things. But we didn't, we closed the café and went about trying to launch Grant's tasting-menu concept, which he wanted to call Evolution. This was where I put my foot down, as that's possibly the worst restaurant name I've ever heard. After much discussion I finally agreed to BHCO (Black Hoof and Company), which I also hated, just much less than Evolution. This whole endeavour was a fiasco.

We kept paying the Café chef two thirds of his salary while Grant hemmed and hawed about his first menu. This was not a fun time. Grant had essentially taken away Geoff's title as head chef, only to ask him to be his sous for BHCO. Terrible move, politically. And I don't think Geoff was too pleased about it, but you'd never know there was ever any bad blood between them because bro code. There was one more cook brought on board who was just clever enough to be wary of Grant. The three of them went on trips to farms, sourcing driftwood for terrible plate ideas, picking up rocks on the beach, again for terrible plate ideas. By the time they put on the first tasting dinner for all the staff, there was a palpable tension among them. I never got the entire story, but piecing together what they told me much later, I got the feeling neither cook thought this was going to work.

They quit on him the next week—both at the same time, clearly coordinated, a coup. And eventually the staff told me how much they hadn't liked the food that had been put out for a staff tasting. I hadn't eaten it all as a whole meal, and I was a bit blindly protective of Grant at that time. Actually, I was *all about* shielding Grant, and being a good partner. So when he called me the night the cooks quit, I rushed to his house to pick up his confidence (and quite literally pick him off the floor, where he lay, defeated). I'd never seen him like that, so obviously full of self-doubt. It was not reassuring. Also, we were hemorrhaging money. It was June 2011 at the time, and he wanted to wait *until the next spring* to try his restaurant again. I was like "Whaaat?" His thinking was that he wouldn't be "ready" until then and didn't want to open mid-winter with a shortage of local produce, which struck me as illogical, as we'd have to deal with winter soon enough. Also, why not maybe aim for September, then, one of the more abundant times of year, produce-wise?

Truthfully, I supported the idea of closing until spring while thinking it was fucking mental. I was trying to be as supportive as possible since he seemed so broken, but when I told Roland what Grant wanted to do, he was not having it. He rightly focused me in on what a terrible business decision that was, and how we'd lose everything if we let this preciousness from Grant continue. It's easy to sympathize with Grant's position in this scenario as the auteur and paint me as the angry money-person, but we simply couldn't afford to have the Café sit empty for ten months while Grant got his groove back.

But this was a real turning point. I was at the end of my rope with the constant fighting and how blasé Grant was about being the reason we now had a building (and all the expenses that entailed) with no business in it. He just didn't seem to care about the big picture, and the seeds of doubt I'd had for years about our partnership were sprouting, poking through. I was starting to fantasize about sole ownership and how wonderful that could be.

The Café space at 923 Dundas West sat languishing, having been empty for months; it was now early July. I told Grant over the phone one morning that I wanted to open a cocktail bar. It would be an easy transition: a new coat of paint, throw in a banquette, done! I was excited about this excellent idea, but his first reaction was to balk, that this would be perceived as a "step backwards." Gee, thanks. I was, at this point, totally used to his negativity and was prepared for him to put up a big fight about it. Roland and I had had a long conversation about how much the cocktail bar idea needed to happen, and it was clearly the quickest way out of a potentially ruinous financial situation. I had fought too hard for success to let Grant's out-rageous "artistic vision," which wasn't even fully gelled, get in the way. We were responsible for a large rent, why should we let a beautiful space sit empty for nine months? It was just plain stupid. So after he continued to refuse to allow me to proceed with the cocktail bar I flat out told him, "We don't have a choice here, so either get on board with this idea, or call a lawyer." This was the first time I'd voiced the feelings about ending the partnership that had been gathering steam all through the summer of 2011. It felt great to say it out loud, and the feeling stayed with me, and since I knew I'd have no trouble running a cocktail bar on my own, and I was starting to suspect that Grant's sous-chef would be happy to stay on and run the Hoof kitchen (even if he would eventually rejoin his "master"), the idea that I could actually do this on my own germinated. I was already running the entire operation. I dealt with everything, every detail, outside of the actual cooking of the food, so I knew as long as I had a good chef in charge I could run the business alone. I didn't know at the time that I would be definitively deciding to do just that in less than two months.

In the meantime, Grant had decided to get on board with the cocktail bar idea, and when he called me the next day (after I'd told him very strongly how I felt) he almost put it to me like it was his idea. "I really think we should open a cock-tail bar." I was like, "Ya, me too." So weird. But I got to work right away with a coat of bright aqua paint on the east wall that didn't work, which I was a bit stubborn about admitting, but then I covered it in the most perfect charcoal grey; I had a banquette built and put up rows of beautiful, meticulously cut wood strapping on the front of the bar that Grant insisted wouldn't age well. It did.

With the Cocktail Bar an instant, unmitigated success, with much higher profit margins than we had at the Café or even the Hoof, the tension between Grant and me cooled, but only slightly and only temporarily, because the normalcy of not stressing about money wasn't enough to repair the damage of that summer. We even booked a three-day trip to Chicago just to try and mend our fractured relationship. The trip was, unfortunately, mostly a disaster. We fought almost the whole time, and I called Roland in tears more than once. Finally, he told me to "just come home." I should have, but I didn't. Instead Grant and I spent the morning after an awful fight peeking out of the previous night's slammed doors and trying to put a mortally wounded partnership back together. We superficially succeeded. I listened to him try to dissect his feelings for maybe the first time ever. And we went home feeling like it was possible to move forward. But by the next week it felt exactly the same as it always had, and I was completely done with trying to fix it.

The final straw was something silly, as final straws so often are. We were discussing work stuff on the bench outside the Cocktail Bar and got into it (about what, I don't remember). We were going back and forth and getting nowhere, and in a rage he threw his coffee at the sidewalk with no concern for how that looked to the cooks who were prepping for service across the street and had, no doubt, seen the whole thing. I got up and left, knowing I was ready to call it quits for good. In that moment I recognized that we were never going to be able to communicate with one another, and that if I didn't make a change now, I'd have a hard time spouting feminist rhetoric without it feeling like a lie.

When I told Roland I was done and planned to ask Grant to leave, he was so relieved. We went over a game plan, what our ideal outcome was, what we were prepared to take as payment for the company, which at this point included Cocktail Bar and another rental property just east of the Hoof that we used for storage, which would eventually become Raw Bar, then Rhum Corner. We decided on our number, figuring that if we could walk away at that price, it was a fair offer.

An hour later, I went back to find Grant in the prep kitchen at Cocktail Bar. Another cook was taking brioche out of the oven and the bartender was grabbing limes out of the fridge. I quietly asked to speak to him. He grunted that he didn't want to. I told him that it couldn't wait, my voice a bit louder, and that it wouldn't take long. We went outside to the street corner and I quickly and clearly told him that I was done with this dysfunctional situation and didn't want to be his partner any more. I didn't go into much detail, only that my decision was final. He said okay and not much else. I plainly asked him if he wanted to buy me out. He didn't. I told him that in that case I'd buy him out. "Let's try and make this as civil as possible," I said. And he agreed that civility was the best course. I genuinely wanted it to be un-messy and tried to make it so.

The few weeks following were unpleasant. Imagine having to see someone you're deep in a cold war with every day. Having to smile at his girlfriend. Having to be polite. And despite an agreement that we would make a public announcement together, citing good wishes for each other but a desire to move in separate directions creatively, blah blah blah, Grant took it upon himself to tweet, out of the blue, that he was "no longer associated with the black hoof." It was such a shitty move. I hadn't even had the chance to tell the staff what was happening, and I spent all day fielding phone calls from hurt employees who just wanted to know what was going on. I couldn't believe he'd ignored our agreement, but then again, I could. By the end of that little battle it felt like a war. I could not have been happier to be out, relatively unscathed, ego only bruised.

After the money had been exchanged, after I gave up the beautiful, vintage-style meat-slicer Roland and I had paid for as a gesture of goodwill back at the very beginning, as well as the Café's forgotten espresso machine that I didn't want anyway, and the countless pieces of cutlery, glassware, plates, and chairs, I felt completely calm. It wasn't worth being petty, despite already having paid a more than fair price for 50 percent of a company I never should have given away in the first place. Lesson learned, I would be very careful before I went into business with someone ever again, and I probably wouldn't do it with someone who was practically a stranger. And I would never let a bully chef rule with such unmitigated freedom, partner or not.

As challenging and scary as it was to go forward without Grant running the kitchen, asking him to leave the company was a first step that would eventually lead me to places in my career I never could have reached in that partnership.

◇ Liquor Forward ◇

Hoof Manhattan $16.00/3oz
Adapted from the Manhattan, Circa 1880's
10 year rye, antica, house bitters
≫ *Will ruin you for other Manhattans.*

Vieux To A Kill $15.00/2.5oz
Inspired by a Vieux Carre and a Revolver
bourbon, armagnac, cold brew concentrate, maple, bitters
≫ *If a Vieux Carré and a Revolver had a mutually desired, highly satisfactory one night stand, this would be what they call their text thread for future hook-ups.*

Whisky Business $16.00/3oz
Cocktail Bar Original
bourbon, rye, jameson, laphroaig, fig liqueur, boker's
≫ *This is not just about jamming all the whiskies into one cocktail to be cool, everything brings something different to the table and it's all very harmonious. Although, maybe it was about...best name ever?*

◇ Wild Cards ◇

Big in Japan $14.00/2.5oz
Cocktail Bar Original
single malt scotch, shochu, orgeat, lemon, sesame oil
≫ *Ironically, this cocktail isn't actually big in Japan.*

Gold Fashioned $16.00/2.5oz
A take on an Old Fashioned, heavily inspired by the Cinema Highball created by Don Lee at PDT 2008-ish
buttered-popcorn brandy, yellow chartreuse, sugar, bitters, cherry coke
≫ *Sounds so weird, we know, but tastes so awesome, just one foot outside the box.*

Sparkling Thing $12.00
Cocktail Bar Original
cava, amaro montenegro, brown sugar, orange blossom water, peychaud's
≫ *You try naming 22 cocktails.*

◇ Bold and Citrusy ◇

Crusta Rhymes $13.00/1.5oz
Based on a Brandy Crusta by Joseph Santina at The Jewel of the South, New Orleans, 1852
calvados, chartreuse, lemon, ginger, mace
≫ *Soooo this drink is based on a Crusta which is some olden times cocktail blah, blah, blah I fell asleep anyway this has mace in it. Busta Rhymes and Ma$e did a song together but, ummmm, we couldn't call it that. Google it.*

Ward 11 $10.00/1.5oz
Adapted from the Ward 8, Locke-Ober Restaurant, Boston, 1898
bourbon, pomegranate molasses, tangerine, lemon, peychaud's
≫ *Three modifications away from a Ward 8.*

Spanish Bombs $14.00/2oz
Inspired by a London Calling, Milk and Honey, London, 2003
caña brava, orgeat, fino, lime
≫ *Poss one of my favourite shaken cocktails of all time.*

◇ Seasonal ◇

Montrose Mule $13.00/2oz
Based on a Moscow Mule created in LA at The Cock and Bull Tavern, 1941
gin, suze, lemon, ginger beer, mint
≫ *Guys it's got mint! You LOVE mint. You're always like: "ummmm, you don't have mint?? Really???" So here. It's MINT. And you can have a mojito, if you ask real nice.*

Absinthe Whip $14.00/2oz
Inspired by an Orange Whip, John Belushi, 1980
absinthe, orange, pistachio, coconut
≫ *Honestly, we seriously considered printing a full colour menu juuust so we could use the sunglasses-wearing emoji.*

Hot Buttered Rum $11.00/1.5oz
Inspired by Kasy Fitch's recipe at Zig Zag, Seattle
rum, butter, ice cream, spices
≫ *If you're lactose intolerant, we have several drinks for you! This definitely isn't one, I'm afraid.*

FOODLINER

Hopgood's
Foodliner

Roncesvalles Ave.

Dundas St.W

Lansdowne Ave.

Grand Electric

Dufferin St.

Queen St.W

Isabel

797

College St.

Ossington Ave.

Bar
Isabel

charcuterie

The Black
Hoof

12: RAW FREEDOM

THE MOMENT I DROPPED THE FINAL BUY-OUT CHEQUE off at Grant's lawyer, it was like I'd unzipped a too-tight dress and rolled off stockings that squeezed just hard enough to indent the skin on my legs. The sense of freedom was palpable.

When the dust finally settled I went through all the "firsts." Like first time walking into *my* restaurant. First Saturday night without feeling eavesdropped on and furtively watched by someone who I thought was perversely hoping I'd misstep in a customer interaction, just so he could be reassured that I was, in fact, a bitch. First time I didn't worry how much abuse the dishwashers had to deal with. But the best was the first time I really noticed how much more relaxed I genuinely felt. It must've shown, because for months regular customers would comment on how happy I looked. And I looked happy because that's how I felt.

In spite of this, I was questioning a lot about myself and the situation I had been in with Grant for so long. I'm the strongest woman I know, so how could someone I had come to have no respect for almost succeed at taking me down? The oppressive environment had been really suffocating. And my response to it, prior to having finally reached my limit, was to pretend it was all okay, to shield Grant from negativity, and to protect the business at all costs.

So it's fair to say that I was extraordinarily relieved to not have to deal with him, business-wise, ever again. I paid a bunch of money to buy back a business that was my concept, and all I can do is wish I'd hired Grant as a chef and never partnered with him. But regret is not a good glass through which to examine one's life. It's not like I didn't learn anything from the experience, but I learned more about myself than about my ex-partner. It was mostly an odd surprise to realize how accommodating I could be for what I believed was the greater good (which sounds like one of those interview situations where you're asked what your flaws are and you say you're a perfectionist, but in this case it really was a huge flaw). Accommodation is such a common thread for women in the workplace, even strong women at the top of their game. They feel a need to adjust and swivel and make space for male partners/co-workers to just keep doing what they're doing, even if it's poor leadership, or worse, abusive behaviour. Because this is both instinctual and learned, and taught to us from such a young age, it's a huge challenge to break away, to decide to say "no, I don't agree with you." And when you find your voice, and say no, instead of being lauded for doing exactly what men have been doing forever to succeed, you are vilified, told to be nicer, told you'll get further with a better attitude, told to be less of a bitch.

In my case, since I am the boss, I'm in no danger of hearing this from a supervisor with the power to take away my job, but the message is delivered anyway by the public's perception of me. My personality, worn by a man, would never have been put through the media wringer that includes fun headlines like "Mean Girl" and describes me every time as "the outspoken

Jen Agg." So, given all my natural instincts toward strong leadership, no matter what the cost, it was very difficult to accept my responsibility in allowing Grant to run half our company the way he had. I had a lot of questions about how I'd allowed that to happen. And I came to a few conclusions: one, that I was terrified I couldn't do it on my own, which enfeebled me; two, that I should trust my instincts, which I'd been ignoring in favour of pretending everything was fine; and three, to stop assuming, in a tremendous arrogance, that I could ever change anybody.

But I silenced all my guilt (which was mostly self-directed, it's taken years to forgive myself for all of it) with dreams of opening a new restaurant in the space to the east of the Hoof that had thus far been used only for storage and firings. (Fun company slang: Taking someone for a talk in "storage," the next door space and the only private area in all of the locations, meant they were being fired—put in storage forever.)

I wanted to do something that would be a complete opposite to the Hoof, and I was excited, too, by the idea of fish and seafood, something with cured fish (or fish charcuterie) as the star and tartares, crudos, baked whole fish, and other lighter stuff, along with a very focused wine list—just whites, pinots and gamays—in a space that was out of my dreams. I also knew it would be a nice complement to the Hoof and was definitely thinking about contrasting the masculinity of the Hoof with more femininity. This would be the Hoof Raw Bar. I wanted to get it open quickly, both as a fresh start and as a way of keeping the Hoof brand in the spotlight. People are fickle and bore easily; if you don't keep doing new shit constantly, they will go to the spot that copied your concept in so many ways but isn't as good, just *because* it's new. So I got to work.

The space had nothing in it. It had been Ferreira's Photography Studio for decades, and had long been a hipster point of reference due to the quirky, retouched photos in the window display. Everybody knew about "NO FACE? NO PROBLEM." But the space didn't even have washrooms, so it was a complete build-out. One very Toronto thing, specific to so many restaurants, is a long and narrow room with basement washrooms. It's just how the buildings were constructed. But this space, at 926 Dundas West, directly beside the Hoof, would be an exception, at least to the basement rule. We needed to build a walk-in fridge downstairs (which left no room for washrooms) and we couldn't get any of the companies who do that sort of thing to agree to it for any sort of reasonable price because it was going partially under a staircase and was full of odd angles, so we built it ourselves, with a little help from our friends.

I love a great washroom, and the area we wanted to use, up a few stairs in the back, was just the right size and shape to do something amazing. I wanted to do separate but unisex washrooms, with a big shared sink outside. But due to some silly bylaw, when there's a proper door involved you have to have sinks in the same room as toilets, which is weird but kind of makes sense, for handwashing and doorknob touching. So we would have to install small sinks in each stall. For the shared sinks that would anchor the whole space, I found a gorgeous pair of old white ceramic wall-mounted kitchen sinks, the kind that have the backsplash built in, where the faucets go, and the rippled drying area beside the sink where you'd rest dishes to drip-dry. So beautiful, but how the hell were we going to install them? Roland and I ran over ideas, but I really didn't want to build a wooden frame, I wanted them to look as though they were floating. There was this old bakers' rolling rack sitting in the small outside space behind Raw Bar and we came up with the idea to turn it on its side and let it bear some of the weight of the very heavy sinks. It worked, and looked so cool. Then I got hooked on wanting to do backstage dressing room lighting around a big mirror. After spending way too long talking to our eccentric electrician, Johnny, about how to do this, I eventually just got fed up and started looking for wall lighting. In the end I found these weird but totally beautiful 1980s-style sconces that have about twenty foot-long solid glass tubes that sit around two bulbs, one upside down, directly below the other; they give off a glowy, perfect light that flatters all. It really is always all about lighting.

White subway tiles, a coat of charcoal paint, and the frames of the wavy glass stall doors in seafoam, a favoured colour, covered the basics. The doors needed a translucent sheet of sticky-one-side plastic so as not to be too revealing, but I like how you can still see movement and shadow—suggestive, while still chaste. And as an unnecessary but beautiful touch, I installed leaded-glass windows above the stall doors.

The main dining area was all inspired by the existing floor, that grey-and-white checkered tile you've seen in every Portuguese or Italian grocery store.

The design was easy because for the first time I was building a space purely for me. The Hoof was cheap by necessity, and the Cocktail Bar, although a beautiful little jewel box, isn't really my taste. This space was grey, white, pale wood, and seafoam green, the colours of my clothes and dreams. And it was a nice blend of high/low, most exemplified by the chipboard bar covered in a pricey slab of quartz.

When it all came together, after a couple of months of doing most of the work ourselves, I basked in the design, just staring at everything, dumbfounded by what I'd made, in the humblest way I could manage. It reflected my taste so directly that it was hard not to take it in as the most beautiful restaurant I'd ever seen, which is undoubtedly how everyone feels about any sort of artistic child, or actual child, I guess. It looked like it was made exclusively from sanded grey and green beach stones, and it felt very oceanic, but without a trace of kitsch—no anchors or boating ropes, not even a singing bass.

While working on the space, I put together a great crew headed by the cerebral and extremely talented Jon Pong. Finding a chef is so scary when you aren't one, and I was maybe a little gun-shy, considering what I'd gone through with Grant. But I had no such fears about Jon; I was very much the boss and had a great working relationship with him. He'd already been manning the *garde manger* station at the Hoof, and I knew he had the organization, dedication, and creativity to be able to not only run a kitchen but make one from scratch. I gave him some parameters for the menu—the cured fish board, a few crudo and tartare plates, house-smoked and house-canned mussels, and whole fish—but he was free to show me anything he wanted, as long as it was fish or seafood. He and Cio, his sous, worked so hard on his first menu. He knew Amancio (Cio) dos Santos from a previous job working for Ted

Corrado, who is perhaps under-credited for training many, many of Toronto's most solid cooks. I helped where I could: finding a framework that made sense, in terms of the menu people would see; tasting; occasionally making suggestions. But Jon got the vibe I was going for: delicate, light, and delicious.

After a couple of months of trial and error, they had really dialled in the salt levels and cure times for the fish charcuterie, which was to be the anchor, and with which I'd fallen in love. The cured fish board was really simple. Just four or five things (pastrami-cured salmon, cured and torched mackerel, scallops kissed with smoked paprika, to name but a few) laid out, with pickled shallots and a variety of accompaniments (we couldn't be nearly as generous with fish as with traditional charcuterie because of wildly different costs). But it was a gorgeous board, and still good value. My favourite plate, whose taste, years after having had it for the last time, I can still call to mind, was a very simple sea bream, raw and lightly dressed with a soy/butter emulsion, a drinkable/craveable mix, surrounding a neat pile of cucumber strands hit with wasabi oil. It was perfection, even with nasturtium leaves subbing in for cucumber. (One terribly sad and ridiculous fact about me is that cucumber makes my stomach revolt. It's an embarrassing allergy, developed in my late twenties, to a thing I adore eating. It's tragic, really.) The whole fish was an impressive platter, with rotating, seasonal sides. And there was always a salad or two. Everything was tasty and I was really proud of it. I ate a late dinner there after working at the Hoof every night for the first couple of weeks of service, ostensibly for quality control, but in fact I couldn't get enough of this kind of light eating and believed lots of other people would feel similarly. And they did.

Raw Bar was busy right off the bat, and I was high on life and winning and the freedom of being in complete control of my businesses. But, of course, control in the restaurant business is an illusion. You'll never be able to wrestle it away from public opinion. And as much as public opinion may lead the media to the story, in turn, it's also led by the media. That's who's really in charge.

13: ON GETTING A BAD REVIEW

EVERYTHING ABOUT THE RESTAURANT BUSINESS is made harder by being in it as a woman. And speaking out about that only makes it worse. I might inherently know this, but I'm repulsed by the thought of staying quiet. It's been a lifelong thing, this need for constant self-expression, and it comes with a prolific suspicion of authority. In this business, the media is the authority, and anyone who disagrees with that probably has enough media attention that they can afford to think something so ridiculous. But if the media is mostly controlled by a populist perspective, by the idea of giving the people what they want, and that perspective is, for the most part, happy with the status quo, how can we make a better industry? If the people like what they're hearing and the content is in some way saleable, there isn't much incentive to change, especially in a once booming media industry that now feels held together by duct tape and hope. Don't forget how much power editors and writers have over what people want just by virtue of being the ones calling for the stories and doling them out to the public. When it's a profile, it can be spun in any way the writer wants; once finished it's out of the writer's hands, and editors—whose main concern is keeping their medium afloat—have all the control, and they can editorialize and package a profile any way they see fit. Even straight-up reporting, which should be completely objective, isn't always.

My feelings about critics, from bloggers to professional writers who are paid for their work, range from disdain to indifference, and then to thoughts of glorious cohabitation in a mutually beneficial house of words. The Hoof has, with a few exceptions, been a real hit with the critics, but even though I understand the economic value of a great review, as it was the unmistakable turning point for the Hoof's quick ascension, it's a fraught relationship, because most of the time, even if the critics get it, they don't *really* get it. And how could they? They are writing about the restaurant, not living it.

The restaurateur-critic relationship is a dance of charm, impotence, and maximum exposure. I feel I've, at the very least, mastered the basic steps, if not a few complex lifts. I have personal relationships with a few prominent Toronto writers and count some as close friends. But I've always felt there's an unspoken fraughtness that hangs over any potential for real friendship. Critics are afraid of having their objectivity impaired or called into question by this friendship, and restaurateurs are always a little smug about what critics actually understand about restaurants, since they often have never worked in the industry.

This brings up the question of whether that ought to be a requirement. Fresh-faced, new-restaurant-me absolutely thought, yes, critics should be embarrassed to write about a world they've never existed in. But, with some maturity, I realized I was approaching it all wrong. Critics aren't necessarily writing to impress restaurant people. Although I'd argue that they secretly do want at least a bit of respect from the restaurant community, that a baseline of grudging admiration from chefs and owners is maybe essential to their success as critics, the fact is that they are actually writing for an audience that also has a limited understanding of the inner mechanisms of restaurants. And with that in mind, critics should be approaching dining as an educated "normal." They should be dissecting the experience as a person who isn't so jaded by restaurants that they've become hard to surprise. As much as I'd like to think it would be a fun job for me when I'm old, and I'm sure I'd come at it with a seriously insider perspective, I basically hate everything, and would be way too harsh.

When Corey Mintz wrote his only four-star review during his two years as the *Toronto Star* food critic and it was for The Black Hoof, I was, of course, elated. It exposed the Hoof to a whole new audience and was the turning point for the explosive growth of the business. Strangely, or perhaps not so strangely, what I had previously seen as his off-putting social behaviours started to morph into intellectual "quirks." There is no doubt that had it been a negative review, our friendship would not have developed, but that's more about common ground than feeling insulted. If someone doesn't "get" or like this thing I've put so much of myself into, how could they possibly like me? Of course, this becomes more convoluted when it's the food the reviewer is negative about, but I'm loyal enough (possibly to a fault) to take that extremely personally.

I remember getting to know Corey over the bar at the Hoof. Sometimes he would read (mostly comics) as a signal that he just wanted a quiet dinner. Other times we would chat about non-restaurant stuff. Although we can certainly go on about food and restaurants, and do, I am always grateful to talk about other things, because being draped in restaurants usually means endlessly talking about them, the industry, and food. I am so appreciative of people who introduce me as "Jen," instead of "Jen, she owns The Black Hoof." Obviously, in a conversation, one's job comes up naturally, but I much prefer it not to be the diving board. That probably seems awfully naive, especially since I have my own biases and preconceived notions about people's jobs, and ultimately want to know what they do, as it is so often revealing of their character. Except, of course, when it's not.

There is great, benchmark food writing and criticism out there—M.F.K. Fisher, Jonathan Gold, Ruth Reichl, and A.A. Gill, to name a few. But there are plenty of writers whose work is so poor, so malformed that it is almost not worth mentioning. It's most disappointing when these aren't just bloggers but actual employed "writers" who get a salary. And as much as it's enraging, it has plenty to do with the Internet and its constant need to feed on new content—it's a baby bird, perpetually hungry, even for food that's already chewed up—which I guess is a small price to pay for complete access to all the world's information. I suppose I can stomach having to read one more "This season's ten hottest vegetables" list if it also means I can look up literally anything I want to know and have an answer in seconds.

Journalism, like any field, is full of apathy: writers just phoning it in, writers who should have retired twenty years ago, writers writing about food trends (honestly, if I never see another prediction for the "top five hot food trends" it'll be too soon). Though our need to eat for survival gives the subject of food a certain importance and urgency, there is a lot of writing about food that is hugely boring and inconsequential. There is no shortage of incompetent writers pitching terrible story ideas, or editors asking for them, particularly in food. It is rare that I read engaged food criticism—writing that elevates simple to beautiful, writing that's laugh-out-loud hilarious, writing that asks hard questions and makes me think about my food choices—in any of our local or national papers. But that doesn't mean there isn't great food writing happening. There is, but it's growing out of piles of useless muck.

If journalism wants to continue to be a real, respected thing, it had better plug the holes in the dam with strong, smart content because there are so many people saying so much stuff it's easy to forget who's getting paid and who isn't. The bloggers are starting to break through the levees with a reckless, insatiable, unaccountable hunger. And that is not good for the future of paid writing.

It is next to impossible to think about food writing and the restaurant business without mentioning bloggers, love them or loathe them. There is no denying the impact these camera-happy keyboard-mashers have had on the industry. They create Internet buzz simply by tweeting about restaurants. They write blogs that are usually glowing assessments of the food, service, etc. Some are beautiful works of art with thoughtful insights and gorgeous pictures; most are mediocre, full of poorly lit shots, under-written with clunky, unedited text; and a few are bitchy whines from sad little people who are just itching for their big break, which will likely never come.

Corey, who, I imagine, spends as much time defending me as I do him, would occasionally write about the restaurant, or

Grant and me. I think when he had us for dinner for his column, "Fed, by Corey Mintz," that was the last straw. His editors forbade him to ever write about the Hoof again, as it was clear we were friends and *The Toronto Star* didn't want any suggestion of favouritism, which I totally get. No biggie, there were plenty of other writers who would be keen to keep us hot under the salamander glow of the media's spotlight. One of them, Chris Nuttall-Smith, became the person I called when I wanted to bitch about the Toronto glossy that happened to be the most influential local food mag, and for which he was head food writer. He was very receptive to hearing about the problems I had with how things were sometimes handled there. But Nuttall-Smith's run was short-lived. He had his sights set on *The Globe and Mail*, Canada's most coveted crown jewel of restaurant criticism, and he eventually got it. I got to know Chris strictly over the many hours we talked on the phone. I found him to be well-spoken, sarcastic, funny, and refreshingly straightforward, except when he was trying to manipulate me into saying what he wanted me to, which was often. I couldn't say how many times we've spoken professionally, but it's a lot. We have more than several friends in common, and I always figured, eventually, we'd end up at the same dinner party. We haven't yet, likely because he is careful about not getting close to restaurateurs, if only to avoid the appearance of impropriety. But it also can't be any fun to say horrible (perhaps wrong) things about a friend.

When Nuttall-Smith came to Raw Bar for dinner, it was a busy Tuesday. Six weeks into being open, the numbers had been steadily climbing every day, we were having busy services five nights a week, and the food was being received very well.

We knew him on sight. He had accidentally outed himself to me years before, when he had come for dinner to the Hoof one night. I hadn't known it was him until he emailed me a thank-you after his visit, complete with an inside joke from a service interaction, like he wanted me to remember him. I planted his face in my memory and recognized him the instant he came through the door. The question of whether recognized critics get better service or food is an unending debate. Obviously, preferential treatment and sending out free stuff are complete (and desperate) no-nos. But it is always helpful to know who a critic is, and, at the very least, it gives you the illusion of control. He came in again the next week so I knew a review would be forthcoming and was stoked for it. I believed in what we were doing. Our mostly natural wine list was many years ahead of its time for Toronto, the room was gorgeous, the service on point, and I had no doubts about the food.

The whole crew was pretty excited for the review to come out. Frankly, it was the only one that mattered to me—Nuttall-Smith's voice echoes from Canada's most respected paper, and he, at the very least, cares a great deal about doing a good job, and generally does. I just assumed Raw Bar would get the three-out-of-four-star review I believed it deserved.

Then, while tending to the plants on the Black Hoof patio, I got the fact-checking call. It started out auspiciously, but he was praising me too much. Telling me how awesome the wine, décor, and service were. I started to sense a "but" coming. And I started to panic. I knew something terrible was about to come out of his mouth and just wanted to flush the phone down the toilet. But I remained on the line, my whole body tensed in anticipation of what I knew would be bad news.

It was the food. He had not enjoyed it, which I couldn't, and still can't, fully understand. Words like "ham-fisted seasoning" and questions like "Why would you cure *that* fish?" (I dunno, Chris, ask ANY Nordic person) started to make me dizzy. He hadn't "gotten" it at all. I sat down, switching the phone from my left ear to my right and then back, feeling a complete loss of control, an unfamiliar feeling I didn't care for. I knew there was no point in saying anything to try to change his mind; the review was written. He told me he was "bending over backwards to try to be kind" and all I could think was, "if that's you being kind, you must be *kind* of an asshole." I felt nauseous. He kept telling me everything would be "fine," which I suppose is easy enough to say when it isn't your $75,000, which is roughly what I'd spent to open Raw Bar—not bad in terms of what it costs to open a restaurant, but still a shit-ton of cash. He thanked me a couple of times for being "so professional" (I wasn't thinking professional thoughts, I was thinking "Fuuuuuck you!")

In that moment, I had the irrational notion that if the conversation never ended, this horrible thing, the bad review, would never happen, so I tried to keep Chris on the phone by making small talk, and I HATE small talk. After he finally extracted himself from my desperate panic, my first concern was Jon. I'm tough, I can take it, but for a chef, with his first menu, to have to hear a critic didn't like it, I was afraid it would be devastating. There was no need to worry, though. Of course Pong wasn't happy about it, but with a centuries-old Chinese stoicism, an excellent attitude, and, I would think, a few sublimated feelings, he just soldiered on and got better and better. That's not to say, "Hey, thanks for pointing out a few of our foibles, it's only made us stronger." Not at all. He would have gotten better just as quickly with a more balanced, constructive review.

I believe we gave Chris the best we could on his two visits to Raw Bar. There is no doubt that there were some seasoning issues with a dish or two, but the scale on which we were judged felt tipped hard, away from our favour. Most of the food was certainly not "awful" as described in his review. In fact, much of it was quite wonderful, avant-garde, and really tasty. I think the name "Raw Bar" caused some confusion, as traditional raw bars have oysters, which we carried, and oxymoronically cooked chilled seafood, which we sometimes had as a special. But the key to the name is "Hoof." It's Hoof Raw Bar. And to me, that implied some licence to go outside the lines. Almost half the menu was raw fish or seafood, done in a myriad of ways—crudo, ceviche, tartare—and we rounded it out with some snacks, like smoked mussels, "canned" salmon, a beautiful cured fish board (the yin to the Hoof charcuterie board's yang), and a few cooked fish dishes. So you could have a full meal, and be exposed to a wide variety of fish and seafood. Hilariously, this kind of menu is currently experiencing a lot of play in Toronto—sometimes it sucks to be the first wave.

The call with Chris was on Wednesday; the review came out late Friday night. Comfily ensconced in my favourite afterservice spot, the red chairs outside the Hoof, with Roland beside me, I took a breath and read it aloud. It was so weird. It basically praised me (to the point of twitchy discomfort) for seven paragraphs (with a strange run-on sentence about the patrons) as a set-up to the smack-down. And smack down it did, hard, with this sentence: "A lot of the food is awful." Although I didn't and don't agree with much of what was written, I tried to pull out some constructive criticism. We worked hard to make sure things wouldn't go out too salty, an unfixable, amateur mistake.

The snarky last line, though, is the one I found most difficult to swallow: "Miss Agg still has some curating to do"— which I did not and still don't agree with, despite how it all turned out. Jon Pong is awesome and I loved working with him. He is widely respected for his talent and creativity, gets the most out of his cooks, and is a pleasure to work with. Also, he is a wonderful guy. His food deserved the kind of one-star review Nuttall-Smith gave a restaurant a few weeks later, one that offered criticism but took the edge off the nastiness, suggesting the chef needed time to fully form.

Over the years, I've given much thought to the reasons behind the review:

Reason 1: Nuttall-Smith needed a big takedown and my restaurant was the perfect fit. This was my first thought.

Reason 2: He was extra-hard on us because the Hoof had been so praised for so long.

Reason 3: He genuinely hated everything we served because his palate sucks.

Reason 4: The kitchen panicked and over-seasoned everything and he did, in fact, have a bad experience.

I will forever believe that he did, in some ways, need a takedown. It was his third review in his new position as *Globe and Mail* food critic, and it would get way more attention as a negative review. But I also believe that he's not someone who would lie about his experience (even to himself), so I think it's very likely that shit went wrong with his food and that he was extra-harsh about it.

It's taken me a long time to get over. I want to be the person who says, "Fuck that shit, it doesn't matter," but the truth is it absolutely does matter. And ultimately, it did matter.

I believe a great restaurant that connects with a lot of people can survive a scathing review, but Raw Bar didn't survive that nasty review, or itself. Turns out the reason so few fish and oyster restaurants exist away from oceans is because it's really fucking expensive. The cost to keep it open was astronomical. And I was emotionally attached, while obviously realizing how stupid it is to be emotionally attached to a failing business. But for plenty of reasons, I was. It wasn't just the aesthetic beauty I was hanging on to, or the fact that I loved the food and the concept and was concerned for the staff; it was undeniably somewhat based in ego, and that clouded my judgment. Hoof Raw Bar was the restaurant I opened right after buying Grant out of the business, and it was partly because of that—I was desperate to succeed, to prove I could do it, on my own.

With its fish and seafood menu, focused in such a narrow way—plates of crudo, everything light and delicate—Raw was so very, very niche that it just couldn't survive. But I wasn't ready to pull the plug yet—there was still a lot more money to be lost! It was a hard winter, both for weather and bottom lines at Raw Bar, and by January I'd decided to bring back the Hoof Café, Thursday to Sunday, in the Raw Bar space. Not because I so badly wanted the hassle of a brunch restaurant, but obviously to bring in more money. It was a nice idea and *not confusing at all* to have two restaurants in one venue, but ultimately it was a last-ditch effort to save a sinking ship.

The resurrected version of the Hoof Café was really good, with instant hits like the blood sausage McMuffin and the sweet/spicy/savoury notes from perfectly fried sweetbreads and waffles, and a French toast with jam and cream that, of course, could be modified with seared foie gras. It was run by Cio, Jon Pong's sous-chef, and it was a really nice brunch. If we'd had the time and money to let it grow and develop legs it would have been a real thing, but we didn't. It was hyper-busy on weekends but not during the week, and after five months it became *almost* clear to me that it was time to shut it down.

But I still couldn't bring myself to do it. I don't know why, it was crazy to keep going. The payrolls were killing us and the bills for only-the-best fish were piling up. Roland was being very vocal about wanting to close it but I was worried about everything, a big part of which was public perception (HEY! Everyone that hates me! Guess what? I FAILED!!! I'm a miserable, loser, giant fucking failure. HAPPY NOW???). But of course I was deeply concerned, also, about the jobs I'd have to cut. There was room to find jobs for a few people in the company, but not the whole staff, and then we'd have to find the money for severance for everyone we couldn't keep—it wasn't much, but it felt like a lot when we didn't have any extra. The prospect of closing overwhelmed me and I just kept stubbornly dragging my feet.

What doesn't work about Raw Bar is the single thing that Ms. Agg can't exercise absolute dominion over. A lot of the food is awful, especially if you arrive hungry for raw, fresh seafood served with a minimum of intervention – the sort of fare you might hope a place called Raw Bar would serve.*

* *The Globe and Mail*

14: BUILDING BLOCKS

EVEN WHILE I WAS PUTTING A LOT OF THOUGHT into how to make the Café work, I was still paying very close attention to the Hoof. I never wanted the quality there to wane. I thought of it as the heartbeat of the company, and I couldn't let it be accidentally neglected as I got more and more wrapped up in opening new places. The Hoof is a challenging kitchen to run, and not just because it's tiny and outfitted with an electric stove that, like clockwork, needs replacing once a year (and in case you're wondering, no, we can't put in a better, more professional electric stove because the building doesn't have enough power and the upgrade would be a hundred times more expensive than a new stove once a year will ever be, plus, we like it the way it is, shut up). The challenge also lies in the kind of food we are cooking. Not only do you have to be extremely knowledgeable about charcuterie, a thing that cannot be fucked with—those moulds are pesky and particular and you need to know how to read them—but you also need experience in handling the odd bits. There are probably fewer than fifteen available people in the country who can do the job, and back in 2012, maybe ten.

After Grant's exit, his sous-chef ran the kitchen for the next two years before giving his notice. Extra-unfortunately, it was to go work for Grant, after he'd told me numerous times he would never do something like that. Knowing what a hard time he'd had with Grant, I'd believed him. It stunned me, shattered my confidence, and scared the shit out of me. I can do a lot of things to make sure the restaurant operates smoothly, but I can't run the line. Right then, I was the most panicked I'd ever been about being without a cook. I made a few desperate phone calls to out-of-province chef friends I trusted who tried to help with suggestions, but nothing panned out. I spent a week just about throwing up from stress. I couldn't eat, I couldn't sleep, and I genuinely believed I was a bit fucked, that I could lose everything I'd fought so hard to keep, everything I'd spent our savings on. Then I remembered Jesse.

We had met a few months earlier in Vancouver. I was there on a wine trip, one of the few I've gone on. Normally I can find various ways to say no to group wine trips. The free trip and education just aren't worth having to hang out with a group that's all but guaranteed to include at least a few insufferable assholes, and likely a high percentage of them—that's just what the world of wine is like. But this time it had been a lovely journey through the Okanagan with one of my favourite wine agents. After four days of being wined and dined by the best producers in the valley, I was ready to spend some time alone in Vancouver.

I cannot overstate how much I enjoy dining alone. It's incredibly relaxing to sit quietly and eat at my own pace. The societal aversion to it, like it's something that should be embarrassing or shameful, has always confounded me. I find it takes a comfortable confidence, especially when I choose a table over the bar—which I do only if it's late enough that I know I won't be causing anyone any financial harm by taking up a deuce by myself. I don't bring books as company. I have this incredibly silly, romantic notion that I'm on a date with the restaurant, and I give all my attention to that, sometimes to my detriment. It's hard for me to "turn off" in other people's restaurants, and I'll often go through an always-rolling mental checklist of all the ways I'd improve on whatever is happening in the room, whether it's by dimming the lights, having the waiters stop hovering, or telling the chef to quit smoking so much during service so he can season properly. That's why I tend to prefer dining alone in restaurants I already know will get it right, places I've been a hundred times.

But this was my first trip to Vancouver, so all I had to go on were recommendations from trusted friends and colleagues. I'd spent the day wandering around the city, a small enough place that it really only takes a day to get geographically comfortable (sorry, Van, but you're a small town, it's just a fact). I didn't really want to head all the way out to Kitsilano; I'd spent a month there as a teenager, when it was still bursting with hippies, getting nearly naked and nearly high on Wreck Beach every night, and figured I could give it a miss. But the one suggestion I kept hearing over and over again was La Quercia—as in, "don't miss it."

I decided to heed the advice, made a reservation for 9:00 p.m., and headed west. The place was hopping, and it immediately appealed to my appreciation of a proper neighbourhood restaurant. It wasn't *cool* by any stretch of the imagination, but it was warm and welcoming. I sat at the small bar facing the open kitchen. It was impossible to avoid conversation with the waiters (not that I wanted to) as they were constantly popping behind the bar to pour wine or mix drinks. I enjoyed watching the scene, everyone working in harmony, somehow not bumping into each other despite the tiny workspace. The bustle reminded me of the Hoof.

I could see just three cooks and a dishwasher in the kitchen, hustling to serve the full room. Plate after plate hit the pass, with many calls for pickups. I settled into my wine and asked the server to just let the kitchen choose my meal, but not to kill me. Being fed too much foie gras is probably the most first-world problem a person can have, but when it's part of your job to eat in restaurants on the rare nights you aren't working in your own, it can get really uncomfortable to shovel in a ton of rich food. And I'm over it. I don't do it to stars of the restaurant world when they come in to the Hoof, and the only place I tolerate it is Joe Beef in Montreal. (You try saying no to an almost-drunk Dave McMillan.)

As it so often goes in these scenarios, because you can just smell your own kind, the server gave me a knowing look and asked me where I worked. We all speak the same language, and if you're an experienced server you can tell by your first drop if you're dealing with an industry person. They might move a glass to make your job easier, or crumb their own table, all clues they are *one of us*. But they'd never stack their own dishes. Servers hate that, and if you do it, it's a dead giveaway that you aren't actually one of us. Despite its benevolent, ostensibly helpful intent, it's just annoying. WE HAVE A SYSTEM.

I told the server I was from Toronto and worked at The Black Hoof. If people ask me where I work, I never counter with something so grossly condescending as, "Actually, I *own* the Black Hoof," so unnecessary, and whenever I hear peers do it, it just sounds so desperately insecure. I saw him turn elegantly into the kitchen and say something in a low voice to the chef. He was absolutely telling him I was industry. This is 100 percent a thing that happens, one of the perks of this business. When you see a table getting spoiled, like, really spoiled? Don't assume they are a table of influential food critics; they are industry.

A few moments later, I was slurping a plate of west coast oysters. West coast is not my preference—I have a bias against them as being slightly too flabby and metallic-tasting. But these Kusshis were delicious, so sharp and clean-flavoured. As he was clearing the empty shells I'd placed back on the quickly melting ice, the friendly server managed to sneak in an introduction and find out my name.

I saw a bit of commotion in the kitchen. I later found out my single-lady-at-the-bar menu of burrata, delicate pastas, and lamb chops got nixed and quickly redrawn into a nose-to-tail extravaganza. It was a wonderful meal. Beautiful, silky vitello tonnato to start, a magical maltagliati, with a slightly spicy classic tomato-tripe sauce, rabbit loin with a deeply nutty crust, seared heart coaxed into deliciousness, course after course of beautiful plates, but thoughtful progression and never too much. And some hard Italian cheese with local honey to finish, which is always what I want.

I noticed the chef discreetly watching me eat, in that chef-ish way, looking for that expression of happiness that comes from perfect bites, perfectly seasoned. That expression is ten times more valuable than any online review could ever be. And all chefs look for it, no matter how big their egos grow or how industry-hardened they appear. They all want to see their food being enjoyed. They want proof. And the only real proof is a happy, swoony face. Words mean shit; faces don't lie.

As I was having a simple dessert of blood orange sorbet with garnishes I'm sure were a perfect counterpoint but which I absolutely can't remember, the chef came out and said hello and we just hit it off from the start. I found out he was the sous-chef, not the chef, as I had presumed, and I told him how much I had enjoyed my meal, a wonderful thing to not have to lie about. I try to avoid ever having to say I liked a meal I didn't, but occasionally it's unavoidable—the polite white lie, so much easier than the truth, which of course I want to tell. I want everyone in this industry to grow a thicker skin and learn to take constructive criticism, but sometimes it just isn't worth it. You gotta pick your battles.

His name was Jesse Grasso. We met up for drinks the next night as I was finishing a delicious if gilded-lily-style meal at one of Vancouver's more gaudily prominent restaurants. It wasn't the right environment for a raucous industry hang, so Jesse took me to The Diamond, a bar in Gastown. We had laughs and cocktails—so many, I almost missed my 10:30 p.m. flight. But I remembered to file Jesse under "Don't Forget." I knew he could cook, and he was the right age and had the right experience to probably be headed toward a chef job next.

My resentment at having to replace the Hoof chef was rooted in feeling betrayed, but despite how I felt emotionally, I intellectually understood it as part of the industry. People get bored and move on. You've always got to be prepared for that as an owner. But when you're saddled with a mostly provincial, mediocre, understaffed food media, the departure of a chef might be described brightly as a good move for a restaurant, with best wishes expressed for the chef moving on to start out on his or her own, or it might be painted in unhelpful tones of failure, with the chef's departure predicted to be a fatal loss to the restaurant. The reader who is paying attention doesn't know what to believe, or how much anyone reporting actually knows about restaurants. But finding a new chef is really just a part of the business. Some partnerships last decades, maybe in miserable lawyer-speak or possibly in marital bliss, but most do not. And the quicker you accept the constant flux, the better you'll be at restaurants.

So, four months after my Vancouver trip, panicked, I took a shot and called Jesse.

He had just returned from a few weeks in Costa Rica, and when I called and asked him if he knew any great cooks who'd want to run the Hoof, letting just a soupçon of that panic leak through in my voice, we both knew that I actually wanted him for the job. I knew I was planting an irresistible seed, running a restaurant with a reputation as respected as the Hoof's, which had now been going strong for four years. It's a dream offer for a cook ready to step into a chef's position. Only problem was he'd have to move halfway across the country.

I could hear that his interest was piqued. I knew he was intrigued, and I knew I could convince him. My expertise is practically built on a firm foundation of extremely honed powers of persuasion. But he asked for three days to consider it. It seemed like a reasonable length of time, given the gravity of the decision he faced. Yes, on the pro side, it was an incredible opportunity, but the con side was full of emotional stuff like leaving behind friends and a life as a big fish to come to a place where the only person you really knew would be your new boss.

But I didn't care about all that collateral stuff; I just wanted him to say yes. I knew he was going to eventually, and I hated being kept on pins and needles waiting for the inevitable.

I hired him via text. I wouldn't leave him alone, sending him dozens of "joke" texts a day, dying for an answer, and at the end of day two, after "jeeeebus, you're KILLING me . . . just say YES," he finally did.

JESSE PULLED UP IN A CAB sometime after midnight in early October 2012, his whole life in three duffel bags and a suit-case. Luckily, the apartment above the Cocktail Bar was available. Well, I made sure it was by going back on my word to a friend of a friend, which I felt terrible about. I justified it by telling myself I had no choice: I wanted to make it as easy as possible for my new chef, who'd moved across three prov-inces with less than two months' notice and basically had two days to settle in before starting work. What a trouper.

It was a very awkward few weeks. The chef Jesse was replac-ing had already mentally checked out, and made sure his cooks had, too. But we were all trying to be polite to each other, as though it was just business as usual. Jesse was basi-cally learning the systems from someone who didn't care about his success, which is the worst way to transition. I felt awful that he had to deal with that at all, but since it was so short-term we all just chose to grin and bear it.

Changeovers, even when they're for the best, are hard. We made a few changes to the menu each week to give Jesse a chance to settle in, and by January the menu was all his, with the exception of three dishes kept on as homages to the three previous chefs, who had each contributed some really great food. One of them took issue with this to such an extent that he put the exact dish on his new restaurant's menu and called it "the original," which struck me as incredibly tacky. I understood why he thought of it as his, but I'd only wanted to acknowledge the history of the Hoof.

It was a stressful winter, but by March Jesse was fully ensconced as a leader and had a whole new team of great cooks. Things were feeling good. Going to work was a joy. For the first time since opening, I felt a true sense of freedom and comfort during service.

While I realize that most restaurants are trying to create a scene of fantasy, I've actually tried instead to create something transparent. Transparency, as much as is feasible, without, say, listing our costs on the menu (nobody needs to know how hard this business actually is), is integral to the feel of the restaurant. You know how your food is being cooked because it's happening ten feet away; you know how the wine is going to taste because we've done our very best to explain it in the plainest terms possible. Jesse's food philosophy fit in very well with this idea of transparency. Nothing was ever too molecular, especially just for its own sake. On the rare occasions when he did a gel or foam, it was because he believed those particular textures were the right choice. It was so fulfilling to watch his growth as he worked his vision into the Hoof's very established style. He managed to give it his own voice, and the menu, under his three-year tenure, was filled with references to his love of Chinese food (picked up from a long stint at Bao Bei, a favourite Vancouver restaurant of mine), the Vietnamese flavours he learned from an early mentor, and his strong love for Southern food. He breathed new life into a menu that people had always thought of as strictly "odd bits," and it became so much more than that, because of him. And for that, and his respect for me, I'll always be grateful.

Eventually, Jesse was ready to move on, and the transition to a new chef was, this time, much easier.

"TEAM" IS A POPULAR WORD in the restaurant business: "Couldn't have gotten our second Michelin star without our amazing team," "Happy Holidays from the whole team!" As a noun it's appropriate—"a group of players forming one side in a competitive game or sport"—because, as much as the industry might project a sense of community, make no mistake, it's a blood sport, and everyone is fighting for a small piece of pie. And it also works as a verb—"to come together as a team to achieve a common goal": a restaurant needs teamwork as precise as a military operation. There's a reason so many military expressions transfer easily to describe restaurant life: being "in the trenches," service as a "battleground," the "war" between front and back of house. It's easy to poke fun at the overuse of the metaphor, but, fundamentally, a team is what a restaurant staff is; teamwork really does make the dream work!

The best way to keep the team functioning in beautiful synchronicity is for the owner to be in the restaurant actually working, even if it's only once a week. Now that I'm not working full services every single shift, I like to languish at home waiting until the last possible minute to hastily spread on some makeup and change from my day clothes to my night clothes (basically the same clothes but with makeup). It's a mental thing, changing, that helps kick-start the transition from day-brain to dealing-with-customers brain. At 6:25, when my phone buzzes on the bedside table—three dolphin emojis, our call system—it means that I'll need to take over hosting from Jake, the manager, so he can focus on bartending.

I'm fascinated by the different responses customers have to Jake and me as hosts. He's polite, but he's not necessarily grinning throughout his interaction with a customer. This is perceived as Jake being polite. But when I host, I've found that if I'm not extraordinarily warm and smiley I'm perceived as rude, even though we are saying the same things in essentially the same tones.

For example, shortly after Jake started working at the Hoof I was hosting every night. I loved greeting people at the door, having a nice, brief interaction with regular customers, saying hello and goodnight to everyone. And obviously at those times I was focusing on the goal of seating customers as quickly as possible, like, why on earth would I want to make you wait a minute longer than absolutely necessary to spend money in my restaurant? But often people would rubberneck to the back of the restaurant and see one or two empty tables and not realize that they were tables for people who had already left their names on the list and gone off to our Cocktail Bar to wait for a phone call. One time, a gentleman got particularly irate and refused to understand the system as I was explaining it to him, and he even went as far as to suggest that I was lying. When he demanded to speak to a manager, rather than haughtily blurt out, "Actually, I'm the owner," I went and got Jake. I thought this was all terrifically funny, but kept an Oscar-worthy straight face.

Jake came over, using his *most professional manager walk* and proceeded to say exactly what I had been trying to explain to . . . let's call him "Dennis." Dennis immediately calmed down now that a fellow man was there to make everything better, and his mortified date just seemed relieved this wasn't going to turn ugly. Jake never smiled once but was able to get his point across easily. I, in my *most demure voice*, apologized for the misunderstanding, and winked (not, like, a sexy wink) at his date, letting her know that I didn't hold her responsible for the embarrassing scene. In timing so perfect as to seem prearranged, a very happy customer was leaving and said goodbye in a way that made it clear I was the owner. Dennis looked sheepishly at his shoes. Loafers. We gave Dennis and his date great service when we were able to seat them an hour later, and everybody won. Except Dennis's date.

That story is extreme and obvious and, sadly, not rare enough, but anecdotal evidence strongly suggests that it's more important for women to *appear* to be warm, even as they are *actually being* warm. I am aware of this double standard, so I'm always conscious of being very smiley while telling people it's an hour wait for a table, and I have noticed over and over that, in general, customers will respond similarly to a smiling woman and an unsmiling man, but will respond negatively to an unsmiling woman. This is just a subtle version of male strangers helpfully suggesting that you "Smile, beautiful" on the street and hissing "bitch" when you ignore them.

Finding Jake Skakun sometime in late 2012, at a point when he was ready to get back into restaurant management after moving from Vancouver, was fortunate happenstance. When he first started it was obvious we have very different ideas about service style, but he is so good and so knowledgeable that I relished the contrast instead of being repelled by it. While I'll boss you into having the menu item I want you to have, Jake will nudge, and when I prattle on about a wine explaining why I love it, Jake will actually tell you all about the wine. I was wholly impressed by the quiet yet firm way he'd manage tables and staff, and even then it was almost a year before I would pass a good portion of administration stuff to him. We got to know each other slowly, over weekly wine tastings.

Tastings are one of the perks of the business. Having a wine agent come in and drown you in bottles of Burgundy honestly never gets old. The agents I worked with regularly loved our meetings as they knew they only had to blow me away with one bottle and I'd impetuously order eighteen cases, or occasionally, wanting exclusivity so badly, I'd take a whole shipment. I needed someone to curb my enthusiasm and to firmly tell me "no" when I'd try to over-order something just because I "really, really liked it." At one of the first meetings where Jake joined in, I tried to order a relatively "small" amount—ten cases—and Jake interjected, "Maybe we should talk about this and email our order in tomorrow?" I played at being crestfallen but knew I had found someone who would help me make smarter, long-term choices and keep our cellar fresh and rotating nicely (some wines can't just sit down there forever—most whites and rosés have a life expectancy, and so do a lot of the super-fresh reds I like to drink). The wine agents, who were all quite partial to my ridiculous, unbridled excess, didn't seem too keen on this new "chaperone" situation.

With Jake now assisting, the wine list at the Hoof experienced an evolution. I am fully comfortable knowing Jake's wine knowledge is vastly greater than mine, and he is completely without pretense, managing to educate about obscure varietals without making you feel condescended to. Some of today's sommeliers are slick sharks—more like used car salesmen focused on competition with other sommeliers than on subtly educating. Their focus ought to be on providing the customer with a bottle they might actually enjoy drinking. And that is much more important than selling a pricey bottle, because once you've gained a patron's trust by showing them something affordable and delicious, they will be more inclined to go outside their palate and wallet comfort zone next time. Being good at selling wine is a long game. Jake has none of those ugly characteristics and all of the positive ones, and eventually I was able to let him completely take over the wine list at the restaurant.

And while I needed time to trust him as a manager and sommelier, Jake took his own time to allow a friendship to take root. He's protective, a slight introvert, and has a lot of layers. At first, I wasn't sure if he and I would become friends, and that matters to me. I can't do what I do with competent strangers. It's perhaps a personality flaw, or a recipe for disaster, but it's extremely important that there's a sense of family, and that means I want to get along, and well, with everyone who's in a management position at The Black Hoof Inc. It's less a necessity with non-management since, these days, we work less closely together, but genuinely vibing with your staff is always a plus. I can't be around people I don't like, and having and maintaining the perfect staff is my constant struggle. I'm a bit less involved these days in who gets hired, but if I don't jibe with the new guy, the new guy probably has to go. That doesn't mean I've absolutely adored everyone who's ever worked for me; the world doesn't offer you those kinds of friendship odds.

But at this point in my career I don't want anyone in the upper echelons that I wouldn't enjoy a long dinner with. And this was a revelation for me. Learning to trust people, teaching them properly what works for the company and what doesn't—which can be tricky, since a lot of what works might be considered "unconventional"—was a huge turning point for me, and has made me a better, more thoughtful leader.

I often hear restaurant life being compared to family life, and I think that's fair. Restaurants are intense environments; kitchens even more so. And when you factor in the long hours, high pressure, and add in chugging wine after hours, it's easy to see why people would bond quickly. But I realize that in most cases owners stay out of it, either because they don't work service or because they are smart enough to keep a cool detachment while still being friendly. I understand all the reasons to do that; it's a lot easier to be someone's boss if your relationship is strictly professional. I'm just not wired that way. I've been in the industry so long as an owner that there was never much time to make friends outside of it. So that's meant negotiating the murky waters that tumble around the complexities of a friendship that exists within an uneven power dynamic. Obviously, this is a much bigger challenge for the people working for me, people I become friends with, than it is for me. It can't be easy to see me in a social scenario after service on a Saturday night, only to have to defer to my authority at work the next day. But it's definitely gotten easier over the years as I've worked full services less and less and maintained a little more distance.

WHEN JAKE CAME ON BOARD AS THE MANAGER at The Black Hoof, he made my life abundantly easier by taking over payroll, running service, and, above all, taking on wine list duties (to name but a few of his responsibilities). And that shone a bright light on how desperate I was for someone with the requisite skills to manage Cocktail Bar. I had always maintained it like a rickety wooden roller coaster—the drinks were fairly easy to duplicate with proper measuring and everything would *probably* be okay without my constant attention . . . but it could ALL FALL OFF THE RAILS at any given moment!

The building that housed Cocktail Bar was directly across from The Black Hoof. This was the flowering cactus that arose from the scorched earth left behind by the Hoof Café. It was meant to be a low-maintenance response to the extremely high-maintenance café, as I knew I couldn't devote that much time and energy to it, so, at first, the drinks were all fairly straightforward. We had some infusions, tinctures, and syrups that I made, and the recipes were not overly complex. It now continues to serve the dual purpose of a prep kitchen and a place to house diners waiting for a table at the Hoof. Aside from that, it's also one of the city's top cocktail bars, but without the weight of a labour-intensive or expensive brunch menu. I still maintain EVERYTHING WAS TASTY under my leadership, but I know for certain I would not have been able to hold on to the acclaim and distinction of being a leader for cocktails in Toronto without the influence and direction of the brilliant David Greig, who happened to also be Jake's best friend, and therefore came vetted.

David was employed at a nearby restaurant/bar while he pursued acting work. I had heard about him through the grapevine and knew he had great experience in London, England, and was, by all accounts, very good at bartending, so I decided to pop into his place of work and check him out for myself. He dazzled me a bit with his skill and confidence, but not in that overly douchey way that's become *de rigueur* for bartenders who want to make a name for themselves. You know the type: full-sleeve of tattoos (one of them is a gold bar spoon!), a hat collection they haven't touched in a couple of years because they finally got the memo re: fedoras (just don't), and a smarmy way of interacting with women. (Let's face it, it's almost always men who fall into this category. It's not that women can't be douchey bartenders; they can. There are just fewer of them.) I was happy to see David was hat- and tat-free and dealt with me professionally. He made me a couple of truly great drinks and I decided it was essential he come work for me at Cocktail Bar.

One of the most frustrating things about this business is how few people are actually good at it. There's a lot of success, a lot of hype, but very little of it is deserved. You don't actually have to be that knowledgeable or talented to succeed, especially at bartending. It's a job that, at its most basic level (pulling pints in a pub), requires little beyond responding to requests for stuff in a timely manner and making change. Even at its most complex (making cocktails in a busy bar), it still isn't rocket science. Yet it is the hardest front of house position to staff because bartenders, as mentioned, tend to sit high on the douche spectrum. So if you happen across a great one, the instinct to go after them aggressively—poach them, if you'll permit the ugly terminology that turns people into animals—is irresistible.

I would periodically pop into David's place of work and have a cocktail or two, and see if I could gauge how happy he was there. He once made me a drink that I can still call to mind, something with mescal, tequila, lemon, Lillet, and egg whites (a variation of which is now in permanent rotation on the Cocktail Bar list), and occasionally we'd nerd out over drink stuff at the Hoof bar, where he'd sometimes hang out and wait for Jake to be done working. For me, this was more like performance because, frankly, nerding out about cocktails, despite my ability to make great ones, bores the hell out of me.

After I'd seen David work a few times over a few weeks in the spring of 2013, I texted him out of the blue: "It's Jen from the Hoof. Want to get a coffee?" Everyone in the entire industry knows this is code for "Want to quit your job and come work for me?" He replied quickly, "Sure. Sounds good. When?" And I knew I had him. Even if he was only looking for the ego boost of being an in-demand bartender, I am very persuasive when I set my mind to something, and I had no intention of taking no for an answer.

We met at my local coffee shop, Sam James on Harbord Street, and had a chat. We'd hung out socially a couple of times through Jake, only briefly, but we'd managed to argue about Bowie covering the Kinks (I am pro) so I suspected we'd work well together. We hit it off in terms of our feelings about the industry and about bartending specifically, both agreeing that there tends to be more hype than substance, and that it's surprisingly hard to find a place to get great drinks, although David is far more diplomatic about such things than I am. We left that meeting with full transparency: David knew I wanted him to work for me, but he needed some time to decide. His job at the time gave him lots of flexibility, which he took advantage of as an actor; I was offering a management position with more prestige, but one that would require him to devote more time. Essentially, I unwittingly put up a crossroads where David would have to choose to focus on bartending as a career or keep going with acting. I knew it was a difficult choice. Normally I wouldn't even consider hiring actors, for that very reason; they'd book a play and want six weeks of weekends off. It's not that I don't love the idea of accommodating my staff's outside pursuits, especially long-term staff, but we are too small a company to operate that way. And once an employee's dream makes too many demands on their reality, it isn't sustainable.

I texted David constantly over the next three days; I felt like I was desperately wooing a crush. I bombarded him with jokey/high-pressure texts, as is my habit in this sort of a situation: "Hi I dropped off keys for the bar at your house and your first paycheque is en route SEE YOU AT 5 TOMORROW" and "SAY YESSSSS JUST DO IT WHY ARE YOU TORTURING ME???" and many, many more. Finally, after he'd had enough, he replied, "FINE, FINE FINE, I'LL COME WORK FOR YOU JUST STOP BOTHERING ME." It was the beginning of a beautiful friendship.

There's no question: I boldly and by all definitions—aside from simmering him in a pot of water—poached David. But can you poach a happy, cared-for employee? And aren't there times when poaching is okay? I think if you take care of your staff—treat and pay them well—they won't find a good reason to leave, providing the restaurant is busy on a regular basis. With young cooks it's different, as they want to bounce around, work under different chefs, and sponge up skills and knowledge. As to whether it's okay: I didn't feel bad about David because I knew I was offering him an opportunity his previous employer couldn't and likely wouldn't, as they already had a passionate bartender running things and David would likely always be number-two there. And I told myself, if I hadn't aggressively gone after him he would have ended up at the Hoof eventually; I'd just expedited it.

Before David's first official shift (he'd given a generous six weeks' notice to his employer) we spent a day or two a week just hanging out and having fun with drinks, working on them, talking about them, drinking them, with the intention of launching a whole new cocktail menu on David's first night. As we began developing recipes together, I found a renewed enthusiasm and excitement for cocktails. I had never had anyone working at the Hoof who I could really bounce cocktail ideas off, so my interest had waned a bit over the years. The bartenders there had all ranged from competent to great, but I'd wanted to avoid dealing with the kind of *bar stars* who only want to make *their* drinks and have no qualms whispering to customers what they hate about *my* drinks, even if *their* drinks happen to suck. Over the years, I'd found that it was better to train great servers to make drinks and follow recipes well instead of bringing in cowboy bartenders with a set (and possibly wrong) way of doing things. It was MY WAY OR THE HIGHWAY. Until David, that is, who is, in every way, better than me at bartending.

Our palates are similar, and within a few short weeks of working together we had developed an easy shorthand. We think about drinks in the same way, and both despise the cocktail culture that's more like a parody. I mean, even my great-aunt knows that wearing suspenders and a holster for your zester is as old hat as, well, hats. You can create a cozy, welcoming vibe for your "hidden gem" of a cocktail bar without beating well-used tropes to death and making it all *so serious* it isn't fun any more. Cocktail Bar is proof of that. And the same goes for the drinks themselves. Drinking should be fun, above all else, and for a decade or so, milquetoast versions of visionary bars (like the now-closed Milk and Honey) were trying so hard to imitate master bartenders/owners like Sasha Petraske (who died in 2015) that they forgot what made Sasha's bars so great: they were fun! Despite the rules and the pretense and the slavish devotion to the cocktail as art form, I never had a bad time at Milk and Honey, or at Little Branch (another of Sasha's bars).

I'm always astonished when people find Cocktail Bar "pretentious"—it's only pretentious if you're comparing it to a hipster dive bar with cheap beer and shots, the sort of place that is slathered in its own kind of pretense, thick as the dust on the indie rock jukebox. On the pretentious scale for cocktail bars, I'd say mine sits at the low end. But then, I'm a total snob.

Out of those first sessions with David came a new menu for Cocktail Bar; with only a couple of exceptions, it was a complete overhaul. One of my favourites is a light (and beautifully textured) mescal-based drink (a reworking of that drink David made me while I was "courting" him). It's mixed with cardamom-infused tequila, Aperol, grapefruit oleo-saccharum (a high-level drink-nerd ingredient, but it's really just juice and zests plus sugar plus time), with egg whites added for froth and lemon for acidic balance. We called it a Mescalero (and seriously, HOW ARE THERE NOT A TON OF MEZCAL DRINKS CALLED THIS? JOE STRUMMER FOREVER). It went on the "Bold and Citrusy" section of a menu that also included "Tall Drinks," "Liquor Forward," and "Wild Cards" (for the serious imbibers) and has grown to incorporate a "Seasonal" section. We also tack on notes about each drink's place of origin and the bartender who inspired or created the originals. It's important to recognize the innovators who came before, and if you have a play on a daiquiri (one of the greatest, most balanced drinks of all time, when made properly) then make sure to tip your hat to Jennings Cox (FIGURATIVELY—you aren't wearing a hat, obviously). We also added a line or two meant to balance out the seriousness of lessons in bar history with something irreverent and funny related to each drink. It was so much fun making that first menu, and almost four years later it hasn't stopped being fun. Every three months, David comes up with a bunch of interesting cocktails and we go through all of them. The drinks are so good I haven't had to make a suggestion in a while, and it's a little annoying.

The wine lists at our restaurants have always come with irreverent descriptions for all of our by-the-glass wines and our featured bottles, descriptions that strip away snobby wine-speak and replace it with modern wine-slugging-savvy-Internet-girl speak. A Riesling we kept on the list for years due to its quality-to-value ratio was accompanied by this note: *"Obvs, I LOVE riesling. It's the best. This lovely number dances on your palate with the tips of a thousand pointe shoes, hitting all your flavour receptors. Off-dry, balanced acidity with bright citrus and green apple notes. And for god's sake, if you're having the sweetbreads, have them with THIS wine. Riesling With Everything!"*

I adore sitting at the bar near the end of a Sunday service, going through all the new wines with Jake and banging out a few words about why I think each one is the "best *ever*." I never spend too much time on it, because I want it to feel off the cuff, like this: *"Jura chard is pretty much my favourite thing. It's nutty, slightly oxidative with laser sharp acidity and green apple brightness. AND IT'S NOT CALI CHARD."* And as time has gone on, Jake has managed to sneak in a few descriptions here and there . . . Okay, fine. We split the list equally, and with Jake being a published poet and long-time wine blogger, I never have to second-guess his beautiful write-ups. He writes in the style of the Hoof (okay, my style) while still making it his own, like this: *"Listen we aren't exactly what you would call 'Chilean wine fans,' but this wine is prejudice-busting and muy tasty. Sourced from 200 year old (!!!) Pais vines, the grapes are foot-trampled through a sort-of bamboo sieve—in fact, nothing here evokes much in the way of 'modern' or 'technologically advanced winemaking.' Think of an odd, yet easy drinking Pinot Noir with some serious rustic charm. Because this wine also comes in a 1-litre bottle, we've nicknamed it 'Big Chile.'"*

When I like someone and I want to work with them, I am at my work-happiest, and with Jake and David in the fold at Cocktail Bar and The Black Hoof, I finally started to see the possibilities that trusting people could lead to. I don't have to micromanage them, I completely trust them both to make good decisions; it's fucking priceless, but still has a price—it is a business, after all.

Gaining new employees who will respect your business and work hard for you, and most importantly share your vision, is the best feeling. At this point, the staff at all locations is so well-oiled that I feel comfortable leaving for a month to finish this book (*goes for swim, drinks piña colada*). And it's been that way for years now, which I can't quite believe. I started with a single-minded approach, and to reach my goals I have made demands, said no, and taken my place in an industry that didn't want to make room for a shouty, opinionated woman. So it really felt like an impossible mission achieved when I was able to find people who could carry on the ideals and practices I'd set up so vehemently; I was finally able to breathe. Somehow, the niche I managed to carve out for myself, within an industry built on a foundation of fundamental maleness, has been exactly the thing I needed, and has led me through doors I only ever dreamed of opening. And I couldn't do any of it without my AMAZING TEAM.

WINE

I LOVE DRINKING WINE.
Not in an ITCHY, DESPERATE way —
in a *Romantic*
"wine is my tonight boyfriend" way.

Of all the world's offerings of things to
drink and I must have had most of them —
hell, I can drink whatever I want from
more than a couple of well-stocked
back bars, shaken up by the country's
best bartenders -- it's wine, I settled
down with. It's not a thirst quencher,
and I don't drink just any old thing
because it's there, I am (now) extremely
discerning about which wines I hook
up with for the *Night*

As a teen it was whatever was cheapest
and back then that meant hovering around
$5 five dollars, so it was most ghastly
BULL'S BLOOD, Hungary's finest
that found its way into my cup.
Sometimes my cohorts and I would snag
Silver Chalices
my mother had in one of her display
cabinets and drink from those,
imagining ourselves to be in a far grander
setting than a dampish Scarborough basement

Even as I learned the difficult lessons about the trashy extravagance of **mike's hard lemonade** reinforced with vodka or just how many cold beers I could suck from the bottle at The Dance Cave, where I lived part time — I mean sometimes it felt that way, for years we ended up there two or three times per week, playing pool and dancing until 3 AM, there was always wine. No matter how many jager shots, ☆ Rye + Gingers ⓟ and draft beers I glanced at, I always came home to wine.

In my 20's as a bar owner and occasional food critic for the long-defunct **EYE MAGAZINE** I got into wine beyond just drinking it. I wanted to understand it, but in the way most young people do, with a rough and ready palate and a small budget.

I wasn't interested in the pale perfection of a delicate pinot noir or the bracing freshness of a lean Chablis, I wanted to be smacked in the face. I wanted

Flavour Town

POP;ME   ELEV 100

I wanted CALI CAB and Aussie shiraz, and I wanted the evidence to stain my lips a purple so persistent it would have to be scrubbed out with **drug store**, apricot kernel face scrub, a product so abrasive it was practically SURGERY

If someone had bothered to tell me how "new to wine" my choices were I would've thought they were crazy! Although it's worth noting how extremely trendy it was, at that time to drink

BIG BALLER REDS

Why would I want a wine that tastes less like wine? I easily replaced my lack of education with assurances that what I liked was what was best, which in a way, I will always hold up as truth, I just had underdeveloped taste in wine back then.

I had to go through that phase of overt, obvious CULTY WINES (and don't get me started on the extreme irony of a rich dude's "passion project" being "culty") to fully appreciate the soft elegant weird, lean, fucked up natural wines that currently pique my interest.

Part of getting there was taking a bunch of classes and learning the language of wine and how to identify and communicate the flavours I was tasting as well as building a sort of

PALATE LIBRARY

what I lack in the mental agility that allows most somms to remember names of producers and a huge roster of wine info and statistics, I make up for in sense memory — I can pick out the smallest FLAWS in a wine.

I'm familiar with and am a fair blind taster, I never let my lack of knowledge about producers intimidate me in restaurants. I know enough to talk about wine and not sound like a TOTAL IDIOT, and I don't care to know more. I have happily PLATEAUED, and drink wine purely for the kind of pleasure that is wrapped up not in bottles, but in wonderful conversations with close friends snorting belly laughs for HOURS and memories of happy summer evenings sitting in front of my restaurants sneaking rosé, but so flagrantly. I grew up with wine. But it was clever enough not to let me anywhere near its most complex and interesting bottles until I was

good & ready.

15: SHOUTING TO BE HEARD

SOCIAL MEDIA, SO UBIQUITOUS AND OF OUR TIME, feels like it's been around forever, even though as a mainstream thing it's barely fifteen years old. It's almost essential to a restaurant's success to have at least some social media presence. Most places run fairly corporate, mundane accounts that lack personality, or perform personality in a slightly wrong way, using off-colour jokes to appear "edgy." But of course there are clever exceptions to the rule, the accounts that set a restaurant apart and highlight its uniqueness. Those are the feeds I follow and admire, and there are very few of them.

The Black Hoof's persona on social media really came alive in year three, when I felt freed from the shackles of a partnership that wasn't working. Our social media presence spans Twitter and Instagram (and Snapchat, which I finally figured out after quitting my job and focusing on it full time) but eschews Facebook. (I just never liked the idea of being found by people I went to middle school with and then being put on the spot to "friend" them. Either you don't like me, or I don't like you, or blessedly both, but if we haven't found a way to reconnect in adulthood, that's probably for the best.)

I am thoroughly addicted to Twitter and do not filter myself at all on it, one time in 2011 tweeting, "Dear (almost) everyone in here right now . . . please, please stop being such a douche."

This, in my defence, was just an in-the-moment reaction to a few Saturday night tables being grossly their own stereotype and acting like assholes. Generally speaking, saying it's a *real* "Saturday night" is common derisive vernacular in restaurants, as Saturday diners tend to be unaccustomed to regular dining out, have generally driven in from the suburbs (known as the bridge-and-tunnel crowd in honour of NYC's original slur), and can sometimes be ill-behaved nine-to-fivers letting off steam on their one big night out. (Obviously this is NOT ALL SATURDAY DINERS.) On this particular Saturday night it seemed like most of the restaurant was made up of variations of this specific subset of diner, and each table was finding new and different ways to torture the servers. A group of young men were whooping it up like they were celebrating the last bachelor party on earth, but also set an annoying baseline of drunken boorishness, and were arguing loudly about the stated bread charge and becoming more and more enraged because we don't take credit cards, also stated. In the front window was a table of regulars who, while being very loyal customers, are especially difficult to serve and would really make the servers work for a pretty lousy tip (we finally started auto-gratting them). At least a few couples were just being generally unpleasant, and table 3 was on the brink of divorce. It was a hard room, and everyone was doing everything they could to make it better. When Justine (one of our head servers for more than six years) pulled me aside to tell me one of the guys from "the bachelor party" had grabbed her waist as she was leaving the table, I snapped, and sent out the tweet that would forever haunt me. I felt pretty, pretty, pretty good hitting "tweet" like I could let off a bit of my own steam in what felt like an innocuous way. I imagined it was fairly unlikely any of the people in the dining room that night followed me on Twitter, and besides, I had used the modifier "almost" to give myself some hair-splitting wiggle room so I wasn't condemning everyone, just in case.

At first the kudos rolled in and I got that endorphin rush of approval, heroin strong, that I can only assume is what keeps us hooked on social media as aggressively as "The Game" held the attention of the Starship *Enterprise* crew, TNG obviously (who, incidentally, had only young Wesley Crusher—whose focus was on Ashley Judd—to save them, as Data had been disabled). *Ping, ping, ping,* THIS FEELS GREAT I AM KING OF THE WORLD, but then, after a good hour of cheers, came the first jeer. "Whatever," I thought, "who cares what one guy thinks?" And then with that, the floodgates were open and the hate started pouring in, mostly centred around what an inhospitable bitch I was for publicly shaming (unnamed) patrons. This mentality caused me to take umbrage. I am extremely hospitable—as are my restaurants, by extension—but not to the point of taking really shitty behaviour from people. I am really lovely until you draw first blood, and even then, it would have to be a deep cut. Anyway, the whole thing ended up on the radio and in our national newspaper, which I was a bit scared about, to be honest, but I held my ground and still believe strongly in defending my staff against extremely rude customers.

It strikes me as strange that so many people think it's fine for diners to go on websites and say whatever they want about a restaurant or the people working there, but that we as an industry are expected to lie down and take harsh, possibly wrong public criticism because of some nonsense like "the customer is always right." Which is an anachronism so ridiculous it's shocking how many people still hold on to it so dearly. (I can only assume they are the same people fighting for their right to bear arms.) At the end of the day, whatever negative attention that impulsive tweet may have garnered me, it was far outweighed by the platform it gave me to speak out about the rights of servers to be treated with at least a modicum of respect. Dining out is a two-way street. So from that point on I decided that instead of being solely focused on food or used as a promotional tool for the restaurant, Twitter would be more like a catch-all for my grievances, a peek into the real goings-on in my brain, a hodgepodge of ideas, sentences, and imagery, made up of all sorts of unnecessary, un-restaurant content just because I think it's funny or artful or clever, plus the occasional food, drink, or design pic, for good measure. The underlying theme of everything we post is the same: the restaurants I own are for *anybody*, but they aren't for *everybody*.

The autonomy of no one looking over my shoulder and judging me really gave me the freedom to just go for it, and my Twitter feed is either sharp, witty, and insightful, *or* the tool that makes me my own worst "Jenemy," depending on who you ask. It wasn't like I made a choice to be more honest, I just chose to censor myself less than I did when I shared the account with Grant, who would sometimes ask me to delete stuff he found too controversial, never bothering to apply the same standard to his own tweets and rein himself in. I loved the immediacy of Twitter; the engagement still excites me, despite all the problems it has in terms of an inability and seeming unwillingness to protect people (mostly women and minorities) from abusive harassment. But I've been lucky that way, and haven't been overly inundated with the rapey death threats received by so many feminists online. Frankly, I'm a little insulted, like, honestly, HOW MUCH MORE AGGRESSIVELY FEMINIST DO I HAVE TO BE TO GET DAILY INTERNET THREATS?

I've been lucky in real life as well. Aside from the oppression of a former partner with a very different world view than mine, I had never experienced the kind of abusive harassment, sometimes even assault, so many women in restaurants, and especially kitchens, have had to endure and continue to endure. In Toronto, sexual harassment in restaurants got put under a spotlight in June 2015 when the extremely brave Kate Burnham came forward with allegations of ongoing sexual harassment and abuse during her thirteen-month tenure at Weslodge, a Toronto restaurant of dubious distinction. The allegations were stomach-churning. *The Toronto Star* published an exposé, and as I read it over and over again I got more and more angry. Finally I shot off a string of tweets, supporting Kate and making it obvious how appalled I was that this extreme abuse was happening in a local kitchen. It's not that I was necessarily surprised, but what she endured was just so nasty. Kate had her face licked, her breasts grabbed, sometimes she would be humped from behind. She was called "angry dyke," squirted in the face with hollandaise sauce (the vulgarity of which is, I assume, self-explanatory), and smacked so hard on the rear with a metal spatula that she could not sit down for days. And this is just a smattering of examples. I tweeted about it all day and the next, and garnered a ton of support from local and international media and a few out-of-town restaurants. But what was starting to become abundantly clear after forty-eight hours was that the entire Toronto restaurant community (with, eventually, a couple of exceptions) was remaining collectively mum. It was really quite shocking. In some cases, there were even unsurprising Facebook posts reminding everybody in an angry, defensive tone that the three men accused were innocent until proven guilty. The whispers that chefs were scared suggested this might be a watershed moment for the industry, yet still it maintained a steely, determined silence that I continued to rail against. It was crazy—here was a thing that was rocking our industry and had brought to light a lot of ugly truths about the dark side of working in kitchens and NO ONE WANTED TO PUBLICLY SHOW SUPPORT FOR THE VICTIM.

So I started in with tweets like this: "Daily reminder that there has still been almost zero support FROM RESTAURANTS in what's basically a plea to stop harassment IN KITCHENS." And I didn't stop there. As is my way, I jumped straight into the volcano and, on a whim, on the train between Montreal and Toronto (more on that later), I decided to stage a conference. The perfect name and tagline popped into my head immediately—"Kitchen Bitches: Smashing the Patriarchy One Plate at a Time"—but of course, not everyone thought it was perfect. I got pushback from helpful bros and moms in Regina wondering if "bitch is really an appropriate word to use in this circumstance." I contend that it was and is (or I obviously would have called my book something else). It's a simple reclamation of a word that has been historically derisive, take-back-the-night kind of shit.

Over the next few days I somehow managed to plan this conference, first getting big-name pals like Helen Rosner (editor of the blog *Eater* and certified genius), Hugh Acheson (*Top Chef* heartthrob), Jessica Koslow (America's Sqirl Sweetheart and AMAZING chef), and Peter Meehan (*Lucky Peach* head honcho) on board to make it easier to get everyone else on board. I was thrilled at the speed with which they responded, eager to help. I called in every possible favour, locking down a venue pretty cheaply and getting the wonderful and talented pastry chef Christine Fancy and wine person extraordinaire Sheila Flaherty to head up organization of food and wine, respectively. The inimitable John Bil donated oysters and shucked them for us. It all came together so fast, I almost didn't notice that I'd been staring at my phone for a week straight, oblivious to everything else in my life. Roland was patient, if not thrilled with the manic devotion I was displaying. And I was high on DOING VERY IMPORTANT STUFF.

The conference was standing room only (over three hundred tickets sold at $50 each in a couple of weeks) and it certainly felt like an overwhelming success. Wine flowed, and I tried to make it as fun as possible while staying focused on the un-fun topic of abuse and harassment in the restaurant industry. Within the first twenty minutes during the "Two-Minute Hits" portion (in which ten people, both women and men, told their restaurant abuse horror stories, in under two minutes) names were being named. It was incredible to feel the audience swell with support, cheering and clapping when abusers were named, and it was something I hadn't been expecting since I hadn't reviewed everyone's final submissions. We did some panel discussions that, in retrospect, could have been tightened up a bit, but I liked that it all felt loose and wild. It went on too long, and by the time I smashed a plate on stage to mark the end, people were ready to get home, which was a shame because the fabulous musicians Leah Fay (of July Talk) and force of nature Amy Millan (of Stars) had donated performances, so the fifty-odd people that did stay got an incredible show. I was so grateful but felt terrible for not organizing it better AND I HOPE THEY BOTH FORGIVE ME. It closed with fantastic indie DJ Raina Douris, from Toronto radio station Indie88 (now at CBC), and me dancing by myself with a stupid grin on my face. I was on cloud nine, just so happy I'd pulled it off, and I celebrated with my best friends and a pile of nachos at Tex-Mex institution Sneaky Dee's, where I've been going for nachos (my death row food) for more than twenty-five years, although somewhat less frequently these days.

The alienation that comes with blowing any sort of whistle is a real thing, as I learned in the lead-up to and aftermath of Kitchen Bitches. For one thing, I discovered that the MRAs (men's rights activists) have a particular fondness for rapey death threats, and they started coming my way (frankly, it was about time). Roland walks away when I read them aloud, while I follow him, insisting they are hilarious, because what other choice do I have? The moment that shit gets under your skin, you're doomed. But these guys have gotten sharper over the years. A popular MRA tactic is to sneak into your Twitter feed as a "nice guy" who's just a little confused about one of your points. I've gotten good at smelling these supposed "nice guys" out. It usually goes something like this:

> *I tweet:* Wouldn't it be great if women could work in kitchens without having to always remember to crouch rather than bend over?

> *Nice guy on Twitter:* That would be nice, but just wondering: Do you think young men also sometimes have a hard time in kitchens?

Seems reasonable, right? So I tentatively engage:

@niceguy165 Yes, totes, of course it's an industry-wide culture
problem and it needs to change from the top down

@theblackhoof thinks abuses women suffer in kitchen is more
important than the more common male abuse

@theblackhoof says she wants equality but actually she hates men
and is the devil

. . . *blah blah blah* blocked.

Or something like that.

And this kind of thing is constant. It's in my mentions and
stains a thousand comments sections. To avoid it, I'd have to
be complacent in the status quo, to keep my opinions quiet or,
at most, muttered only among friends. And I simply refuse to
do that, even at a huge cost. By expressing dissatisfaction with
my industry, of the culture it supports, of my problems with it
in a general and specific sense, I open myself up to an unending stream of whispered dismissals and all sorts of ugly
descriptives. But aside from anonymous trolls on the Internet,
none of this is ever directed at me openly. If (LOL "If") cooks
and restaurant owners are saying terrible things about me, it's
behind the kitchen's closed doors; I just get to hear about it
through the industry's endless need to fill itself with gossipy
games of broken telephone.

But even sensing rather than actually knowing that your
entire industry wishes you'd just shut up and go away is very

isolating. I feel like I'm hanging out on a limb all alone. And some might say I did that to myself—by what? HAVING OPINIONS AND THE GALL TO SHARE THEM? Obviously I have enough objectivity to fully get that I'm not for everyone, that some people just straight-up dislike my particular brand of shouty snark, but I have enough lived experience to know the difference between dislike and misogyny. And when I see men with huge platforms saying whatever the fuck they want with no real consequences, I can't help but feel alienated. I can't help but think it's completely unfair.

The conference is something I'm very glad I did and something I will never, ever do again. I got a sped-up lesson in the mechanics of politics, including but not limited to all the people who are supposed to be on your side but who come with their own set of agendas (which, of course, they wait to spring on you until it's too late to turn back). But I wasn't fully prepared for how closely what I was doing resembled activism. I have no interest in subjecting myself to public scrutiny, where you put yourself unwittingly under a microscope the moment you call into question the behaviours of others. Even if you aren't specifically calling anyone out, just challenging the status quo is enough to get a target painted on your back (metaphorically, I mean—the actual death threats haven't started . . . yet). This is just a thing I care about. I have maintained a fierce and loyal relationship to feminism my whole life, and as I saw it intersect more and more with my life as a restaurateur, I couldn't just shut up about it. And now I'm in so deep, my two existences have no choice but to exist together. This is a terrible way to run a business, but a great way to sleep well at night.

16: RHUM COMES

THROUGHOUT OUR LIVES TOGETHER, and perhaps sparked by that long-ago first visit to Café Habana, Roland and I had often talked of opening a Haitian restaurant, something really fun with super-tasty food and lots and lots of rum, something that would be an emblem of our lives together. We had been kicking around the idea of having it somewhere on Dundas West for almost the whole time Raw Bar was open. I really wanted a spot with a patio and saw that as 100 percent necessary for the type of restaurant I envisioned (the yet unnamed), Rhum Corner. And, naturally, I was being really particular about it. "But piña coladas NEED to be drunk on patios, which is as close to a beach as we can get!"

Raw Bar was putting a strain on us financially and emotionally, mostly because I was refusing to let go. One night in June 2013 we went out to one of my favourite spots, 416 Snack Bar, and drank a bottle of rosé, and finally, finally, Roland found the words that worked, words that erased my insecurities about closing and forced me to see that if I let my ego continue to rule me I'd be putting us in financial jeopardy, and just how stupid and selfish that was. It called back the time he'd convinced me bankruptcy was my only option. "Honey, we have no choice. If you don't let go, it's going to drown us." And then and there, we decided. We'd close Raw right away and try and have our long-dreamed-about pet project, Rhum Corner—which we named on the spot, a reference to Roland always hanging out in the corner of Cocktail Bar ("Where's Roland?" "Oh I just saw him, he's in the rhum corner"), giving rum to friends—open by October 2013. And in that moment, it became real.

I was surprised to find myself very quickly over the sadness and shame of having to close Raw Bar. Sometimes shit doesn't work out the way you want it to, and no amount of hope and will can change that. That's just how life goes. But I am terrible at coming to terms with platitudes like "That's just how life goes." I am controlling and stubborn, and when faced with circumstances beyond my control, after trying everything possible and still not getting what I want, my next reaction is to panic. And I had been panicking, right up until the moment I switched it off and chose to stop trying to make something work that simply was not working. My mantra was: Just because you fail at something doesn't mean you have to *be* a failure. JUST KIDDING, I don't really do mantras, but it's a line of thinking that helped. I had spent my whole adult life believing in my infallibility, because I had to teach myself that I was just as capable as a man, despite all the subtle and not so subtle cultural signals to the contrary. So when I was faced with an honest-to-goodness failure (for many reasons it felt bigger than the slow death of Cobalt, which had run a respectable eight years) that was mine alone to bear, I almost couldn't swallow it, until, suddenly, having dug into my "so what?" reserves, I could. This failure does not define me or my career, it's just a thing that happened. My reaction to it would have to be bigger than the failure, and it was.

The prospect of the new build also thrilled me. It's my favourite part, and I find the constant stimulation more exciting than stressful. I've often wondered if I have an abnormally high tolerance for stress-induced thrills, because nothing blends my love of making shit, doing shit, and designing shit better than building restaurants. I'd never hired designers or architects (other than to sometimes have drawings submitted to the city, because my ability there starts and stops on a cocktail napkin), which I think shows in the look of all my places. Sometimes designers can really cut the heart out of a place. I understand the need for designers in the restaurant business, and if I were ever planning on opening something with more than 750 square feet I'd strongly consider working with an expert, but I like the rough-and-tumble-ness of doing it myself, and I like the total control.

The first thing was painting. I had this can of turquoise paint left over from a Cocktail Bar fail, so I tried that on the back wall and it set the mood perfectly. A deep aqua, it needed three coats to look even, but it just feels Caribbean.

I wanted a neon sign of the Rhum Corner logo, but I wanted it in amber. Guess what colour neon absolutely doesn't come in? I went back and forth on colours with the neon guy—who constantly deferred to Roland, to the point where I had to tell him in no uncertain terms that Roland didn't care about the neon, and he'd just have to accept that I was in charge—and finally decided on golden yellow. He seemed to clue in only when I signed his cheque. But this wasn't some special, isolated incident. I had gotten very used to contractors being dismissive and assuming that because I'm a woman I don't know anything about construction, and it was a common occurrence with new people. It always enraged me when plumbers would just start talking to Roland, even though I was the one asking questions; subcontractors would call me "honey" before they knew I was in charge, then once they found out, they'd just stop making eye contact. I was constantly having to prove my expertise to workers who assumed they knew better. I knew exactly how I wanted the plumbing to be done, and what was and wasn't possible, so the moment I got a whiff of condescension in any situation that involved tradespeople, I just wouldn't hire them, or I would stop hiring them, because even if they were able to be respectful for a time out of an obligation to a well-paying job, the misogynist's true colours would eventually shine through. Just ask Romeo, the A/C guy I never called again after a nonsense-filled rant that culminated in him telling me to calm down—while *he* was yelling at *me*. I highly, highly doubt he'd ever have spoken that way to Roland in the same circumstance, but he felt perfectly comfortable ranting at me, a long-term client.

In another instance, a contractor told me to "calm down" (men commonly speak this way to women who are merely expressing themselves) when I was rightly dissatisfied with some tile work. I was *very calmly* explaining why it wasn't acceptable, so being told to "calm down" just got to me. I'd heard it countless times, used as a dismissive weapon meant to undermine whatever it was I was claiming. I called him the next day and explained, again *very calmly*, why he shouldn't speak to a client like that. He apologized immediately: he'd told his wife what had happened, and she'd refused to take his side, and only after that was he able to see his error. I really appreciated his genuine apology, even if it had taken prompting from his wife, and nothing like that ever happened on that job again. But that was a rare situation of actually getting through to someone. Money talks, and you're never going to make a sexist asshole not a sexist asshole, but you don't have to work with them.

I focused on painting the walls that needed Caribbean-izing while Roland worked on a large-scale mural of a nude black woman reclining on the beach under a big pink-and-red umbrella, with the Barbancourt rum logo in the background. It was an homage to a very different Barbancourt mural painted on the side of the Port-au-Prince Hotel Aux Cosaques—where Roland's mother was a cook—by the incomparable Geo Remponeau. Roland had never done a mural before, and the bricks of the wall were so uneven that he spent the first week swearing at them, full of anxious regret. Eventually he figured out how to work with the bricks and use the depth disparities and crevices to his advantage. Over the two months it took to complete the mural, he developed an even stronger appreciation for Diego Rivera. All the struggle and frustration was worth it—it's beautiful, and it transports you to another world. I'd watch him work and be blown away by his patience, as in life he is less that way. He takes his time with his art, not only with the physicality of it, he'll spend time falling in love with it. He could lie down in a room with his work and lose six hours. Such a beautiful thing to observe, with only occasional moments of frustration from me, but if I sense myself wanting more of his attention when he's working, I remember how generous he is when I hole up and write for ten hours a day.

I wanted to transform all obvious Raw Bar design features into something else, so we needed the back wall mirror in the dining room to become something different, to serve as another point in the room that could act as a portal that would instantly lift you out of the winter doldrums of Dundas West and hurl you somewhere dense and hot and full of art, somewhere that felt, if just for a second, like Port-au-Prince. We took an image Roland had painted of an African king and queen, printed it on transparent plastic, and glued it—just on the edge—to the big "aged" mirror that had previously anchored the back wall of Raw Bar. The way the transparency ended up being a bit loose on the angled-down mirror created this incredible 3-D effect from the reflection. It's hard to see in the dim light, but it's so cool.

Which brings me to lighting, always the most important part of any good restaurant design. Yes, string lights have been done on patios to beautiful effect, but I wanted them inside—because I wanted the inside to feel as outside-ish as possible, while still having walls. We hung them with just the right slouch—it took three tries—back and forth in diagonal rows. It looks great, very Caribbean-patio, exactly the look we were trying to achieve. The only problem was the neon—it had turned out perfectly in terms of being well formed and evenly lit, but it was way too bright, it just ate up the dim glow, and it was almost blinding. Since you can't dim neon, we had the sign company down the street whip up a brown, translucent plastic box to sit overtop, which was a simple and effective solution.

A big improvement in making it feel more like a rum bar and less like a Raw Bar was removing the front banquette and turning that area in the window into more bar seating. It's amazing how a little adjustment like that can totally change the room.

This was a fun renovation. The bones were all in place, and it was really just a matter of a few aesthetic changes and the small structural one that expanded the bar seating. I had a very clear idea of how I wanted the finished room to look, and I based the colour scheme on the colours of the Haitian flag—red, yellow, green, and blue. There are accents everywhere that reflect that, from the bar stools to the many hanging planters that Roland thought he was going to hate: "No plants!" I just hung them anyway and he had no choice but to concede that they look great.

In addition to the beautiful mural he created, we found ways to insert art in as many places as possible. In the washroom we wanted to hang 1950s-style pin-ups featuring black women, but the images were hard to find—a racist failure to find black models attractive for the mainstream—so Roland did a bunch of drawings. As he was working on them, I got the idea to balance out all the boobs with some dick—it's only fair—so he inked two guys in varying states of undress to complement the four women, and we created a repeating-patterned wallpaper using those templates, à la Warhol. And it's the best thing about the room. A dude once called to complain, on behalf of his girlfriend. They "loved everything, but found the wallpaper vulgar," which perfectly highlights what I find so unbearably repressed and uptight about this culture—that nudity is vulgar. It's insane that gun violence in movies is okay for teens and nudity isn't. And it's the basis of how fucked up we are culturally about sex. If you've been around kids you know it's not their natural instinct to cover up, they have to be told, and when we make our children feel shame about their bodies, we, as parents, are the first to enforce an idea, based firmly in Judeo-Christian values, of what's "proper." Why are we all so ashamed? It certainly hasn't done any good for anyone, especially women, who take the brunt of it with ridiculous double standards about nipples in social media, and who have to watch movies that display female sexuality with a blasé casualness while mostly protecting men from the embarrassment of having to acknowledge that not all cocks are created equal. I mean, if you want to dissolve a group of men, start talking about dick size and watch them change the subject or scatter.

But, on a positive note, many, many people have told us how much they love the washroom wallpaper, and it hasn't been covered in graffiti, which is a very good sign.

The other prominent work of art is a large chalk drawing of Baron Samedi (one of the Loa of Haitian Vodou) done by Virgil Baruchel, who, aside from doing an excellent job bartending at the Hoof, is a hugely talented artist. The plan was to change it every so often, but I am very attached to the Baron. I just know someday I'm going to walk in and Virge'll be wiping it clean, prepping for the next one. Ephemeral art. (The Baron Samedi is often depicted wearing a black stovepipe hat perched atop a white, skull-like face, and showing off all the trimmings of a dressed corpse. He represents fun-loving and enjoyment of overindulgence, but also is said to appear at the bedside of the near dead, to usher them into the underworld.)

Rhum is a vibrant room that reflects the art and culture of Haiti while also being perfectly at home on Dundas West, which is exactly what we wanted. But the room is just the canvas. Sure, it's nice that it's beautiful, but a place called Rhum Corner has to have spectacular drinks. That's where Cocktail Bar manager David Greig comes in. Ever since he came along and made Cocktail Bar into what I'd always wanted it to be, I knew I'd met my match. He is, quite simply, the best I've ever seen at cocktails. His knowledge is encyclopedic, his creativity boundless, and his technique flawless. I still contend that I have a slightly better palate, but he's got me beat in every other conceivable category. So we dedicated a couple of days each week over the course of a month in the summer of 2013 to absolutely nailing the rum-based cocktails that would anchor the opening list for Rhum Corner.

We started with the plain lime daiquiri slushie that would be one of two frozen slush cocktails. It was too easy. We knew we had to make it a bit sweeter than a non-frozen drink or it would be off-balance, as freezing vastly changes our perception of sweet. So we started with a very basic, simply proportioned recipe containing white rum, lime juice, and simple syrup, and got it just right on the first try. (This actually happens more than a lot of bartenders would care to admit. There's this mythology of tossing a drink out and remaking it over and over again until it's perfect, sometimes fifty times, but honestly, if you're throwing out more than a few drinks, maybe you aren't that good at this.) With the confidence of a well-slushed daiquiri under our belts, we tackled the other chamber of the slushie machine, figuring we'd bang out the perfect piña colada in no time, but it was not to be. We tinkered with it for days, finally settling on a combination of a few different rums, fresh pineapple, fresh lime, and coconut cream. It should have been so easy, but getting the balance just right so the flavours worked together instead of fighting for attention took four or five tries. It was frustrating, but we eventually figured it out.

We tried rum-and-Cokes in many different proportions, with many different base rums, finally settling on Barbancourt, and lots of it, with a full glass of dense ice and a generous splash of Mexican Coke (used for its real cane sugar, instead of the corn syrup that ruins otherwise perfectly good American Coke), obviously all carefully measured out. None of that cowboy free-pour shit in any of my spots! It's the most delicious rum-and-Coke I've ever had and it's turned me on to drinking them regularly, often topped with a decadent swirl of whatever's in the daiquiri chamber, which led to a Franken-drink called a Daiq'd Up. It's off menu, and you should absolutely order one.

We also came up with a bunch of larger-format "Pour Deux" drinks, including the dangerously delicious Zombie. I honestly don't know how we jammed 4.5 ounces of booze in there but you almost can't taste it. It is, for real, a two-person sipper. It's flamingo pink, as in not actually pink but more of a deep salmon, and its crushed ice base forcefully peaks out of the top of a curvy hurricane glass, with two pastel straws (different colours, obviously). And just to give it *presence* we fill a squeezed-out lime-half with over-proof rum and set it on fire. So far, surprisingly, no one has burned off their bangs.

With the drinks nailed, we looked to getting the food right, and turned to Hoof chef Jesse Grasso to figure out how to make delicious, slightly tweaked Haitian food with modern methods. A research trip to Haiti was the thing to do, so Roland and Jesse did just that. Jesse came back inspired and full of ideas and put together a great menu, centred around the idea of hearty plates that all come with rice and beans, fried plantains, and pikliz (the spicy cabbage slaw ubiquitous to Haitian food). There was griot (fried pork shoulder), goat, cashew chicken, and a whole fried fish, with a few snacks and smaller things to round it out.

All the elements were there, and in October, Roland and I opened the doors to our dream restaurant, and thrilled at watching the kids connect with something that represented so much of us and our life together.

17: FIRED UP FOR MONTREAL

I AM COMPLETELY OPPOSED to the idea of my hormones ever owning me, and I try very hard to be aware of all aspects of my cycle (including using the Clue app) so that I don't start to believe my own self-generated bad press when one morning I wake up filled with loathing and self-doubt. One or two days before I get my period, every other month, following the release of a withering egg from the real asshole ovary, I am capable of extreme emotional highs coupled with the lowest of lows. And I hate the perception that it's "nothing," it's "just hormones." I get so sad that the weight of it pushes down any logical thinking that it's *just* hormones. If it's just hormones, then why can't I get out of bed except to go buy two flavours of chips? It doesn't feel like "nothing" when its ugliness burrows into my deepest insecurities and makes me think, however briefly, that the worst of who I am (selfish, controlling, impatient, an asshole) is *actually* who I am. And the darkness of those thoughts can bring me to messy tears, the kind that hurt your whole body—sometimes all I can manage to do is watch marginally good TV for hours on end while waffling between shoving in chips and shoving in gummy candies—a cliché lacking only ice cream, but one that comforts my desire to be alone, destroying junk food instead of my relationship. Because in a continuation of "clichéd period tropes," the brunt of my dark-cloudiness is felt by Roland, who, to his credit, has really learned to be sensitive to my mood swings and feelings of worthlessness in the delicate days leading up to a bloody reinforcement of my femininity, which frankly, I could really do without. I used to hate having him smugly point out the obvious connective line between my rage over his trail of toothpicks scattered on the bedroom floor and PMS ("the garbage can is *right there*"), but through many, many discussions, we've gotten better at dealing with the fire in my belly: dormant coals for twenty-six days, ninety-second-pizza hot for two.

This destructive yet predictable cycle (me being short-tempered, Roland being bothered by it, and one or both of us realizing the best solution is kid gloves and television) was in deep rotation when Roland called me from Rhum one warm August night in 2014 to tell me Win and Régine (of Arcade Fire) were hanging out there and I should get my shit together and come say hi.

I am a big fan of Arcade Fire's music and never seem to get bored by it. Criticisms that their sound is "arena-friendly" or "bombastic" never struck me as very thoughtful. Their music perfectly encapsulates my love of well-constructed pop that is far too intricate and unusual to be categorized as "pop." The songs always have twists and turns and fucked-up key changes that mark them as distinctly Arcade Fire. I'd seen them play a couple of times and had been captivated by their live shows— the pageantry, the enthusiasm, and the complete lack of ironic detachment so emblematic of most indie rock bands. It's hard to overstate the crackling energy and magic of an Arcade Fire show: they are consummate performers and have fine-tuned their shows to the taut ping of a slapped conga drum, but still manage to project a crazy, high-energy spectacle that feels uncontrived, like it could all tumble apart, but it doesn't, it just drives forward, rhythmic and hypnotic. They're the kind of band that can sell out Madison Square Garden and still manage to keep their indie cred.

I'd be hard-pressed to pick a band I admire more than Arcade Fire (maybe the Pixies, a love nurtured from the age of fourteen), and I've adored every album they've put out. Even Roland (who has really only learned to *tolerate* and not love indie rock) always liked them—in fact, we fell in love over the swells and restraints of *Funeral*, which had dropped a few months before we met. I had been listening to it obsessively, while Roland had heard it through staff at his bar, Cocktail Molotov. He would make his nest of blankets in the old apartment and we'd just lie there, listening to music and fooling around (which, twelve years later, is still pretty much what we do—love is nice).

I'm not necessarily a big fan of meeting celebrities. I don't think it's of much value to meet your heroes, especially when there's a huge distance between career arcs and one party is way higher up the ladder. It often features the kind of non-starter conversation that leaves a fan feeling "handled" and a celebrity feeling bothered, and it has always struck me as pointless. But after some cajoling Roland talked me into it, so I peeled myself out of the little phone-chips-blanket nest I was cuddled up in— even in the middle of the summer, I can always intertwine with a comforter—and thought about next steps. When I'm feeling shitty like that, the simple act of putting on clothes seems overwhelming, and I've often imagined it's what depression feels like (NO OFFENCE TO CLINICALLY DEPRESSED PEOPLE), except I'm able to sleep it off, for which I'm very grateful. I can go to sleep questioning every choice I've made and wake up feeling invincible. I've often wondered how I'd cope with waking up to a dark-cloud perspective every day and simply can't imagine it—it's hard enough a couple of days a month.

Thanks to Roland's insistence, I managed to throw on some clothes and get my face to a state of public readiness—which actually took multiple attempts. Shrouded in PMS, I can never quite find myself body-comfortable, my corrected vision obscured by waves of feeling sorry for myself and fat. But makeup helps. Honestly, I fucking love makeup for moments like this; like a mask, it hides even feelings.

I made the under-a-minute walk over to Rhum feeling heavy and not at all like talking to anyone. Even as I rounded the corner at the church steps, I thought about turning back, running home, and restarting whatever HBO hole I'd fallen into, the whole time feeling slight resentment toward Roland for pressuring me into leaving the perfection of being alone in a room. My mood was set, and I knew it would be challenging to interact with people. I popped into the Hoof to grab an extra-large pour of lean-and-mean rosé, as the options at Rhum are decidedly more rum-focused.

The vibes of the Hoof and Rhum are so different and distinct, yet so complementary. The Hoof had by this time settled into its role as an institution, attracting a mixed crowd of travelling food enthusiasts (WILL NOT SAY "FOODIE"), regular customers who came in once a month or more, and restaurant people on Sundays and Mondays, or late at night on the weekends. To me it feels very comfortably like a hangout place. If I have to meet a journalist, I'll do it at the bar of the Hoof over some snacks and a few glasses of Pinot. Rhum has more of a party vibe and attracts a much younger crowd. The food is relatively cheap, the space feels summery (which is nice in the dead of a Canadian winter), and it's great for larger groups of six to eight. And after 10:00 p.m., it really ramps up and is just a super-fun room to be in. They are both joint efforts in some ways, as Roland had built Cocktail Molotov and I used the leftover imprint to inform the Hoof's design, but Rhum is distinctly our baby: the perfect culmination of our marriage, our very different cultures, and our long-held dream to open a cool Caribbean restaurant.

Calling Rhum Corner "Caribbean" automatically immunizes it from claims it isn't "authentically" Haitian. It isn't meant to be. This whole idea of "authenticity" in restaurants is sort of ridiculous. Should we have spotty electricity and toilets that only flush sporadically for that genuine Haitian feel? We try to emulate the flavours of Haitian food, but we use some modern techniques, because, frankly, they yield a better result, and we are literally in the business of making food taste as "better" as possible. All the griot I've eaten in Haiti has tasted great while suffering from dry, overcooked pork. Why wouldn't we sous vide it for 24 hours, then quickly fry to order? The result is a tender, juicy nugget of pork shoulder with a taste that's related to the original dish but is different in a way I think is better. And of course I am aware of the criticisms of imperialist leanings this process might evoke: "Why is your modern white-person technique better, asshole?" I understand that thinking. I just like it better, and I believe in the marriage of modern techniques to the bold flavours of Haitian food. People who don't like it can go eat griot in Haiti for a truly "authentic" experience (and they should, it's a fascinating, beautiful, fucked-up place), or they can take our versions at Rhum Corner as the loving homages they are intended to be.

The Hoof is generally a bit more sedate and controlled, despite the loud thrum of indie rock, and I just wanted to stay there that night, sucking on my rosé, but I knew Roland was expecting me.

Out of the corner of my eye, I noticed an available window stool at Rhum with a view; Dundas West was bathed in street lights, it was a moving portrait of Friday night traffic and the unending promenade of tipsy teens and buzzy hipsters. When I slipped in, Rhum was filled with the electricity of a culturally diverse, rum-soaked bunch of kids, so, clutching my rosé as surreptitiously as possible, I avoided eye contact as I gently pushed through the crowd and made my way toward the corner stool oasis, the perfect place to hide. I sat there, curled over my wine glass, amidst the chaos of a thumping Friday night, trying to make myself as invisible as possible, neglecting the schmoozing and smiling I should have been doing. I felt like I was being a pretty lousy owner, which of course made me feel even worse. If every night in the restaurant business is like hosting a party, a sullen me in the corner was a real hosting fail. But I just didn't care and I slurped at my wine, slowly feeling its effects, which were at least a little positive.

Eventually Roland came to change the music—his corner "DJ" stool was directly behind the front-window-adjacent spot I'd snagged—and saw me.

"My love! You came! How are you? I was worried about you. Okay, come say hi to Arcade Fire."

"Nahhhh, I don't want to. I'll do it in a bit," I said, genuinely feeling like I could not, at that moment, make polite small talk with rock stars. But Roland was not having it, so he went to Win and Régine's table and dragged them through the over-capacity throng of people to come and say hi to me. As Win towered over me slumped in my stool, and Régine and I were smushed into the corner, I pointed out the absurdity of *them* coming to say hello to *me*, but they were so warm and charming that it didn't even matter. For a while the four of us chatted, and I made the wise decision to move on to rum. I could feel myself perking up and my mood getting better, especially after a Daiq'd Up, which that night had a slushie Negroni to top the rum-and-Coke.

Eventually Win asked Roland if he could plug in his iPod and DJ, and obviously Roland said yes. I mean, it wasn't like "open mic night," and Roland is not the kind of person to kowtow to celebrity, but he liked Win. They DJed back and forth, Roland focusing on live recordings of kompa, the music of his youth, and Win on rara, a faster, more frenetic carnival music. The room got more and more electric.

And the volume inched up.

Régine, a true artist who I don't think ever stops thinking about music, was dancing in the doorway, and the bar just pulsed with fun, laughter, and rum-addled happiness. All the Friday night regulars were being treated to a pretty rad DJ set, and even if half of them had no idea Arcade Fire was in the house, the room hummed with a frenetic, manic energy.

And it got louder.

Régine took her infinitely watchable twisting and twirling out to the sidewalk where the music could be clearly heard, and Roland and I danced in the tiny space by the entryway.

The volume kept creeping up.

The PA's needle was inching into the red and it was getting really hot. Roland kept telling Win to keep it in check, but it was too late. Abruptly, the amp cut out, mid-chorus. Everyone took a second to notice the music had vanished as we rushed to put a fan and bags of ice on the over-heated amp, but it was going to be a while before it would be cool enough to push music back through seven speakers, turned up to eleven. It turned out not to matter as Arcade Fire's touring musicians, some of the finest percussionists in the world, were in the room. One of them rhythmically clinked a spoon to a glass, while another hit the table like a pair of congas, and like a wave crashing ashore, more people quickly joined in. Win hit a rum bottle with a knife and Régine and Roland chimed in, singing a traditional Creole song at top volume.

It felt like such a natural progression for the night and it was absolute magic. What a beautiful way for music to fulfill its purpose of bringing people together under its spell: if there was no recorded music, real musicians, people who have no choice but to make music, would do just that, make it. As I watched it all unfold from my perch on the stool, the hairs stood up on my arms, and I was so glad that Roland had forced me to pull myself out of my shitty hormone hole and buck up. I would've been so pissed off to have missed it. It was truly one of the coolest moments I've ever seen in a bar, as well as a moment that perfectly and totally illustrated the modern Haitian vibe Roland and I had dreamed about creating all those years ago in New York.

But that kind of moment felt so exclusive (in terms of Toronto spots) to Rhum. We had made our love into our restaurant. It's food, art, and commerce all tangled up in a space that hums with the energy of real inclusiveness, where any given night there are more non-white people than white crammed around the bar. And for a hipster bar in a hipster neighbourhood to have achieved that on a continuing, regular basis is a testament to Roland's presence there. He's a beacon for young black kids who, used to their parents' strict, sometimes religious leanings (NOT TO GENERALIZE), recognize his lack of conservatism and just want to be around him. It's amazing to watch him hold court, share his rum, and just hang out. Black culture has been liberally borrowed (STOLEN) from by white culture for markers of "cool," and marginalized instead of lauded (many, many much smarter books and essays have been written with authority about this cultural and actual genocide, but it's pretty "duh" obvious as far as cultural appropriations go). We want to celebrate black culture in a way that's different from how white, western people usually do that: i.e., an appreciation for rap music. There is so much more to black culture than black American culture (OKAY, I'LL STOP WHITESPLAINING BLACK CULTURE). We have tried to create a space that recognizes just that—a hive of the new normal that we are supposed to have achieved already but haven't. It's a little drop in the bucket, but it's something. For Toronto—and, for that matter, America—to actually turn a corner and be any kind of "post-racial," any kind of integrated, culture needs to change. White people need to stop appropriating black everything. Republicans need to stop being assholes. Democrats need to be more action-y, less sympathy. And everyone just needs to be way less racist. Basic.

Finally, fifteen minutes later, with the system now cooled down, we picked up where we'd left off when the amp faltered. Everyone slowly put down their spoons and resumed drinking and nodding along to the music.

In that moment, and in so many more, Rhum felt like the future instead of the now.

OWNING AND OPERATING A SUCCESSFUL RESTAURANT (or two or three) is a fuck-ton of work. It never, ever stops being that, but if you surround yourself with talented, trustworthy people, you can maybe lose the "fuck." Along with all the stress, the long hours, and the razor-thin profit margins of restaurant ownership, though, there are a few pluses: I almost never have to pay full price at other restaurants (this is not something I ever expect, but it sure is nice); I can get a last-minute reservation almost anywhere; and there's the much-taken-advantage-of perk (less "traditional" and more "me specific") of bringing my own wine to dive bars that I love more for the ambiance than the wine on offer, and paying only corkage. The best and the most surprising perk, though, is the door to other worlds that opens to you as a restaurant owner. I've met so many amazing people through the business, and not necessarily just other restaurant people—people in the arts, countless writers, and, sometimes, a favourite band.

A few days after that night hanging out with Win and Régine at Rhum, I opened my email to see "Régine Chassagne" in my inbox. It was just the loveliest note and it included a wish to continue discussing our rum-sprinkled idea to open a spot like

Rhum Corner in Montreal. I had two simultaneous reactions to this. The first was a humble and excited "Holy shit oh my god what the fuck, I mean, ya, we sorta talked about it, but this could be a for real thing?! DYING!!!" The second was decidedly less humble and excited: "Well, this is a perfectly normal thing to happen to me. I am extraordinary and therefore should OBVIOUSLY be working with extraordinary people. Perfectly normal."

Almost too quickly, Roland and I were on a train, hurtling (but not fast enough, I'd really like fast Euro/Japanese-style trains, please) to the heart of one of my favourite cities, to see Win and Régine, the heartbeats of one of my favourite bands.

Montreal has always held my gaze. Its architectural beauty alone puts Toronto to shame. It's the Sophia Loren of cities, designed, almost specifically, for living well and being admired. Each street is more tree-lined than the last, bike lanes are clearly separated from cars, oversized flower pots sit in the middle of residential streets to slow down cars, well-tended parks pop up everywhere, and there are more great restaurants than you could ever wish for, wine bars that sell *only* natural wines, and you can *buy* wine at the corner store. Montreal is great, truly great. Culturally it's a better city than Toronto, whose WASPy underpinnings—the elite, grossly moneyed, buying only blue-chip art, living on gin martinis and canapés—will eventually bore you to death. Live there long enough and you'll wonder how you got so uptight. It's not your fault, man . . . it's Toronto. So I escape to Montreal as often as I can, for refresher courses in proper urban living, underscored by traffic lights that prioritize pedestrians over cars. I find it in the ham plate of Le Vin Papillon, and at the bottom of the great bottles that pack the lists at Joe Beef. I realize my views are very rose (rosé?) coloured, and that your favourite city will seduce you way harder if you're there as a visitor. I don't have to stress out about the French-English tension or the political corruption (not that there's any of *that* in Toronto), or worry about how the mob runs EVERYTHING. How backwards the hydro and gas companies are is of no concern to me. As a short-term guest in Montreal, my only concern is fun. As I've spent more and more time there, things like the crumbling infrastructure, inefficient systems, and slow-moving government offices (especially slow) have started to colour my rosy perception, but in the beginning, I was in paradise.

Roland and I would go often to visit my stepson, his youngest, Jamal, who's there for school. We'd always stay at Casa Bianca, one of the very few hotels in the Mile End, Montreal's coolest neighbourhood, although, as is always the case, it's getting slightly less so by the year. It's stunningly beautiful, and its six rooms all come with claw-foot tubs and the modernity of great linens in a rustic, yet cleanly decorated space, across from Jeanne-Mance, a beautiful park in a city full of beautiful parks. All I really care about in a hotel is a comfortable, king-sized bed with really nice sheets, and a bathtub— because I'm *sooo* no-fuss—so Casa Bianca is really perfect, and somehow it's also not crazy expensive. (It's funny how quickly you become accustomed to nice things. As a teenager I stayed all over North America in hostels and never thought twice about sleeping on the top bunk in a room full of girls for $22 a night, all my possessions jammed in a little locker, but now I can't imagine sleeping in a lumpy bunk bed, or how I ever fell asleep in a room full of strangers.)

Whenever possible, we'd plan to stay in Montreal from Sunday to Wednesday; I prefer not to be away from Hoofland on a weekend if I don't absolutely have to be. That day, as we passed the "FARINE" factory sign and pulled into the downtown train station, I was already bristling with excitement. The first thing Roland and I did when we got to the hotel was have a nap and fuck—because that's how you start a vacation. That night we ate a truly fantastic dinner at Derek Dammann's Maison Publique—it may be backed by Jamie Oliver, but it's pure Derek, with rustic pastas and piles of fried quails and perfectly made charcuterie. Other highlights from that dinner included a giant baked oyster in kind of a Welsh-rarebit-y sauce that I still dream about—it's so good that I made Roland and Jamal share so I could have one all to myself. There were fried green beans with chilies and anchovies, so simple and delicious, and a super-tasty, moist, smoked fried rabbit.

The next day I woke up excited, knowing we had this big-deal dinner planned with Win and Régine. It wasn't weighing on me or making me nervous; I was just looking forward to hanging out and eating at Hotel Herman (a newish spot, stunningly beautiful, with a lovely horseshoe bar and twinkling lighting, serving great wine and food from a super-tight kitchen team) and seeing if the four of us got along. I mean, as thrilling a proposition as opening a bar with Arcade Fire was, I knew we'd have to like each other or it would be awful—a lesson I had already learned, the hardest way.

That night, the vibe was very "just feeling each other out," sniffing around the new relationship. I was drinking wine at what I'm sure looked like an alarming rate but was just a little sped up compared to my usual intake. As the beautiful whelks and scallops hit the table, Roland said he didn't want to open something "folkloric," which I think got Win's hackles up. When you are all about modernity in your art, it's always offensive when people don't assume that's how you'd be across the board. Ironically, Roland has taken offence over similar assumptions many times. But really, it was a minor thing. The major stuff was an aligned sense of humour between Win and me, and Roland and Régine's profound connection to Haiti, passed on to her from parents who escaped Duvalier's regime to settle in Montreal. It was a fun dinner, but both Roland and I left with the uneasy sense that we might not be completely on the same page. It was important that we all have a similar vision for the project.

As exciting as the prospect of a partnership with indie rock stars I actually admired was, there were obvious reasons to at least try to be cautious—not my strong suit. I'd had a partnership with a virtual stranger go terribly wrong and didn't want a repeat of that. Thinking about it, though, I realized we wouldn't be working all that closely day to day, and fears of not getting along were likely unfounded for that reason alone. But we still spent hours that night after dinner working out what we wanted to get across at our lunch meeting with our prospective partners the following day, at their house.

Win and Régine's home is lovely, a perfect mix of modern and family: in the art on the walls, in family pictures, and in the complete normalcy. It was exactly right. Win offered to bang out an omelette for us but we politely declined, which would later, as the afternoon wore on and hunger tore in, prove to be a stupid decision. We all talked bar potential in a pragmatic way, and I pretty much just laid our fears on the table and emphasized that we needed to continue to make cool shit that's economically viable, because that was our livelihood. I worried I was being too direct with them, but a well-placed, encouraging nod from Régine assured me that I wouldn't offend with straight language. And right then and there we found ourselves on the same page. We would open something that functioned as a restaurant. We'd make sure to hire Haitian staff and work with Haitian suppliers wherever possible, and just do as much as we could to make it a place for the Haitian community to gather. And we would call it Agrikol, after the agricole-style rum (which was made from pressed cane juice rather than molasses) produced in Haiti, and with the Creole spelling.

After coffee, Win wanted to show us their studio. I was like, "Sure, cool . . . that'd be nice," but inside I was actually more like fireworks/rollercoaster/prolonged scream. We got into the car and started driving, eventually pulling up to a nice but ordinary-looking house. I had no idea that what lay inside would send shivers down my spine and make my hair stand on end all at once, because the space was pure magic. The band had just finished a long tour, and equipment was strewn everywhere, dumped on the main floor. But once you climbed a flight of stairs, you entered a high-ceilinged, almost church-like room with beautiful exposed beams, stained-glass windows, gorgeous lighting, and the requisite sound-absorbing Persian rugs. We were completely surrounded by stuff that made music happen: a giant mixing board, sets of conga drums, and many, many synths. To us it was new and different, but to them it was just their normal.

Régine playfully hit the drums a bit as she hummed quietly

to herself, hitting notes octaves higher than my most strained high note. It was awe-inspiring, and I was so grateful to have seen the studio, but she was excited for our next destination, a potential space for our restaurant, "the Leonard Cohen spot," so dubbed because it's just across the park from his famous residence, off Boulevard Saint-Laurent. (RIP, Mr. Cohen—you were the best of the best.) And when we got there, I could see why, neighbourhood- and vibe-wise, Régine was into this location. It was an expansive, long-abandoned garage covered in the best graffiti, with roll-up doors and a musty, mouldy smell snaking out the broken windows. There were old painted-on maple syrup ads and weird signs. It was so fucking cool, but it would also cost millions of dollars. It was an old building, and I highly doubted that we would be able to preserve any of what made it cool, as it looked awfully condemned. And even if we could, it would still be a total gut job. My instincts told me it was far more likely that the building would have to be demolished, which would inevitably crumble all the vibes it had. But I really liked the idea of it.

Finally, we made our way to the spot they had their eye on more seriously, right in their neighbourhood, which was beautiful and not totally gentrified yet. We stopped for coffee and I marvelled at how easy it was for Win and Régine to just exist in Montreal. People gawked occasionally when they recognized them, but no one really bothered them, which was contrary to what I'd seen in Toronto, where people constantly asked for pictures and autographs. I assumed this was partly related to what an ingrained part of the scene they are in Montreal, but it also probably has something to do with the generally laissez-faire attitude of Montreal citizens (if not the government, which couldn't possibly interfere more with business, as I would come to learn).

I've done enough restaurant renos to know a perfect space on sight, and as we pulled up to the white building on Rue Amherst, contrasting against a cerulean sky, light shimmering off its polished tin roof, I knew immediately it was perfection, a dream space, full of charm and potential. The moment we stepped inside I could instantly see the reno in my head. I was mentally cutting out half the ceiling and taking down all the unnecessary walls. I looked at Win, my face frozen in awed shock, and tried not to squeal in front of the current tenants. They probably weren't all that into their landlord selling the building, even though their business didn't, let's just say, completely utilize the amazing space. In its current condition it didn't seem all that amazing from the inside, but the exterior was painted white and cottagey and needed nothing. Never mind the absolutely glorious patio starring a giant, bushy oak shading a space big enough for fifty people, marked with one of Montreal's famous circular metal staircases, which served as a fire escape from the apartment above another storefront, which was included in the rental. All of a sudden, I was seeing a restaurant and a smaller bar, connected by a lush patio, and I was already picturing it teeming with life, hearing the sounds of glasses clinking.

We couldn't stay long, but we (or maybe it was just me) skipped back to the car, and we were all talking at once about how perfect it was. It was the right size, it had an amazing patio . . . all it needed were some aesthetic changes, and that was my very favourite part of the process. (Lies! Turned out it would need to be completely rebuilt from the inside as the roof was caving in, but that was news for after we'd committed to buying the building.) Win and Régine had just allowed me a small peek at the jewel of the Nile, and now I WANTED IT. And, recklessly, I didn't bother to wonder why the building was so cheap—by Toronto standards, it was practically free—or if the structure was sound.

By this time, we were all getting a bit hungry, and they wanted to take us to their favourite Haitian lunch counter. Called Pâtisserie l'Irréductible but subtitled Pan pi Bon (Creole for "better than yours"), it was a bit north of downtown but totally worth the trek, if only for the legumes, which is a dish that translates to "vegetables" but is always packed full of meat, as Haitian food isn't super vegetable-heavy. We do it with goat at Rhum, but in this case it was beef. It was fantastic. We sat around a small table under buzzing fluorescent lights and scraped every last delicious bit from Styrofoam containers.

It was getting late in the afternoon, so Régine and Win dropped us off on Saint-Laurent at quite possibly the best, coolest lighting store I've ever been to, and we spent an hour poking around, admiring the perfectly curated fixtures. Then Roland and I picked our way down the street as the sun slipped behind the low-rise buildings, arm in arm, stopping wherever we wanted, so happy.

18: FUCKING THE PATRIARCHY

OUR DAYS IN MONTREAL were slowly becoming a part of our life and routine. We'd taken a really lovely light-filled apartment near Agrikol, in the Gay Village—that's literally what it's called ON THE MAP—one complete with a balcony overlooking a lush garden, and large enough that Roland could use it as a studio. It was an area just about to peek around the corner of gentrification, an abrupt turn that I imagined Roland and I and our restaurant would be the engines of—though that, of course, was not our goal. The Montreal Village had been slowly pushing out its scruffiness for years, and what I liked about it was how insistently that scruffiness held on—the economic and cultural mash-up made it a vibrant place to live, and I revelled in the sensory perk-up of high alert my body naturally tuned in to when I occasionally walked back to the apartment alone after midnight.

A primary reason for my thus-far-unchecked love for Montreal is the glorious dining scene. It sometimes seems as though the restaurant hubs there have popped up like mushroom clusters in late-spring dampness around centrepieces of bountiful markets, but it's mostly the unstoppable, inimitable force that is the Joe Beef empire that makes it look that way. Since opening in 2005, Joe Beef has taken over what feels like a whole block down the street from Atwater Market. I routinely make a point of heading west from our east end apartment to be on that lovely block, tipping back bottles of wine in any one of their spots almost weekly. I can't emphasize enough how firm is my belief that the Joe Beef restaurants (currently including Liverpool House and Vin Papillon) make up the best restaurant "group" in the country, maybe even the continent—they consistently blow me away with their attention to detail, deep and delicious wine lists, and food that strives toward and achieves perfection. I could sit every night on the back patio of Vin Papillon chugging weirdo perfection wines, staring out at the baseball field that sits across the alleyway, wondering how the sports lighting is somehow bright yet undistressing. Every. Single. Night.

Even though Roland doesn't excitedly exist in the details of restaurants and dining out as much as I do, he has learned to enjoy our Montreal routine, and as we go again and again to the same places he becomes more comfortable, learning what to expect. We will linger over many plates at a two-top along the wall of Hotel Herman, in the heart of the Mile End, or take in the candlelit din of Le Bremner's Old Port patio, or sit as close to each other as possible at a cozy booth in the perfectly curated Nora Gray in Little Burgundy, holding hands and talking about how much we love each other and all the complexities that exist within a long love. And those same complexities can lead us to argue in restaurants: snapping at each other in a way that's polar opposite to the strained awkwardness of the typical WASP outbreaks that have been burned into our collective consciousness by shows like *Mad Men*, heavily based on the reality of a generalized ad man, sixty years ago, in a double-breasted suit, clutching a glass of whisky, chastising his perfectly coiffed, red-lipped wife for daring to ask him where he was the previous night; they fight in the plush corner booth of their favourite restaurant in a discreet and distinctly middle-class-1950s-white-people way, an archetypal couple that, hilariously, still exists, but of course dresses differently. Some couples' public disagreements are pained, thin-lipped attempts at seeing who can yell the most quietly. I've seen it at the Hoof too many times to count. Both people looking down, limited eye contact with staff, usually one of them wearing the embarrassment more obviously. Everyone knows you're arguing; trying to hide it in hushed whispers and lowered heads is just humiliating. On the rare occasions Roland and I do have a public spat, it's usually sudden and explosive, and over just as fast; occasionally, though, it will drag out overnight and into an anguished morning. We are both people of extremes, and as much as I detest the idea of strangers seeing a slice of something so private, I hate the silence of unanswered fire more.

When I can convince Roland to walk back across town from lunch at Larrys in the Mile End, cutting diagonally southeast, we'll linger on a bench in Square Saint-Louis and somehow still find more to talk about. Both of us firmly identify as lovers, preferring that to the much-touted middle-class idea of marrying one's "best friend," yet a friendship has entwined us. While sex will always be our primary way to connect, all the hours we aren't having sex or cuddling in bed are filled with unending, meandering conversations that string together and repeat and somehow never bore.

Almost twelve years of togetherness has only bound us closer, intensified our sex life, and torn away walls protecting even our most closely guarded ideas about ourselves and each other. I have learned things about my stubborn personality and how to manage it more thoughtfully that, ten years ago, I would not have thought it possible to learn. I've learned how to un-defensively get to the other side of dreadful rows. I've learned to tell someone I love the truth in an unvarnished way, and how to be patient with a man who is worth being patient for. But I've mostly learned that love, for all its twists and turns, is really, really nice.

And we fuck all the time.

I HAD FOUND ALL THE THINGS in our Montreal neighbourhood that I needed to make me feel at home: a coffee shop (where we drank tea), a community centre (whose gym door I still haven't darkened), and the organic *fruiterie* around the corner (to provide me with all the things I need for my oatmeal bowl). In a panicked fit over the winter, after realizing that I'd been really lucky to make it to thirty-nine without ever having to worry about what I put in my mouth, I'd given up bread, pizza, pasta, cookies, and cake. Metabolism-wise, I'd long been able to demolish a plate of veggie nachos at 2:00 a.m., peeling up every last bit of cooked-on cheese, without ever exercising. But as lucky as I had been, as I approached forty, I realized quickly that this luck wasn't going to hold, and if I didn't do something, the little belly softness I'd grudgingly accepted was ready to take over and spread lazily around my midsection and seep into my thighs, like pastry cream. This realization and my attention to it is troubling to my vanity, which, of course, exists within the also troubling, suffocating confines of the patriarchal beauty standards I've been inundated with my whole life. And even if I don't desire an intense, focused thin,

I also don't want to be fat. So I exercise a bit (cardio, Pilates, and weights) and I eat a lot of steel-cut oatmeal, cooked with apples and broccoli and topped with a thick blanket of old cheddar and toasted almonds. I tell myself it's health food.

AS SUMMER 2015 EASED INTO FALL, and we settled more and more into a Toronto-Montreal life, our dreams of opening Agrikol in August crashed and burned in a fire fuelled by garbage bureaucracy and Montreal perhaps being allergic to money (while actually taking *all* of it). Want to close down ten city blocks on a major thoroughfare to sell trinkets? No problem. Want to open a revenue-generating restaurant that will bring jobs and promote tourism? Good fucking luck. *Bienvenue à Montréal.*

So, I began making the weekly trips to Montreal on my own. There were always on-site meetings to have and sconces to pick out and windowsills to paint and distress, but Roland didn't necessarily have to be there for those minutiae. Despite getting used to our Montreal life and creating our own routine there, the back-and-forth was hard on him. He is very used to our Toronto routine. Every day is the same but different. We almost always start it at Sam James Coffee Bar, waffling between the curvy window bench that anchors the Queen Street West location and the outside bench of the Harbord Street shop for morning coffee. Roland always has cappuccino and I have restricted myself to mostly green tea, sneaking in the occasional perfectly made cap. I love coffee, but it doesn't love me back; it makes my heart palpitate and it even keeps me up if I drink it past noon. Lunch is usually a sushi or salad-y affair, but it's a constant struggle to find the food I want to eat in the afternoon, and I'm usually too busy to go home and cook; we really could use a Sqirl L.A. here in Toronto. After we eat we will do whatever errands need taking care of, and then Roland will go to the studio to work. Evenings are most often spent between the Hoof and Rhum, with occasional pop-overs to Cocktail Bar. Roland is a man comfortable in routine and doesn't enjoy it being upset. I, on the other hand, know it's good for us to be apart. As much as I love him, I need time away from our life together in a real way. I adore being with Roland in every sense, but I also really need time to be alone, to do whatever I want, to eat oatmeal and chips in bed binge-watching HBO, or go out and dine alone at a bar.

I need time to have no one to answer to or accommodate. And not for nefarious reasons, although there was a time when I couldn't stop thinking about all the things I didn't have freedom for, because *marriage*. It's not that being married and committed to fidelity don't come as natural instincts to me; it's just that I sometimes find the idea of monogamy a conundrum intellectually, if not so much emotionally. It's hard for me to know what I really think since I'm not sure I'd ever want to test our relationship by making it open. I believe in my ability to separate sex and love in the same way I believe I'd be a hero in an apocalyptic war zone, but I haven't been tested on either front. So, as much as I can construct a fantasy based around how I think I'd behave amidst the entanglements (both literal and figurative) of an open marriage, I have no way of really knowing. I would absolutely *Eyes Wide Shut* it if I weren't so repulsed by what that actually means—gross rich people turning sex into something that lacks empathy and encourages a sad broken-ness all gussied up in ball gowns and petrifyingly cold masks. Sexuality is complex, and mine exists on an incredibly satisfied plane, but if the societal pressure didn't balk so judgmentally at the idea of "open relationships," or if I weren't so insanely picky about where my attraction falls (because it's on practically no one, and Roland takes up so much room in it and has ruined me for other men forever), I might be comfortable outside the constraints of monogamy. I am so grateful for a husband who can hear me talk about and explore fantasies of many-cocked sex, S&M-light, and a million other un-vanilla things. But as glorious as the orgasm from hard fucking swirled with vocalized ideas about being prodded and poked by three cocks might be, the idea of setting that up and the awkwardness of actually getting to that point horrifies me. I mean, do you hire two dudes from Craigslist (I'm aware that, yes, this is what some couples do) and then, like, talk to them? Ugh. Sounds awful. And decidedly like a thing I never ACTUALLY want to do. This is why they are called "fantasies."

Years ago, in a moment of restless confusion, based probably on the way-too-regular pitfall of a "seven-year itch," I almost stepped off the cliff once, giving in to the idea of my attraction to another man. We knew each other from years past, around the restaurant scene. He and I found ourselves drunk at the same time in the same place one night, it was late, and I asked, incredibly inappropriately, if he was attracted to me. I just really wanted to know, even knowing fervently that I would never actually want to do anything to compromise my very happy relationship with Roland. And I am grateful to this man for his strong moral compass. Thanks to him I didn't have anything to take back. But the fantasy, the thrilling idea of "otherness," still clawed at me, distracting, terrifying. Roland could feel me drifting away into the idea of this unformed lust for a first taste of someone else. Despite our unending happiness, he could never provide me with a *first* kiss, a *first* fuck. I was desperately missing the short-lived sparks offered by single life, by dates that creep past 3:00 a.m. and offer nothing but possibilities, even knowing the truth is more like awful small talk with idiot strangers. And there was no reason for this longing. Nothing had changed in my marriage. I suppose if I dig deep enough, my id was scratching at my ego's door, convinced there was a way to both have my cock and eat it too™. (See above-mentioned many-cocked fantasy.) But there isn't for me, I am a person of extremes, and of whole, complete love; there was no way I could actually and happily juggle two men, and I didn't even want there to be. Never mind how dreadfully unappealing the idea of Roland being attracted to someone else would be. This just wasn't a door I wanted to open.

It was all in my head, but it was driving me crazy, and it was making me a disconnected, shitty partner, and Roland was getting tired of it. Tired enough to engage me in a difficult and emotional conversation. One afternoon, sometime in summer 2012, after a few pointed questions about whether I had fallen in love with someone else (I hadn't, but the questions were understandable, I was prioritizing my needs over Roland's), I finally admitted I was struggling with an attraction. It came out in a terrified wail and felt like a punch to the gut as the words left me, words I knew I could never retract. But Roland didn't yell or judge me too harshly. He empathized. He fucking *empathized*. He told me he imagined that must be a hard, painful struggle. And, as selfish as it seems, it was. I was torn up by it. But I wanted to keep my marriage far more than I wanted to kiss someone else, and in that moment, within that beautiful conversation, that fact became incredibly, finally clear to me. I kneeled beside him as he sat, shell-shocked and exhausted, on a stool, and through tears, both of our tears, I swelled with love for him, hugged him tightly, and begged him not to give up on me, to trust our love and my commitment to him. And he didn't give up. Not for a second.

After that conversation I felt better, but not completely cured of desire. So I did the only logical thing to kill the fantasy for good: I fucked a woman. Up till then, my interest in vaginas had been strictly limited to my own. Sure, I had kissed a few girls as a teenager, for kicks, but, like, who hasn't? I had known her for years. She had always worked at the coolest, busiest bars and had a traffic-stopping look that I had seen literally stop traffic. I never found much common ground with her, but I was attracted to her sheer physicality. And I loved tinkering with the idea of our separate motivations: I was there to kill a fantasy, and though her motivations were less clear to me, I had no doubt we'd both noticed each other for reasons outside the naive purity of interest. We were each the other's pawn, maybe . . . who knows? She was beautiful enough that it was easy to kiss her and be turned on by her, but far enough away from my interests that I wasn't actually interested in her. And I'm sure I made a pretty lousy first-time lady-lover, so her gaze, whatever the reason for it in the first place, was short-lived.

I had finally snapped out of it. The very next day I told Roland every detail, and it 100 percent brought us closer. There is no question that it's worth examining why he wasn't jealous of a woman, and trust me, we examined it. Looking back, it seems crazy that *actually* sleeping with a woman felt like less of a betrayal than *considering* sleeping with a man. But it did and probably for horrendously sexist reasoning like there was no dick involved, but mostly, it never felt like anything other than just sex. It only happened twice, but it was exactly what we needed at the time, because although Roland didn't participate (and I realize how incredibly, selfishly tone-deaf this sounds), I did it for us. Within an objectively perfect union, this thing, this completely mundane thing that happens to almost everyone in long-term relationships—noticing a person who isn't your partner and maybe wanting to kiss that person—was the biggest test of our marriage. And even though I scratched whatever itch I had in a very unconventional way, it worked. All those complicated feelings lifted away like a fog, just disappeared. I was so glad I had told the truth, all of it; even if it wasn't something concrete, it was crushing me.

I knew this all had to do with hitting some sort of late-thirties beauty/sexuality crisis that I needed to address. Our culture does not make it easy for us to age. Hollywood actresses are deemed "too old" at thirty-four to play the love interests of actors well into their fifties; models are pushed to retire at the ripe old age of twenty-five; and May-December romances (mine included) almost always consist of an older man and younger woman. Men are "allowed" to age with an implied elegance, and the perils of aging (grey hair, wrinkles, the need for reading glasses) are presented as "distinguished" qualities they should be happy to grow into. Women, on the other hand, are expected to do whatever is necessary to remain tight and fresh, like we have a "Best Before" date stamped on our ass. If it's illegible due to sagging, it helps you know you are too old! The Amy Schumer sketch pointing out our "Last Fuckable Day" works for a reason. With all these societal pressures weighing down on us, it's a miracle we, as women, can develop any sense of self that exists outside our relationship to beauty.

I wasn't surprised by my need for some sort of reassurance from someone other than Roland that I was still sexually viable, despite my well-developed ego. I'm surprised that (ostensibly) straight women sleeping with other (ostensibly) straight or less-straight women isn't a more common phenomenon, a new rite of passage, a perk of aging we can use to remind us we are beautiful while the world is telling us we are dried up at forty, along with our over-poached eggs. I realize there's an implication that I think that lesbians and bisexual women are there solely to help straight women out of their marriage slumps, and that's not at all what I mean. Sexuality is becoming more and more fluid. Young people are having all kinds of non-conformist sex—it's like the 1970s out there, but more modern—and it's absolutely glorious and hopeful. Although it's still, I think, a bit easier for straight women than straight men to find the idea of same-sex fucking appealing. So I gave in to my need for an ego boost, but somehow managed to walk out the other side with my marriage stronger than ever.

Everyone has fleeting moments of being attracted to someone outside their relationship, but our culture is such a goddamn prude that most couples repress and bury feelings that should be expressed and explored. And having the freedom to tear apart the feelings I was having with my husband—to unpack all of the shame and ugliness of being scared in front of Roland instead of hidden away, tucked under a bottle of wine for a friend to find—has always made me feel incredibly lucky and grateful. He has never looked away, has never let me fall, and he fucks me with a ferocity of intent that has never been uninteresting or left me wanting.

As I approach my forties I have given much thought to how my sexuality will be affected by the inevitable, unstoppable chugging of time. I live a very youthful life, unencumbered by children (wonderful as I'm sure the experience is, and I literally can't resist a cute baby, I still haven't decided if I want to dive in). I'm a stepmom to a kid I love like he's my own, and I'm surrounded by my staff, who—ranging from twenty-two to thirty-five-ish—make for excellent substitute children. Plus, I can still pull off the shortest shorts and clingy, unforgiving fabrics, and I will keep "dressing young" for as long as it doesn't look like I am "dressing young." I never gave my looks much thought in my twenties and thirties. I see mine as the kind of unusual attractiveness that always kept my wit razor-sharp and is wrapped up in *who I am*. In other words, I never found myself in the Venus flytrap of being so conventionally pretty as to not have to try. This is an afflicting gift that's equal parts curse, and I've seen many women in the restaurant business accept it too wholeheartedly. And obviously there are tons of exceptions; I'm just speaking to occasions where I've seen women not develop skills outside yoga and makeup, believing in the myth of their own beauty, being swallowed up by it. But despite my comfort in my own attractiveness, I was taken by surprise at having any thoughts at all about aging. I always assumed I'd do it with—how is it society suggests is the best way?—with "grace" and "humour."

And while I'm succeeding at the humour part, I'm disturbed by how much I imagine I'll be unwilling to let go of youth and what it stands for: fuckability. So as much as I want to fuck the patriarchy, it seems I still want to know it's at least a little interested in fucking me back.

A LOVE LETTER

The first time I stumbled into Sneaky Dee's in the mid-90s, it was after a night of sucking every last drop of Budweiser from every last bottle at the Dance Cave and dancing hard enough to somehow only be half drunk. Everything about the place spoke to teen me—the booths, not just markered with excessive graffiti, but etched with it, a pocket knife's punk rock response to even the permanence of a pocket Sharpie. The washrooms were a disaster and to be used only if absolutely necessary and the décor can best be described as kids-paint-every-available-surface-with-the-same-kind-of-imagery-tattooed-on-17-year-olds-in-the-nineties. It's the type of place that you either grew up in or didn't, that you either get or don't, and it's an excellent litmus test for who the cool 40 year olds of Toronto are, not that you can be 40 and cool.

The smell hits you right away, and it is still the exact same smell, a potent blend of fajita sizzle, the intoxicating scent of deep, golden-fried chicken skin so specific to wings, and the distinctive tang of their house nacho sauce. As teens, naturally we had spent almost all our money on beer but managed to pool our funds and had just enough for a platter of plain nachos (the austere purity of tomato, cheese and chips), which cost something like $9, that the three of us could share. What simple perfection! A single layer of chips on a huge platter with just the right ratio of cheese to sauce and no naked chips, cooked to a paragon of melty and crispy. (In a piled situation, I prefer some chips to be free of toppings and bring the crunch necessary for a complete nacho experience, but piled was out of our budget.) I was the one using my thumbnail to scrape up errant bits of Monterey Jack

the smell hits you right away and its still the exact same smell

the dance cave

A HOT MESS OF BEEF

HOT GOOEY PILE

A POCKET KNIFE'S PUNK ROCK RESPONSE

eventually, after getting a job... I could go

LESS

JA + VN

SNEAKY DEE'S

that had splooshed onto the metal platter and cooked to a texture that was soft and yielding in the middle and edged with lacy crispness, which gave me a snack idea that has settled into permanence, to just skip the vehicle for cheese and fry it up in a non-stick pan if I ever found myself in the kind of mood that demanded cheese, and cheese alone.

Eventually, after getting a job, I didn't have to scrimp and save when dining at the Sneaky Disease (as we all called it). I could go lux. I tried the King's Crown, a hot mess of beef, beans and all the usual toppings, but always found it too soggy, and kept returning to plain nachos, until one day, with a vegetarian, we ordered the veggie nachos to share. And I fell in love. I have indulged in veggie nachos at Sneaky Dee's many, many times. I have had them at their worst (over- or under-baked, too little cheese or too much sauce) and I have had them at their best, ratios and baking times in perfect balance. They come topped with crisp, cold iceberg lettuce and a generous gloop of sour cream. The biggest complaint I hear is about the lettuce. People are very divided on whether it belongs on a hot, gooey pile of nachos. It does. It absolutely does. The perfect bite is a chip full with toppings and cheese, underpinned with a partly naked chip for support and texture, dipped into sour cream, topped with chopped jalapeños (ALWAYS REMEMBER TO GET THEM ON THE SIDE, TRUST ME) and a tangle of lettuce for a delightful temperature contrast.

I still get cravings every so often and will go in (mostly by myself, but sometimes with pals) and put back most of an order, and it always makes me feel very, very good.

I SHOUT OUT CRAVINGS

FAJITA SIZZLE

ERRANT BITS OF MONTERREY JACK THAT HAD SPLOOSHED ONTO THE METAL PLATTER

NAKED CHIPS

WAGON OF MELTY & CRISPY

1/2 DRUNK

19: BASICALLY . . .

THERE IS AN INSANE DOUBLE STANDARD applied to men and women in life and in work. It is the root cause of every business frustration, outside of pesky financial ones, I've ever had. It envelops relationships I've had with employees, contractors, and customers. At least once a day I'm given the opportunity to imagine how any one, in any of those groups and more, would be communicating differently with me if I were a man. And why should I ever have to think about that?

Yes, in conversation, women who are perhaps more successful than their male peers are constantly trotted out as examples that sexism is over and we are living in a post-gender world. In the realm of indie rock, someone might point out how obviously Liz Phair's record sales trump Ryan Adams'—maybe . . . someone fact-check that—and one could certainly find many examples of successful women in pop music, while of course ignoring the male executives that still run the music industry, and the fact that the cultural impact of PJ Harvey isn't at all proportionate to her monumental talent. In literature, Joan Didion may outsell many of her male peers (but we'll have to ignore how few Didions even get the chance to compete in the heavily male-dominated world of words on a page that aren't about female friendship, vampires, or witchcraft). In art, if you're the next Cindy Sherman you may outsell some dudes, but you'll never really be as critically acclaimed, and if you are it will be under the belittling banner of "female artist." And in food we still have the embarrassing title "Best Female Chef" announced each year by the even more embarrassing "World's 50 Best Restaurants," a list that HILARIOUSLY was meant to be an antithesis to the stuffy *Michelin Guide*. The only place there should be a gender separation is in sports, where the test is physical strength. In the modern-day world of food, it's often the same couple of chefs who are trotted out over and over to suggest that everything is totally okay and equal now. And if, against all odds, as a woman you some-how do become "legitimized," "critically acclaimed," the questions to ask are "Who's doing the legitimizing? Whose approval are we seeking?" It's mostly white men, sadly. They hold so much of the power in media. It's changing, but too slowly.

The media have a responsibility to take the gendering out of their coverage, which they mostly fail at (*cue helpful peo-ple telling me about all the exposure I get, to totally negate my argument*). It is their responsibility to think about who they are most often choosing to support with lilting, prolific praise, and how objective their choices really are. But, of course, it's complicated by there being so few prominent women in food in the first place.

And obviously it's not just media, it's our entire culture, built to accommodate and prioritize the needs of men. But under the umbrella of the patriarchy and within its themes is day-to-day life. And that's where it becomes death by a thousand cuts. It's the little things, like how new contractors constantly defer to my husband, even when I've booked the appointment with them and detailed the work I want done, until Roland exasperatedly throws up his hands and says, "I don't know where the sink is going, talk to my wife, she's the boss." And then the contractor says something awesome and conspiratorial to Roland, like, "I hear ya, chief. Happy wife, happy life." Or when customers are talking to me and ask if they can "speak to your manager" (I MANAGE ME, ASSHOLE). These erasures of talent happen ALL THE TIME when you're a woman. And they happen even more in a job that requires the ability to make tough calls over and over again, at lightning speed. Men don't have to worry about being disliked for incisive business decisions; they are lauded for their hand-on-the-tiller leadership style. Women, on the other hand, are endlessly criticized for actions that are objectively the same. I've lost track of how many times I've heard through the grapevine that someone we tried out at one of the restaurants hates me for the egregious sin of not hiring him or her. That's not even a real beef—hate me for my politics, hate me for personal animus, but don't hate me for running my business the same way men have been running theirs forever. Friends in the industry have gone to bat for this idea. Peter Sanagan, of the popular local butcher shop Sanagan's, offered this quote to an *Elle* magazine profile: "I can name five Toronto chefs and restaurateurs who are a little difficult, and all people say is, 'He can be a bit of a dick, but we respect him.'" So plain and simple: men who are perceived as difficult still get "respect," women don't.

Look at the way I'm portrayed in the media. It's consistently "the outspoken restaurateur Jen Agg." Doesn't sound so bad, right? Until you've seen it over and over again, and it occurs to you it's not meant as a compliment, and it's never used to describe equally outspoken men who own restaurants. They, by contrast, get awesome adjectives like "rebel," "mastermind," and "the innovative ———." What the writers actually mean when using "outspoken," even if they aren't always fully aware of it, is "rabble-rouser," "shit-disturber," "troublemaker."

Expressing one's opinions ought to be an obvious freedom. But in our culture women learn early to shut up: on the playground, in classrooms, on dates, in boardrooms, and of course on the athletic field, where we are meant to be cheerleaders for the men. This holds true even when the men are doing egregious things like regurgitating our ideas/ jokes/plans of action back to us, presenting them as original and having the gall to explain what they mean. If you're a woman with a job, this has happened to you at some point over the course of your career. And to have women in leadership roles stand by and do nothing, benefitting from the privilege they've achieved, supporting a system they too had to fight against, but not wanting to disrupt their place in it by rocking the boat—that's an integral part of why nothing ever changes. Which, sadly, I can totally relate to. When I felt like I was "winning" at restaurants, even if it was alongside someone whose leadership style I didn't agree with, I had a hard time speaking out and putting my foot down. I felt like I had to adjust my demeanour to exist within the structures of an oppressive relationship, a relationship that conformed to the status quo. I'm also not surprised that women who've reached the pinnacles of their careers in restaurants claim to have had little to no trouble with sexism. Maybe that's willful blindness—they're fully aware of how shitty it is but unwilling to point it out for fear of being kicked off the mountain. Or maybe they've just been able to navigate through the system by playing the game, and eventually they come to believe that there is no "system" because the success they've achieved is obviously merited. I don't know, and I never will. But I do know that both those attitudes foster a perpetuation of the status quo, and that's no good.

We are the pressers of our own brakes, the authors of our own fates, or any other metaphor that will help fully drive home the message that we could really do a number on the patriarchal structures that engulf our culture if we'd stop being the primary supporters of those walls. If women would stop scurrying up the ladder to dutifully patch the cracks in the glass ceiling we could smash that thing for good. But as long as women un-ironically state that they've "never really noticed a boys' club," or helpfully suggest that kitchens are worse for young men than for young women, or run magazines that continue to glorify men's accomplishments while diminishing women's, we just won't get anywhere. The status quo is a worn old hammock, and even when its taut strings are uncomfortably restrictive, we lie there, comforted by its familiar shape, lulled by its familiar sway. Even when it becomes obvious we must get up, we lie there, while our circulation gets cut off and we become motion sick from what once seemed like a pleasant way to take a nap.

It's a yarn I'm so tired of winding round and round, and my metaphorical swift is bulging with enough to make onesies for a thousand lumberjacks, but despite everyone inherently *knowing* the oft-repeated woes of the modern bourgeois feminist, it bears repeating. The most obvious example I can reinforce all this with is Hollywood, which is basically the restaurant business with less food, more makeup, and much bigger profit margins. There, men are allowed to fail over and over again with ill-performing, ham-fisted filmmaking, while women who are perhaps better directors (or could be, given the chance) must hit it out of the park on their very first try or they'll never get another shot. And when a famous actress complains about wage disparity, which she has only become aware of because of a hack, maybe the world isn't so sympathetic, because what could a woman making $20 million a film have to complain about? And that's really the crux of it, this "how dare you be ungrateful?" attitude.

Yes, it's slowly changing, but most women still find ways to couch their language when expressing themselves, or voicing their dissatisfaction with systemic problems; they caress their opinions with smooth add-ons like "I feel if we consider the options" and "What about looking at it this other way?" while men are given the freedom to just bluntly state their thoughts. The more I say, the more my image gets wrapped up in something that people see as politics—as if my wanting true equality for women is somehow political and divisive. Crazy. Simply by saying what I think, I open myself up to closer examinations of my decisions, to criticisms of my language choices, and to comments sections that would make your eyes bleed. This isn't because I'm actually the worst and am constantly screaming faux controversial things from the rooftop of city hall; it's because of the patriarchy. And when you're a woman, living in the stifling confines of a historic system in which you've only relatively recently been allowed to vote and own land (calm down, I said "relatively," as in relative to when time began for humans), having opinions always translates to "outspoken." But at least I can own my home. And *that's* kind of the problem: "at least." "At least" stops us in our tracks, throws a spoke in the wheel, and grinds us to a halt. And it's often women saying or thinking "at least": "At least I wasn't forced into marriage missing a clitoris." "At least I'm not someone's property." These comparisons don't do any good. I mean, it's obvious that feminism is a worldwide issue, and the degree to which women are emancipated depends greatly on where they were born and live and the colour of their skin. It's like someone slapping you in the face and then saying, "At least I'm not hitting you with a hammer." Yes, great, that's true, but I'd REALLY like you to stop slapping me.

So what are my options? If hosting another conference proves to be too laden with metaphorical landmines, and a strong lack of desire to repeat it, how do I take steps in redefining what it is to be a woman in the world, and in the world of restaurants? I honestly don't know. I think putting words on a page helps tremendously, though. As much as I love the restaurant business, and as much as it's been good to me, if I end up with "restaurateur" on my tombstone, I will have woefully fucked up my forties.

The Glass Ceiling
fig. 1

The Glass Ceiling
fig.2

20: GREY GARDENS, BLUE SKIES

BACK IN 2009, I went on a trip to New York with a friend. We had a fun, restaurant-filled Tuesday and Wednesday planned (at that time I couldn't be away from the Hoof, ever, so any trips were short ones, on days we were closed).

After we made our way to Manhattan from the Newark airport, we dropped our bags and freshened up for a bit of exploring. We walked through SoHo over to First Avenue at 10th, stopping in used clothing stores that caught our eye, but were careful to not be late for our 9:00 p.m. reservation at Momofuko Ko. It had been such a pain in the ass to procure, we didn't want to fuck with it. Ko's reservation system, back then, anyway, was a democratic yet annoying online game of fastest-fingers. (This was years before it moved around the corner to fancier digs, with glassware by Zalto and chairs WITH BACKS ON THEM, all in a setting dripping with David Choe's mural and graffiti art.) A few weeks prior I had set an alarm for 9:59 a.m. to remind me to start fighting for two seats when online reservations opened at 10:00, and somehow I'd lucked out and landed them on the night and time I wanted.

Walking into the original Ko was, for me, like walking into the platonic ideal of a restaurant space. I loved its minimalism—even if it was necessitated by size constraints rather than a thoughtfully considered design choice—and instantly started connecting the dots between the anti-ness of it all (anti white tablecloth, anti quiet jazz, anti bright lights) and my aesthetic at the Hoof. If New York streets were my pilgrimage, Ko was my Mecca. I felt immediately at home, and the feeling was reinforced by dim lighting and by Talking Heads pumping on the stereo.

Behind the spare, wooden bar, a skinny cook stuck out among the three who were all busy with something. He was wiping down a cutting board and subtly singing along to "This Must Be the Place." In his heavy-framed glasses and buttoned-all-the-way-up white shirt, he looked less like a cook, more like an intellectual, complete with an aloof vibe that made me want to charm him with my sparkling charisma. It's really quite a feat to maintain any kind of aloofness while singing along with David Byrne, but somehow he did. My friend and I were seated in front of his station and I settled in, knowing the hard, backless stools would seem more comfortable as wine glasses were drained. I looked around at everything, taking it all in while trying to hide my excitement and trying to play it cool.

The food dazzled, especially the shaved foie dish, which seemed designed to be unforgettable. A "Ko Klassic," it even turned up on the menu at Ko 2.0. It was a pretty straightforward dish that relied, so oddly, on canned lychees, with hits of pine nut brittle, Riesling gelée, and a blanket of frozen, shaved foie gras—an incredibly smart way to fool diners into believing they were given a much larger portion of pricey foie gras than they actually had. It was a little sweet, undeniably delicious, and without a doubt sent many a cook to wrap up torchons of foie and put them straight in the freezer, including at the Hoof, where, after visiting Ko a few months later, the cooks used it to great effect as a garnish for a bison tartare dish. Another plate that sticks in my memory, whether because of its unwavering tastiness or its fame as "the dish," was the slow-cooked smoked egg and caviar, also a total crowd-pleaser. I was able to sneakily grab a grainy pic with my trusty BlackBerry despite chef-owner David Chang's "no pics" policy, which he has since (smartly) abandoned (like I have my BlackBerry). It wasn't for anything but my memory. I knew if I didn't take pics I would forget the details of what I ate, and I wanted to be able to tell the cooks at the Hoof about every sauce, each garnish, because I knew they'd be interested. Somehow I equate not remembering with not caring, which it isn't, I just happen to have the memory of a tipsy goldfish (unless you've wronged me, then my memory works fine).

But it wasn't just the food, or the abundance of pretty good wine (much better now at Ko 2.0), that made this dinner stay with me. It was the cooks, who dropped the plates and explained them to you, who made the experience so special, so memorable. Chang had hit on something big with this, to go along with all his other big ideas (he may not have invented pork buns, but he undeniably made them ubiquitous), and the effects continue to ripple outward and settle into restaurants as far away as Wichita, Kansas and as close as London, England.

Mitch Bates was our guy, the cook who most often dropped our plates, although I didn't know that was his name or that he was in charge, or about to be. He kept our interactions to a minimum, at first. He'd be as brief as possible. "This is a smoked egg and caviar." "Okay, cool," I said, while sinking my spoon into some serious egg porn. The deep-gold yolk leaked out and swirled into the onion soubise (a sauce of slow-cooked onions thickened with béchamel) creating a perfect, rich foil for the salty brightness of a generous portion of (affordable, yet truly delicious) American hackleback caviar, with new potato chips for crunch. Fact-checking this with Mitch, I found it hilarious that the dishes that stood out for me were the super popular ones everyone remembered—well, two of them were. The other was one of the most perfect pasta dishes I've ever eaten: three corn ravioli so abundant in pure corn flavour it was like I'd never had a corn purée before, the buttery richness offset by chorizo, pickled tomatoes, and cotija cheese. It was thoughtful, somehow both obvious and subtle at the same time, and in stark contrast to the in-your-face, look-at-me-I'm-a-rock-star boldness of the pre-Instagram yet highly Instagram-friendly foie and caviar dishes. I ate it way too quickly and gushed at the skinny cook, hoping overt praise would curry favour, perhaps crack open a smile.

As our meal wound down, the cook started being a bit more chatty, made a few jokes, dug out cold beers from an ice well to pass around to the guys in the kitchen, and they were all guys. He hopped up onto the counter and we had a great chat—which he, when we eventually met again in Toronto, claimed to not remember but which had of course stuck with me as highly significant because NEW YORK CHEF—about restaurants, the business, and our favourite indie rock bands: LCD Soundsystem, Arcade Fire, and all the Brooklyn kids that had strapped on guitars in the early 2000s. I paid the bill after accepting a couple of after-dinner drinks and getting a little giggly. It was the most expensive meal I'd ever treated myself to (sadly, it has long since lost that title), and yet I felt completely comfortable with the cost, the experience having been so enjoyable. We stumbled out into the almost-midnight and somehow managed to squeeze in more drinks at bars scattered around the Lower East Side, me flush with excitement about such a fantastic meal, my friend secretly hoping the next day would be full of big salads and grain bowls. (It would not be.)

Years later, sometime in 2013, I was delighted to see none other than Mitch Bates, the skinny cook from Ko, wander into the Hoof with a group of four. He had moved to town to head up Momofuku Shōtō, which was to be Toronto's Ko, but made with someone else's money and therefore many shades shinier than the Ko I remembered. The venues hadn't even opened yet, but the city was on fire with Momofuku fever. Many restaurants got left with huge holes in their front and back of house as what felt like the entire industry collectively dropped their order pads or kitchen chits and raced to be considered for the chance to be on the opening team at an arm of the worshipped empire of David Chang. I felt very fortunate to not have to suffer such a blood loss and reminded myself to make sure to let all my staff know how grateful I was for that with an especially lavish staff party. The Momofuku complex now looms over University Avenue and houses an ambitious four concepts—a Noodle Bar, Daishō (for large-format meals meant for sharing), Nikai (a bar), and Shōtō.

Mitch's group (of Momo staff) settled into charcuterie and terrine while I quietly oversaw the service at their table, watching to make sure we showed off our well-honed skills but didn't flaunt them. It's always fun to serve your peers, especially if you really respect their work. I eventually made mention of my meal at Ko and our nice chat, to which I got almost no reaction. I read it at the time as cool snobbery, and I was totally hurt to be considered so forgettable, but eventually I learned this was attributable more to Mitch's innate shyness than any kind of "too big for his britches" ego shit. And he ultimately admitted to remembering serving me at Ko, because how could he forget someone "so loud and obnoxious." By the time he told me this, we were already fairly comfortable in a friendship and the beginnings of a partnership. I was relieved. Be disliked, be controversial, but never be forgettable.

Mitch is a thinker's cook. As I learned over the course of many amazing dinners at Shōtō, his tasting menus are imbued with a thoughtfulness I've rarely seen elsewhere. Each course is army-precise, the flavours dialled in and the salt just right, enough to highlight without overwhelming; salt should always be used very judiciously, despite the current trend to "salt everything, even dessert"—while I agree that salt brings out the best in things, it must be done with care. His sense of place-ment is so honed that the meal unfolds naturally, each course leading perfectly into the next, never too much of anything and always bright and lifted flavours, using richness as a note rather than the whole chord—really masterful cooking. I'd sit at the polished black granite counter and watch him pull six pieces of beef cheek off the grill when only four were needed and get rid of anything that was next to perfect. It was perfect food, and there was only room for perfect protein.

He was the best I'd ever seen in my life. And I couldn't shake how much I wanted to work with him. Everything I did was to that end. I mean, I loved going to Shōtō, and as we got to know each other over many Daiq'd Ups at Rhum or post-service gin-and-tonics at The Communist's Daughter, I was just biding my time, waiting to see if we could actually talk about it, waiting for him to hint at wanting to open his own place. I had no idea what his plans were, but I could see how ambitious his food was and assumed that ambition was not limited to food alone. It turned out my instincts were correct, but it was really Roland and Caitlyn, Mitch's wonderful girlfriend, who brought about a serious discussion to partner up. Mitch and Caitlyn came by Rhum to hang out one Saturday and, pretty much out of the blue, Roland said, "When you two going to make a restaurant together?" (the chef/restaurateur equivalent of "You gonna fuck, or what?"). Caitlyn basically echoed the question, and before you could say "dim sum" we were having a clandestine meeting at a Chinese restaurant in a mall north of the city, where we were positive absolutely no one from the business would see us. Courting cooks in a paranoid industry is very much like having an affair. But once we started talking about it, it was very obvious this was to be a short courtship.

Mitch already had a space in mind. He'd seen a "For Rent" sign in a building on Augusta Avenue, in Kensington Market, which was hugely exciting to me as those vibrant few blocks I'd been exploring since I was a teenager had never stopped being full of charm and unpolished mystery. It was exactly where I saw us putting our unnamed restaurant. So what if it was across from the druggers' stoop and needed a complete build-out? Nothing could stop me from seeing it as perfect. I wandered through with the real estate agent, mentally building my dream restaurant. At over 4,000 square feet, it was more than enough room, almost too big. And that's when the light bulb lit up. My restaurant with Mitch would take up most of upstairs, and be outfitted with a proper dish pit, staff room, and even a garbage fridge to store, well, garbage (all luxuries compared with the bare-bones-ness of the Hoof's cramped space). Then the basement would be split between a private dining room and wine cellar, plus all the washrooms, and we'd still have almost 1,000 square feet left over, plenty of room to house the pub idea David Greig and I had been nurturing since year one of working together.

IN MANY WAYS, WHEN MITCH, DAVID, AND I signed the lease at 199 Augusta, the timing could not have been worse. The drawn-out and expensive construction of Agrikol had gone on from May 2015 to February 2016; it was the hardest build of my career, and with only slight hyperbolic inflection, it almost killed me.

But as with childbirth (SO I'M TOLD) once that little bundle of joy looks up at you and smiles, you forget you're torn from your v to your a, and all the pain and frustration just melts away. And after a few weeks of having Agrikol's doors open, that's how I was starting to feel. I was falling in love with my kid, and it wasn't hard, because she was absolutely perfect.

Agrikol is a space that unfolds itself slowly as you make your way through it, and there's a lot to take in, even though it's not huge; the double-height ceiling that soars up in the back half of the room, whose white-stuccoed wall is broken up with three custom stained-glass windows backlit by soft bulbs, makes it feel bigger. As does the overlooking upstairs balcony, which, in one journalist's perfect description, "breezily conjures the tropics, without kitsch or affectation"—that was just about the exact compliment I was looking for. A space like that could so easily veer into overdone camp, as Caribbean places outside the Caribbean so often do. We definitely went with a more-is-more approach, but the room is transporting and warm and exactly the vibe I was hoping to achieve when faced with a huge demo and rebuild.

As Agrikol was finding its feet as a restaurant—meaning every day was a new lesson in how much stress we could take, as staff would turn out to be a wrong fit or we'd have consistency issues with the food—I was also having to shift some of my focus to the raw space at 199 Augusta, which was awaiting permits. So I'd spend four weekdays in Toronto sorting out and coordinating quotes from electricians, plumbers, and HVAC, then jump on the Thursday train to Montreal to help try and make sure Agrikol was managing to not drown under the swells of people rushing to check it out. It was extremely hectic. But with Julio Mendy, a strong manager who learned from David (who had agreed to assist in the operations over the first three months, for which I'll be forever grateful), and some help from Roland's sister Monique, who taught the chef proper Haitian seasoning, it would eventually settle down into a proper functioning and very busy restaurant.

I could turn my focus to building what would likely be my last restaurant, my dream restaurant, my swan song—which I sincerely believe I mean. There's an understanding in the restaurant business that people who open more than one restaurant treat openings like crack hits, can't really stop, and likely won't, but right now, the restaurant I would open with a team of people I adored, the restaurant that would make me want to work full services again, really feels like my last big project. Perhaps that is a direct result of 2016 being so intense, to the point that I developed stress rashes and genuinely wondered, on occasion, if I were exhibiting signs of a nervous breakdown.

I wasn't—I don't think—but I was most definitely at the upper limits of how much stress I could handle.

This was all compounded by feeling like I was the restaurant industry's unofficial mascot for feminism, a pretty thankless job, unless you count retweets as reward enough. I knew, because of how drained and conflicted the Kitchen Bitches conference had left me, that I wasn't cut out for traditional activism. I'm too reactionary and too unwilling to adopt the "play nice" attitudes of the mainstream to ever be someone who could change the perspectives of the unconverted. A politician I'm not. As a foul-mouthed shrieker at the choir, however, I was all but a perfect fit. And I enjoyed many parts of that role: the rush of banging out a few kernels of truth on Twitter; speaking engagements where I had the freedom to talk about whatever I wished; and, most of all, having trickily manoeuvred myself into being introduced as a restaurateur AND a writer. But I didn't want to box myself into such a narrow place, despite how necessary I know my voice to be for women in restaurants (if not me, who?). I never wanted my fight to be so single-minded that I would lose sight of objectivity, that I would become unable to see nuance. When your subject matter is oppression, the waters are murky with all sorts of special interest groups (LOL to women being "special interest," and LOL to anyone being "special interest"). I wanted to remain unencumbered by the boundaries of a "movement" while still being a part of it.

But I just can't help but be constantly checking in with the current climate in restaurants. I want to know if things are getting better. Whenever I travel to new cities and inevitably meet new bro chefs (who don't fully understand my brand, so they are always really nice to me) I am still shocked by their ignorance.

I have had so many conversations with white male chefs circling in and around the same theme: that most white male chefs don't even recognize that there's an equality problem in the restaurant business (and in the world). I can't even count how many times I've casually broached the subject with a simple question on what they think about women in the industry—my basic litmus test for who I'm dealing with. Most will start by lavishing praise on all the "bad-ass female" cooks and chefs they've worked with and for, implying that there is clearly no issue as "these bitches are so much tougher than the guys." Maybe they had no choice but to be? Maybe it's internalized misogyny? If I push a bit (and I usually do) and ask if they think the industry is at all sexist, I'll often get a very sincere, "I dunno, I've never noticed any sexism," to which I'll reply, "Well, no. You wouldn't, would you? I mean, you're a white dude." This, of course, invariably makes them defensive. They'll start telling me how hard they've worked to get where they are, how good their food is. And I have no doubt; those are both so often true things. Everyone works hard in the restaurant business. But what's so galling is the willful ignorance. These men can't even conceptualize what that means for women, who, I feel very comfortable asserting, must work twice as hard for half the platform. If I try to point that out, even if I'm delicate and kind about it, I am almost always met with, "I just don't think the industry is sexist." And what do you even say to that?

That I'm surrounded both personally and professionally by men who actually "get it" and who understand that the world is designed for white men to succeed is, of course, not an accident. But it is also very insulating when all the men around you are feminists. You forget that so many men (and women) aren't.

BEFORE MITCH AND I TEAMED UP, Roland had asked him a question, a little exploration, almost to make sure Mitch knew what he was getting into.

"Mitch, you know who my wife is, right? You're not scared to partner with her?"

"What do you mean?" Mitch said.

"You know, my wife does her own thing, lots of people don't like that."

"Ya, but that's what I like about her. I do my own thing too."

A more perfect response I could not have written myself. And in a turn of good fortune, Roland really liked Mitch, and I've never known a better judge of character than my husband.

Talking about food with Mitch always assured me that we had similar ways of thinking about it. When I asked him where he stood on the art versus craft of cooking, he said, "For the most part I believe it's a craft, but as with all crafts it can be something more. There are nice tables and there are beautiful ones." This is partly why I felt such immediate kinship with him, his thoughtfulness. He isn't at all like me (although we both have vast collections of music and great palates), but he is very much an island in the restaurant business, and I imagined that together we would be unfuckwithable. Or at least it felt that way in the months before we actually opened the doors to our restaurant—those glorious weeks when everything is possible and nothing is set in stone.

Shortly before we'd signed the lease, we'd gone over everything, how we both saw our restaurant, the structure of money versus ownership. Despite my history, I still trusted my gut and was eager to make this an equal partnership. I was positive it was the right choice. But it wasn't just my gut. Some might think it's crazy to almost fully finance a partnership ("Keep control, keep 66 percent" is what good lawyers say), but as a dyed-in-the-wool cashmere socialist, I truly believe that, in an altruistic sense, the investment of "sweat equity" is of equal value to literal money. And I think it's a worthwhile risk that will pay off in true symbiosis, true equality. I want my restaurants to be an antidotal oasis to the bro-chef way of life. If I can prove over and over again that you can create a beautiful, quality experience for people while existing in relative harmony with (ideally) happy staff, all the animosity I feel directed at me from inside the industry (the call is ALWAYS coming from inside the house) will have been worthwhile. And I sincerely hope that it will rub off on my employees and on outside observers. But for now, I know I am choosing excellent people to expand with.

MITCH AND I WENT BACK AND FORTH about the name. For a minute, The Grey Lodge was a contender, liked for its vague reference to a sort of halfway between *Twin Peaks*'s Black and White Lodges—halfway between good and evil. Mitch felt "lodge" was too evocative of something far woodsier than what we were aspiring to, and eventually I agreed. But I was insisting on "The Grey" something, and after sitting with it for a few days, could not detach myself from the idea of "Grey Gardens." I was thrilled when Mitch liked it too. I worried that people would think it was a direct reference to the documentary *Grey Gardens*, as a kooky homage to Big and Little Edie, but it was, in small part, my own personal inside joke about being far more able to see the world in its intended shades of grey than in the black-and-white, less nuanced perspectives of a younger me. In a larger sense it was a connection to the idea of being outsiders. Because, for all of my success and acclaim in the restaurant business, I didn't at all fit into it, at least not in the way I felt was expected of me: the quid pro quo, hypocrisy-laden style most restaurateurs drown each other in, one giant circle jerk. I'm just not built for those kinds of false, yet profitable friendships, and I (technically) have nothing to jerk. I understood that my isolation was self-imposed. You can only criticize chef bros so many times before they won't support you any more, either literally or figuratively.

Obviously I love making restaurants. I might complain about the red tape or tradespeople being insane or a myriad of other problems that show themselves along a road I always think might be free of hurdles *this time*—it never is. My weeks early in the summer of 2016 were split between designing and opening Agrikol's very beautiful *terrasse* (not bragging, it's gorgeous) and getting moving on the mechanical for Grey, which I'd hoped would be quick and easy but, due to an electrician who could most kindly be described as "quirky," was neither easy nor quick. It wasn't nearly the insane challenge Montreal had been, but it wasn't exactly a walk in the park. When we were finally at the end of an involved and complex hood installation I thought I could see the light, I thought we were getting to the best part, finishings. But there was one more surprise! After finally getting the landlord to contact the city about upgrading the gas meter (a fairly simple process, we thought) we were very disappointed (I almost cried) when the local gas supply company showed up to tell us that there might not be enough gas being pushed from the city line to the property. If this was the case, it could take up to four months and cost upwards of $40,000. We would have to gather BTU (British Thermal Units) specs for all of our equipment and wait a very tense four days. We got approval, only to realize we'd forgotten to add the BTUs of the return air heater. I chose to spare Mitch the even more tense three days of wondering if we'd be okay, which was undeniably the ethically right choice. I almost jumped for joy on the train when I received the email assuring me all was well.

With all of that finally in order, I was able to start to really focus on making the space into exactly what I saw in my head. I was excited for the opening of what I truly saw as my last great effort for the restaurant business, but even more, I was excited to do it with people who had become my family, people I deeply trusted.

Working with Jake and David while navigating a friendship complicated (only slightly) by power dynamics was a highlight of my restaurant career. They made me realize my limitations and allowed me to become better at leadership by letting go of some control and learning to delegate. But I would often wonder how they felt about what we all wanted to believe was an equality-based friendship made unequal by the plain fact that I was the boss. It was obviously less of a problem for me—I never felt like I had to bite my tongue or withhold criticism, but perhaps they did. And wondering gnawed at me, not in a way that damaged the psychology of our friendship, but in a way that helped keep my natural inclinations toward absolutism in check. I would sometimes ask them about this and if they ever felt like subordinates outside the walls of Hoofland. I was happy to hear they didn't, and believed them, but remained hyper-aware to never carelessly make them feel like anything other than respected equals.

I had been making all the decisions and running things for so many years and really enjoyed the autonomy. If something needed to be taken care of I just took care of it. If I wanted to buy new washroom doors with leaded-glass details, I just bought them. I wasn't necessarily in a hurry to enter new partnerships, but I also understood that if I didn't offer ownership to such hugely talented and loyal people, I risked losing them. With Mitch, it felt absolutely necessary to toss my fears out the window and dive into an equal partnership, despite how poorly it had gone the last time I dove. I trusted Mitch as a person, as a leader, and most especially as a chef, and I wanted Grey Gardens to be reflective of both of us. But it was more than that. I'd been overseeing the kitchen staff at the Hoof for years—which, as a non-chef, was a huge challenge. No matter how much time and attention I devoted to checking in with the cooks, tasting new dishes, I was always an outsider, never really "one of them." And even though I felt that most of the cooks who'd run the Hoof respected me, there was a certain level of respect I couldn't access, one reserved for their "mentors." I understood it, to a degree—they might realize/grudgingly accept that I have a good palate and could maybe even make worth-while suggestions to improve the plates they presented, or make them more "Hoofish" (which I certainly did, especially at the beginning of a new chef's tenure). But I knew that with Mitch as a partner in Grey Gardens, I'd be largely relieved of these stresses, and it was something to look forward to.

Having David act as opening bar manager for Grey, and then eventually downstairs as my equal partner in our pub, General Public, had been an understood goal for a long time. I had no doubts about our ability to run a business together—we have complementary skill sets, and where I am, say, not super-diplomatic, David is the U.N., and while I will avoid small talk at all costs, David will happily engage with people. Conceptually, General Public was pretty straightforward: great beer, cider, gin-and-tonics galore, and a few well-made cocktails, with imported "crisps" and a small menu of very British food, or, at the very least, proper Sunday roasts. The idea had sprouted from one of my many thorough searches through Toronto's second-hand and salvage stores. I'd been on a mission for new patio chairs for Cocktail Bar, and found them in the Junction. As I piled them up by the checkout desk, I saw they were hiding a beautiful wooden door with a glass window advertising the business it had once guarded. The lettering was slightly worn, gold and blue, and it said "General Public." It flipped a switch, because a more fitting name for a pub I still can't think of. A quick Google search revealed (shockingly) this wasn't already the name of a million pubs, and I immediately registered the company.

Jake would come on board as GM of Grey, with a firm understanding that we'd eventually partner for a future project, something small. I knew for certain that we'd have an incredible wine list, which I wanted to be a big part of Grey Gardens's identity. Jake has knowledge to back up the passion and an ability to remember all the details about a producer, details that would drip through my understanding—pushed out by my refusal to learn any more than whether I like a wine or do not.

I only felt good and excited for these partnerships, and particularly with Jake and David, I knew them so well and trusted them so much that I didn't have any lingering doubts about how it would be when we were existing as true equals professionally—I'd been thinking of them as equals for so long, it wouldn't be much of an adjustment. When I'd hired Jake in 2013 I'd realized quickly how much I'd always needed people to help me run my business, and how much easier it was to let go of the urge to control every little thing. Without Jake and David to lean on (as well as long-term front of house staff Julia Gilmore, Lee Evans, and Stu Sakai) I never could have *considered* opening Agrikol. With such talented future partners, I was starting to see the full potential of what we could achieve as a group. Mitch as a chef, Jake on wine, David on cocktails, and me designing and contracting the build would be a pretty unstoppable consulting group. I just don't know that I have it in me to execute someone else's vision, no matter how great the financial reward.

While I'm excited about the goals within this partnership, I can't wait for Mitch and David to really understand money stress. As managers they are very careful to keep costs in check, but the truth is that nothing will teach you to tighten up money drains faster than watching your own money draining out. But with those hard lessons about the economy of restaurants also come rewards—rewards I couldn't wait for Mitch and David (and eventually Jake) to reap.

The idea of attaining any sort of success is highly unappealing if you do it on an island. I don't want to have a financially secure life studded with occasional luxuries while my friends scrimp and save. I want to create an environment where we succeed together, because really, what's the point otherwise?

MITCH AND I WANTED A PLACE that would be bustling and casual while still respecting very high standards. A place you could pop into for a glass of pét-nat and a quick bite, or reserve a table for a limited set menu at the kitchen bar on your anniversary. A place you could feel comfortable frequenting in sneakers and a T-shirt, knowing there is a deep (and deeply weird) wine list waiting for you. A wine bar and a restaurant all rolled into one, which, for whatever reason (*cough* THE LCBO) hadn't been properly done in Toronto yet. If you wanted that experience, you still, even in 2016, had to go to Montreal, New York, or Paris. Grey Gardens was a way for me to make a slightly less narrow version of the Hoof, because, philosophically, there would be a very strong connection to the same ideals that first motivated me there—build a place you want to be in—only now I was in my early forties instead of my early thirties and working with a much bigger budget and a like-minded partner.

It's early December 2016. I'm sitting on the floor inside the still-unfinished Grey Gardens, leaned up against the south wall, legs carelessly splayed out in front of me, eyes darting from the newly constructed bar to the recently installed lighting fixtures, marvelling at the beauty appearing before me, as if by magic, forgetting for a moment how stressful the build has been. I instinctively touch my inner elbow, where an anguished stress rash is retreating and pulling back into my arm in response to construction having finally turned a corner from dust clouds and grinding steel toward the joyous peace of deciding where to hang a gilded mirror and which wallpaper to use in what washroom. For now, the visuals of Grey Gardens remain my secret, a manifestation of a long-held dreamy vision, slowly put together, piece by piece. Design isn't art, but I can almost trick myself into believing it is, especially when it's an empty restaurant space with only impressions of its future self—still unencumbered by the dining public's expectations, unfussed with by customers crowding the doorway. The build really is the best part—despite how specifically stressful it can be.

My gaze rests upon the muted jewel tones of a mural that spans the entire north wall, a reference point for the whole look of the place, a miscellany of tropical and English garden, sanded away in parts to appear as though it has always been there. I absentmindedly push my finger around a patch of concrete floor in small, concentric circles, leaving behind a sheen of vanilla-scented lip balm that permanently resides on my right forefinger from near constant dipping and applying. Hours go by. I change positions, moving to different parts of the room to really see it, every detail. I have spent all year picking out lighting fixtures, chairs, fancy faucets, vases, and everything I need to make the finished space match what is in my head, to assert that this is a restaurant both wild and restrained.

For all my fears of being defined as a restaurateur instead of as an artist, Grey Gardens is in fact the canvas that has offered me the most freedom for my mashed-up ideas of clean-lined modernity and beautiful wreckage, a lens through which I can amplify everything I've learned about existing in the restaurant business my own way, a vehicle driven strictly by the motivation to draw the art and commerce of running restaurants ever closer together.

But within my created world lies a deeply rooted understanding that running restaurants was never exactly for its own sake, it was always a path to freedom—freedom to build a fantasy, freedom from a boss, freedom to choose how love and marriage work best for me—to leave all the ropes of a suburban childhood and a patriarchal culture unwound at my feet.

GLOSSARY

AGRIKOL: The Haitian Creole spelling of *agricole*, the style in which the rhum of Haiti is made.

AUTO-GRAT: You are being auto-gratted at most places if you are a party of six or more. This means the tip (usually 18%) is added to the bill for you, lest you manage to bungle it as you divide the bill six ways.

BACK BAR: Liquor on display on shelves behind the bar.

CHARCUTERIE: Blanket French term for a variety of styles of prepared meat products, including cured (salted and aged), terrine, sausage and pâté. This term is a bit broader than the Italian *"salumi,"* which is specific to dry-cured meats.

DEUCE: Slang for "table for two."
USAGE: "Nice job squeezing those three tiny girls into a deuce."

DROPPING FOOD: This is not, as it appears to be, the mishandling of plates that causes them to tumble to the floor, spilling food. This is server-speak for delivering food to a table.
USAGE: "The new bartender is really great with people, but he needs to seriously work on his drops."

FIRE: The term for the kitchen going ahead and starting to prepare the next course; usually used interchangeably with "pick up," but it's more of a kitchen term.
USAGE: Chef to line cook: "I fired the heart ages ago, where the hell is it?"

GARDE/GARDE MANGER: Directly translating from French to "keeper of the food," this is the cold station, or salad station.

NORMALS: People who don't work in restaurants.
USAGE: "Table 2 is awesome—super-keen normals."

OCTOPUS HANDS: Gripping the glass from above, with your fingers grasping around the rim of the glass, and serving it this way, as an octopus might carry a cocktail in a life and death situation, because HOW ELSE WOULD HE DO IT?
WHY IT'S BAD: From lived experience, not too many minutes go by that I'm not poking around in one of my holes. Whether it's taking my time with a delicate and thorough nose-pick (or a necessary quick and secret one) or pulling my underwear out of my butt-crack with lightning speed as I walk or perhaps I've found the perfect nest on which to cup my hand while watching TV. The point is, everyone (this is not me-specific, right?) is always picking at themselves and no one is scrubbing up, doctor-style, before every drink served. So, just keep your grubby little fingers away from where my mouth goes.

PÉT NAT: Shorthand for pétillant-natural ("naturally sparkling") and a catch-all term for wine bottled before primary fermentation, known as méthod ancestrale (as opposed to méthod champenoise, a more common wine-making practice) is complete.

PICK UP OR PICKING UP: Unrelated to dating. This means to let the kitchen know to fire your next course.
USAGE: "Hey, Virgil, can you pick up bar 3/4 for me?" Also used by chefs as an alternative to "hands, please," to let servers know plates are ready at the pass: "Pick up, please."

QUALITY CHECK: A way of making sure the customer is enjoying the food without constantly asking them the impossibly worded, yet extremely common, "And how are you enjoying that?" How do you even answer that? "I am, um, enjoying it with *fervour*?"

ROLL-UPS: The neat and tidy way diners and many casual restaurants keep forks and knives together, mostly for ease and speed in resetting tables.

RUN THE LINE: Vernacular for the position of whoever is in charge of the kitchen. This is usually the chef, but in bigger kitchens it could be the chef de cuisine or even the sous-chef.

SALUMI VS. SALAMI: All terriers (salami) are dogs but not all dogs (salumi) are terriers. Make sense?

SEAT NUMBERS: Assigned numbers for every seat in the restaurant so that food always goes to the person who ordered it and the server doesn't have to stand there, haplessly, auctioning it off ("Annnd, who had the salmon?"), which is the height of amateur hour.

SERVICE BAR: Either a dedicated bar or bartender who only deals with what the servers on the floor need.
USAGE: "Got crushed tonight, bro. Was doing the whole bar PLUS service bar."

SOUS VIDE: Meaning cooked "under vacuum," this is a newer technique that cooks were going mad for in the early 2000s, but that has only recently settled into its rightful place as just another kitchen technique.

SOUS: Short for sous-chef and meaning "under," the sous is the second or third in command, depending on whether there's a chef or a chef de cuisine and an executive chef. All very French, all very militaristic.

STAGING: An anglicized version of "stagiaire," a term I have no doubt you are very familiar with by now, but just in case you aren't, it's an unpaid internship, usually applying to cooks (but bartenders have been known to accept stages, too). The transaction is one of labour for education, as well as for bragging rights, in the case of Michelin-starred places.

THE MARKET: What Torontonians (maybe specifically West-enders) call Kensington Market. Sometimes simply "Kensington," but mostly "the market."

THE PASS: the connection between back of house (BOH) and front of house (FOH). All food goes through through the pass to get to diners.

TRAINED UP: Fairly obvious, but in case it's not, this is the process by which a new hire goes from zero knowledge to most of it over the course of a couple of months.

TURNS: The number of times you can re-seat a table during the course of service.

USAGE: Server to host: "Holy fuck, dude, we got slammed tonight. Did like four and a half turns." Host: "Turn 'n burn, baby, turn 'n burn."

ACKNOWLEDGEMENTS

WRITING THIS BOOK was sometimes the easiest thing in the world. I'd feel smug satisfaction as the words poured out of me, only to be reminded of writing's tedious underbelly during the editing process, throughout which I was the most stressed I've ever been about making something in my life. It's a solitary pursuit, writing, and for me required conditions to be exactly right. I could write on the beach, but only in a shaded hut and only if waves were the backdrop (as opposed to loud, smoking Russians—no disrespect intended, but these happened to be Russians, in this particular case). I also was able to work on the many train trips I took between Toronto and Montreal; something about the white noise of the tracks would lull me to type rather than to sleep—I'm on the train right now! But I accomplished the most, had the most significant "breakthroughs" at the Ghent, New York home of my dear friends Stephen Metcalf and Koethi Zan. Their beautiful place looks out to the rollingest of rolling hills and I'd spend hours and hours a day getting words on the page and the evenings cooking, drinking wine and laughing, totally bucolic. I will be forever grateful for their immense hospitality, and our many "writer's camps."

Thank you to all the artists who took the time to really understand the ideas I had in my head, and also who came up with wonderful extras that made each piece that much better.

It was amazing to work with so many talented women, and, of course, Roland, who started his incredible portrait on just my face, only to ask me, hours later, for "a close-up of your pussy." We talked about the pros and cons of a nude, and then just decided to go for it. As a woman, you're so "damned if you do, damned if you don't" regarding your sexuality, which is endlessly frustrating, so fuck it: here's my vagina.

Many thanks to my friends who were *almost* as supportive of me as I would have been of them, had they been running three busy Toronto spots while building and opening Agrikol in Montreal, as well as Grey Gardens in Toronto, all while trying to write a goddamn book. I love you all, you know who you are (what a cop-out . . . but you do!).

Thank you to my amazing staff and especially to the front of house managers/best pals I know I can rely on and trust. I would fall apart without you, and the restaurants would too. David, Jake, Julia, Lee, Stu and Julio, you are invaluable and I hope I tell you enough just how much you're appreciated, and tell you with money.

I'm incredibly grateful to Mitch Bates, who sees the restaurant business through a lens similar to mine and confirmed my suspicion that there's a more human way to run a kitchen, and who is, truly, one of the best cooks I've ever seen in my life. He continues to blow my mind with his thoughtful, precise, and above all delicious food.

Without the constant nudging from the great Jared Bland, I would never have met the great Kristin Cochrane, and this book might never have come to be. After we shared much wine and more laughs, she said, "You've got a book in you," and suggested I get an agent right away, so I did. Based on both

Jared's and Patrick McGuire's recommendations, I chose the best, Martha Webb, who helped me shape and unravel what it is I was really trying to say, and still does that for me (as well as matching me glass for glass, an impressive feat, for anyone, let alone a woman much, much, tinier than me). And how fortunate I was to end up under the Doubleday Canada imprint, headed up by the impressive, lovely, Amy Black.

And as I really got into it, it was Bhavna Chauhan who took so much care in dissecting every line and pushing me to realize that the reader didn't live in my head and that I'd need to really explain things. It was such a great experience working with her. When she called me to tell me she approved the book for copyediting (a huge hurdle) I almost cried, I was so happy. But the copy editing process was less awful than I imagined it would be because Catherine Marjoribanks was extremely generous regarding my abuses of language. Also, I learned about "stet" and made a number of increasingly ridiculous "stet puns": "stet right up, Catherine, welcome to my stet class. r u having fun yet?!"

It's really nice that basically everyone who was intimately involved with the making of this book is a woman (exception, Roland).

So much love and thanks to my parents, who raised me to never for a second doubt that I could do the outlandish things I set my mind to. I wish so badly that my mom was here to hold this book in her hands (she'd be immeasurably proud), and that my dad didn't need reminding every day that I have actually done okay for myself. A little bit of my heart died with my mom and a little bit of my brain died with my dad's. Better parents I couldn't imagine.

But most of my appreciation, as it so often is, must be heaped on my remarkable husband, who dances with me in the morning, hangs out with me at night, and makes me feel so loved every day. I can't believe I get to spend my life with someone so ridiculously cool and smart and compassionate, and who is, without a doubt, the most handsome man I've ever seen. Je t'aime.

PHOTO AND ART CREDITS

Tree planting (page 47); "Vodka is Stupid" essay artwork (page 80-81); Toronto map (page 203); Raw Bar (page 212); Kitchen Bitches (page 264, design by Unspace—Meghann Millard and Jorge Villabolos); Montreal streetscape (page 296); Grey Gardens (page 342): Chloe Cushman

"A Love Letter to Sneaky Dees" essay artwork (page 310-311): Ilona Fiddy

Bogart and Bacall Kissing (page 98): Getty Images

Charcuterie board (page 11); Hoof bitters and Manhattan (page 183): Julia Gilmore

Portrait of the author (page 143); Nudes (page 276-277, photo credit to Jenna Marie Wakani): Roland Jean

"Balls are Weak"; "Wine" essay artwork (page 250-253); "The Glass Ceiling" (page 320-321): Michelle LeFade

Cobalt menu (page 127); The Black Hoof sketch (page 166); Cocktail Bar menu (page 202): courtesy of the author